ST. LOUIS SOCCER

AN ILLUSTRATED TIMELINE

DAVE LANGE

FOREWORD BY CAROLYN KINDLE

REEDY PRESS

DEDICATION

For Janet and Will

Reedy Press
PO Box 5131
St. Louis, MO 63139, USA
reedypress.com

Library of Congress Control Number: On File

ISBN: 9781681066509

Cover and Interior Design: Eric Marquard

All interior images are courtesy of the author or believed to be in the public domain unless otherwise noted.
Back cover images: Top: Kutis, 1957 US Amateur and Open Cup champions (Rich Meisemann Collection). From left: Roman Bürki (St. Louis CITY SC), Al Trost (Bill McDermott Collection), Becky Sauerbrunn (Getty Images)
Front cover: Harry Keough (left) and Frank Borghi, USA vs. England, 1950 World Cup (Frank Borghi Collection)

Printed in Canada
26 27 28 29 30 5 4 3 2 1

CONTENTS

JOSEPH S. CARENZA, SR.
"BRONZE BOOT"
PERPETUAL TROPHY

FOREWORD

ST. LOUIS is America's first soccer city.

For more than 150 years, St. Louisans learned to play the game as children, watched it as adults, and taught it to their families and neighbors. An unusually large number played soccer for their schools or parishes, in professional leagues, and for their country at the highest level.

The book you are about to read recounts their many amazing achievements. Among them is a team of local players, sponsored by a hat company, who won the first of 90 national soccer championships for St. Louis. And it describes the United States side with five St. Louis starters who stunned England in a 1950 World Cup match. Most importantly, it tells the stories of more than 75 men and women from St. Louis who have played for US national teams.

That winning spirit continues today, not only in pickup games in neighborhoods around the region but also in our local stadium restaurant partners, local artists and musicians, and most importantly, our fans. Soccer has become, and remains, a universal language.

CITY SC is proud to foster that spirit by providing free soccer training for children, developing the next generation of great players through our youth academy, and making Energizer Park the best and most accessible fan experience in Major League Soccer. We see soccer as a way to unite our community and bring people together to support the vitality of our neighborhoods, ignite civic pride, and be part of the increasing number of St. Louis organizations and individuals who dream big for our future. CITY's vision is to become part of the fabric of St. Louis—just like soccer has been in St. Louis for generations. We are proud to be one chapter in the long and ongoing story of the beautiful game in St. Louis.

Sincerely,

Carolyn Kindle
CEO/Part Owner
St. Louis CITY Soccer Club

Previous page: Bob Guelker (left) and Harry Keough, US Soccer Hall of Famers and legendary college soccer coaches, eye the Bronze Boot trophy awarded to the annual winner of the regular-season match between the men's teams of Keough's Saint Louis University and Guelker's Southern Illinois University–Edwardsville. The image was taken before the 1982 game at Busch Stadium. Guelker, who started the soccer programs at SLU and SIUE, coached teams to more NCAA men's soccer championships (seven—five at SLU, two at SIUE) than anyone. Keough coached SLU to five NCAA titles and was one of the greatest players in the history of St. Louis soccer for his roles on the 1950 US World Cup team and on the national powerhouse Kutis teams of the 1950s. The Bronze Boot series began in 1971 and continues today. **RICK STANKOVEN**

Josh Sargent scores the first goal by a St. Louisan in England's Premier League on January 21, 2022. His spectacular goal on a "scorpion kick" came for Norwich City against Watford.
GETTY IMAGES/CHARLOTTE WILSON/OFFSIDE

ACKNOWLEDGMENTS

PRINTED AND online sources, individual interviews, and personal and archived collections served as important sources for this book. But it would not have been possible without the assistance of many individuals, especially Bill McDermott and Jim Leeker, who read the manuscript and tracked down missing materials; Carolyn Kindle and Marc Abel, St. Louis CITY SC, for providing this book's foreword and CITY photos; Erin Bova, Stephen Peck, and Marie Self, Jefferson College; Charles E. Brown, University of Missouri–St. Louis; Mike Carpenter, Chris Mackenzie, and John Schneider, Quincy University; Shelly Clark and Patrick Longo, current St. Louis Ambush team; Lindsay Kennedy Eversmeyer, Fire & Ice Soccer Club; Ed Farnsworth, Society for American Soccer History; Jan and Joan Gettemeyer, Jeff Kuchno, and Ruth Harker, UMSL and 1985 US women's soccer materials; Joe Hamm, 1972 US Olympian and son of Central Brewers goalkeeper Johnny Hamm; Davina R. Harrison and Janice Hovis, St. Louis Community College, for Meramec Community College materials; Laura Inlow, Lewis & Clark Community College; Les Jones, Canadian soccer historian; Ursula Kittner, J.B. Marine Soccer Club; Karen Lombardo and Mike Sorber for information about and photos of Florissant Valley Community College's men's and women's teams; Bridget McCann, Washington University; Dennis Northcott, Missouri Historical Society; Glen Pariani, son of US Soccer Hall of Famer Gino Pariani; Steve Pecher, St. Louis Scott Gallagher Soccer Club; Joe Pott, Southern Illinois University–Edwardsville; and Brian Roth, past St. Louis Ambush team.

This book would have been far less visually appealing without Rick Stankoven's Steamers, Granite City, and Steve Trittschuh 1980s images; Dave Preston's 1990s Ambush photos; Paul Bryant's 2000s Steamers pictures; and Tim Vizer's Maddie DiMaria image.

Finally, a big thank-you goes to Josh Stevens, Barbara Northcott, and Jaime Bourassa at Reedy Press for turning the idea for this book into reality.

My sincere apologies to anyone I missed, and my deepest gratitude to all.

— Dave Lange

MAY 28, 1875

SOCCER IN ST. LOUIS BEGINS WITH "FIRST GAME"

ON MAY 28, 1875, the Grand Avenue Base Ball Park, soon to be renamed Sportsman's Park and the future home of the Browns and Cardinals, hosted the debut of another sport that St. Louisans would embrace. The crowd on that cool, overcast Friday afternoon saw the first reported soccer-like game in St. Louis.

Local lawyers, divided by the color of their pants into teams called the Blondes and the Brunettes, played an advertised charity "foot ball" game. Proceeds went to the Newsboys Home for indigent boys who hawked newspapers on the streets.

Accounts of the event described a match that failed to follow soccer's Laws of the Game, published in England in 1863. But a decision early in the game made this a soccer-like match: Hands were not allowed to be used to advance the ball.

Although the Blondes won the game, both sides agreed to call it a draw.

Earlier "foot ball" games certainly had been held in St. Louis. "Foot ball" games to be played by boys were advertised as early as February 1872. But the Blondes–Brunettes game is the first account of a soccer-like match actually played in St. Louis, thus making it a starting point for America's first soccer capital.

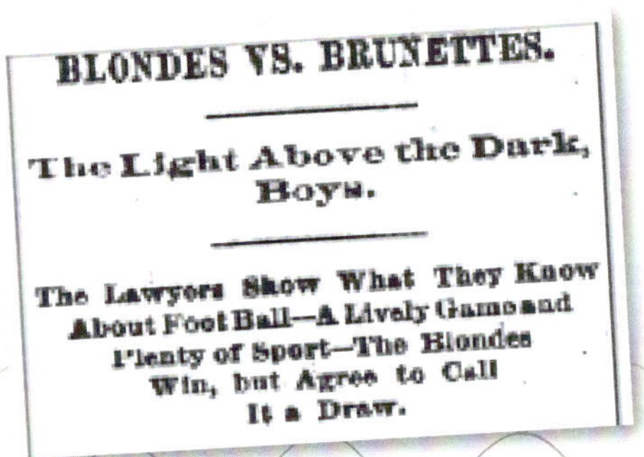

BLONDES VS. BRUNETTES.

The Light Above the Dark, Boys.

The Lawyers Show What They Know About Foot Ball—A Lively Game and Plenty of Sport—The Blondes Win, but Agree to Call It a Draw.

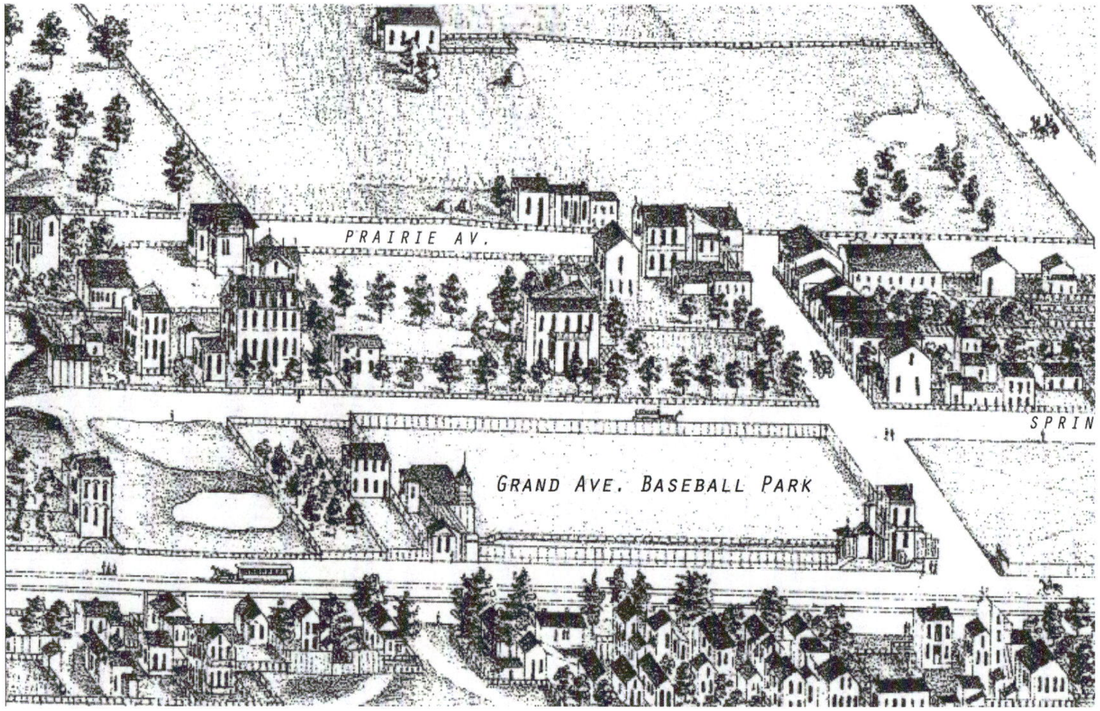

Headline in the May 29, 1875, edition of the *St. Louis Globe-Democrat* (left), **NEWSPAPERS.COM**; a sketch of the site of the game made in 1875 from an aerial balloon (above)

DECEMBER 25, 1884

ST. LOUIS SITE OF FIRST INTERNATIONAL GAME IN US

SOCCER BEGAN haphazardly in St. Louis as one-off games or as part of community fairs.

That changed in 1884 thanks to two events.

The first happened on October 21, 1884, when four local teams formed the Western Foot Ball Association, the first soccer league in St. Louis. The league scheduled its first match at Sportsman's Park on December 7, 1884. The Western Association gave local soccer its first structure and predated the Football League in England by more than three years. Although the Western Association folded before the end of its second season, other leagues soon followed.

St. Louis soccer reached its second milestone on Christmas Day 1884. At the invitation of the Western Association's Thistles, a team representing Canada's Western Football Association visited St. Louis for the first of three scheduled matches against St. Louis opponents. Historians have concluded that the game on December 25 was the first international soccer match played in the United States.

The Canadians, said to be the best players from Ontario, routed the Thistles, 9–0, on December 25. Bad weather forced cancellation of game two. In the finale, the Canadians prevailed, 5–3 against a combined Thistles–St. Louis Hibernians team on December 28.

In what may be the earliest known photo of soccer in St. Louis, Canada's Western Football Association team poses in December 1884. Although none of the players are identified, the player seated above the player with the ball likely is David Forsythe, known as "the father of Canadian soccer."
COLIN JOSE/CANADIANSOCCERHISTORY.COM

SEPTEMBER 29, 1893

SEED PLANTED FOR CYC SOCCER

CATHOLIC YOUTH Council soccer, the greenhouse that has grown generations of high-caliber St. Louis players, traces its beginnings to September 29, 1893. Organizers active in the city's Catholic churches formed the Sodality Foot Ball League. Young men from six parishes joined Christian Brothers College to comprise the seven-team league.

Juvenile leagues followed around 1910, creating a process for older boys to learn the game and graduate to the city's men's divisions. Teams representing St. Louis parishes competed in these leagues until 1946. That's when the CYC, formed at the national level in 1937 and started in St. Louis in 1941, started its own high school and senior leagues.

The CYC added younger age groups for boys over the next two decades. By 1966, the CYC had become the USA's largest soccer organization, with 447 teams in eight age groups from under-8 boys up to senior men. The CYC's vast youth organization is largely credited for creating a production line of players that dominated the sport in the United States from 1959 to 1979: Teams of St. Louis men won 15 US Junior Cups and 13 NCAA, nine NAIA, and eight NJCAA championships.

Sodality Foot-Ball League.

The standing of the clubs in the Sodality Foot-Ball League is appended:

	Won.	Lost.	Drawn.	Av.
St. Theresa's..........	2	0	1	1,000
St. Alphonsus'..........	3	1	0	750
College (P. A. Club)....	2	1	0	666
St. Malachy's	2	1	1	666
St. Kevin's......	1	2	1	333
St. Bridget's........	0	2	1	000
St. Patrick's......	0	3	0	000

The standings early in the Sodality League's first season were published in the November 26, 1893, edition of the *St. Louis Globe-Democrat.*
NEWSPAPERS.COM

APRIL 18, 1897

6,000 SEE ST. TERESA'S SOLIDIFY STATUS AS CITY'S BEST

A CROWD of 6,000, the largest yet for soccer in St. Louis, saw a match between the city's top two teams: St. Teresa, winner of four city championships from 1893 to 1896 with an almost all–St. Louis squad, and the Cycling Club, a soccer team predominantly from Great Britain and champions of the 1896–97 Lindell League.

Local soccer supremacy, a $100 wager, and 75 percent of gate receipts were at stake.

St. Teresa won at least 57 of 60 games during its four championship seasons. (One season's record is unknown.) The Cycling Club featured Scottish-born Benny Govier of Chicago, considered the nation's best player, and Welsh international Dick Jarrett. The teams had been intense rivals since the Cycling Club started its team in 1895. Their matches "were downright pitched battles."

St. Teresa's fielded the best team in the early years of St. Louis soccer, winning four consecutive city championships.
LOUISA H. BOWEN UNIVERSITY ARCHIVES AND SPECIAL COLLECTIONS, SOUTHERN ILLINOIS UNIVERSITY AT EDWARDSVILLE

The Cycling Club featured outstanding players such as US Soccer Hall of Famer Benny Govier, a Scottish native by way of Chicago.
LOUISA H. BOWEN UNIVERSITY ARCHIVES AND SPECIAL COLLECTIONS, SOUTHERN ILLINOIS UNIVERSITY AT EDWARDSVILLE

But St. Teresa's Ted Guinan scored in the first minute. Phil Kavanaugh and Frank Tighe added second-half goals as St. Teresa won, 3–1. Kavanaugh scored the Cycling Club's only goal when he inadvertently headed the ball into his own net.

The victory cemented St. Teresa's legacy as the best team in the early years of soccer in St. Louis. A side note to the match: It outdrew a Cardinals' home exhibition game the same afternoon.

St. Teresa 3, Cycling Club 1

Friendly at South Side Park, Missouri and Russell Avenues

ST. TERESA (first names given if known): GK William Robinson; FB Harry McNamara, Frank "Stump" Kavanaugh; HB McCarthy, Moynahan, Frank Tighe; F James Daly, Mike Corcoran, Ted Guinan, Phil Kavanaugh, Arthur Granville

CYCLING CLUB (first names given if known): GK McCormack; FB McDonough, Patrick; HB Dan Daly, Joe Myddleton, Milne; F Dick Jarrett, Benny Govier, Orrack, Connie Reed, Billy Kane

GOALS: Guinan (ST), Tighe (ST), P. Kavanaugh (ST), P. Kavanaugh (ST) OG

REFEREE: Rodgers

GOAL LINESMEN: Harding, Church

ATTENDANCE: 6,000 (estimated)

NOVEMBER 17, 1904

CANADA'S GALT MINES OLYMPIC GOLD AT FRANCIS FIELD

THE MODERN ERA'S third Olympics came to St. Louis as a sideshow to the 1904 World's Fair. Soccer, with only three teams, exemplified the shabbily run Games.

Soccer's gold medal was won on November 17 by the Galt (Ontario) Football Club, representing Canada. Two teams representing the United States competed from St. Louis: Christian Brothers College (then an elementary school, high school, and college for males) and St. Rose.

Organizers had pondered a more proper soccer tournament at World's Fair Stadium (today's Francis Field) with local pro and Ontario amateur teams. But it was decided on November 4 that only amateurs could play. Ontario teams, citing either lack of money to travel or confidence to beat Gault, dropped out.

The St. Louisans faced a far superior team. Galt, three-time Ontario champions from 1901 to 1903, ripped CBC, 7–0, on November 16 and St. Rose, 4–0, in the gold-medal clincher the next day. On November 23, the silver medal went to CBC, which won a rematch against St. Rose, 2–0, after they had played to a scoreless tie November 18. Olympic records thus credit the USA with winning two medals (silver for CBC, bronze for St. Rose) in soccer, a team sport.

Galt's Olympic gold medalists. Back (L-R): John Fraser, Robert Lane, Albert Johnston, Parnell Gourlay, George Ducker, Albert Ernest Linton, Otto Christman, John Gourlay. Front: Tom Taylor, Frederick Steep, Alexander Hall, Gordon McDonald, William Twaits, Albert "Red" Henderson. **SPALDING'S ASSOCIATION FOOT BALL GUIDE (1904-05)**

Galt (Ontario, Canada) 4, St. Rose 0

Olympic Games at World's Fair Stadium (today's Francis Field)

Victory gave Galt the gold medal.

ST. ROSE: GK Frank Frost; FB Cormic Cosgrove, Leo O'Connell; HB Claude Jameson, Harry Tate, George Cooke; F Thomas Cooke, Henry Jameson, Joseph Brady, Edward Dierkes, Martin Dooling

GALT: GK Ernest Linton; FB Tom Taylor, Frederick Steep; HB Alexander Hall, Gordon McDonald, William Twaits; F George Ducker, John Gourlay, Albert Johnston, Robert Lane, John Fraser

GOALS: Taylor 2, Henderson, own goal. Time of halves: 30 minutes

REFEREE: Paul McSweeney

ATTENDANCE: Unknown

SEPTEMBER 23, 1905

FIRST VISIT BY ENGLISH TEAM PACKS LEAGUE PARK

ABOUT 3,000 PEOPLE watched the Cardinals–Boston Braves game on a Saturday afternoon at League Park in north St. Louis. Many more waited outside for the second attraction: the first visit to St. Louis by an English soccer team, which played St. Louis opposition after Cardinals games September 23 and 24.

The English drew the biggest crowds yet for St. Louis soccer. About 10,000 watched on September 23. The next day, two or three times as many (estimates vary) sat or stood for the rematch.

The visitors—called the Pilgrims and created to popularize soccer during a US tour—humbled St. Louis all-stars 10–0 on September 23 and 6–0 the next day.

The crowds saw one of the era's top players, the Pilgrims' Vivian Woodward. Woodward scored 29 goals in 23 appearances for England from 1903 to 1911 and tallied 91 goals in 237 matches for Tottenham and Chelsea from 1901 to 1915.

The Pilgrims of 1905. Right back Fred Milnes is No. 10. Identification of other players is unknown.
SOCIETY FOR AMERICAN SOCCER HISTORY

PILGRIM ASSOCIATION FOOTBALL TEAM DEFEATS ST. LOUIS ELEVEN, 10 TO 0

PILGRIM FOOTBALL TEAM OVERWHELMS LOCAL ELEVEN.

BUSY MOMENT DURING INTERNATIONAL FOOTBALL CONTEST

MILNES PRAISES ST. LOUIS PLAYERS.

POINTS ON THE BIG FOOTBALL GAME.

The September 23, 1905, edition of the *St. Louis Republic* covers the first game played by an English team in St. Louis. **NEWSPAPERS.COM**

The Pilgrims returned to St. Louis in 1909, with results similar to those in 1905: They won all four of their games in 1909 by a combined score of 31–2. But the most important outcome was that local teams adopted the Pilgrims' skillful playing style, making St. Louis soccer a better game.

Pilgrims of England 10, St. Louis All-Stars 0

International friendly at League Park (later called Robison Field), Natural Bridge and Vandeventer

ST. LOUIS (first names given if known): GK Jack "Gas Pipe" Tully; LB Corcoran; RB Ricksteiger; LHB M. Devaney; CHB D. Devaney; RHB John "King" Finnegan; OL Cunningham; IL Tim Daly; CF Phil Kavanaugh; IR John "Butch" Ammann; OR Johnny Comerford

PILGRIMS: GK Sir Charles Kirkpatrick; LB F.S. Walmesley; RB Fred Milnes; LHB W.H. Nuttall; CHB J.D. Barnesdale; RHB Cuthbert Storey; OL J. Bryning; IL C. Coopland; CF Vivian Woodward; IR Tommy Fletcher; OR Jim Raine

GOALS (exact details unknown): Fletcher 2, Woodward "more than half" of the goals, Raine at least one

REFEREE: Paul McSweeney

ATTENDANCE: 10,000 (estimated)

The December 18, 1926, edition of the *St. Louis Athlete* shows fans at Sportsman's Park watching a St. Louis League match.
DUNN FAMILY COLLECTION

NOVEMBER 3, 1907

PRO SOCCER RAISES CURTAIN ON 31-YEAR RUN

THE ST. LOUIS Soccer Football League played its first games, beginning a 31-year run of professional soccer in St. Louis.

About 3,000 fans watched a doubleheader at the new Athletic Park in north St. Louis. St. Teresa topped the Thistles, 3–0, in the opener. The second game ended 2–2 between Innisfails and St. Matthews. Innisfails and the Thistles used players primarily from Benld, Illinois. Innisfails finished first and St. Matthews second in the 1907–08 season.

St. Louis leagues operated as early as 1884, but the St. Louis Soccer Football League paid players from gate receipts. Players occasionally earned more money from big crowds than players in England, where wages were capped at four pounds per week.

The St. Louis Soccer Football League experienced a mutiny of two teams that formed a new league, also called the St. Louis League, for the 1913–14 season. Confusion reigned until the leagues merged into one for the 1915–16 season. The new St. Louis Soccer League, usually with four teams playing Sunday doubleheaders primarily at Sportsman's Park, continued until 1938.

League teams reached the US Open Cup finals 13 times, winning five: Ben Miller (1920), Scullin Steel (1922), Stix (1933, 1934), and Central Brewers (1935).

St. Teresa 3, Thistles 0

ST. TERESA (first names unknown)**:** GK Dooling; FB Coppinger, January; HB Thornton, Devoy, Zarchell; F McNiff, Hoffman, Peltier, McNamara, Haggerty

THISTLES (first names unknown)**:** GK Reid; FB Donald, Weakes; HB Cairus, J. Gunn, C. Gunn; F Wotherspoon, Murray, Bingham, Corlett, Brady

GOALS: McNamara 2, Peltier

REFEREE: Dick Jarrett

Innisfails 2, St. Matthews 2

INNISFAILS: (first names given if known)**:** GK Sam Robertson; FB A. Ricksteiger, J. Robertson; HB Pete Harris, J. O'Berty, J. Frew; F Pepper, George Fincery, S. Harris, Yates, C. O'Berty

ST. MATTHEWS: (first names given if known)**:** GK Behan; FB V. Harris, Mike Corcoran; HB McNamara, Mike Devaney, Clancy; F Eddie Ryan, Sullivan, McHugh, Tate, Flanagan

GOALS: Frew (I), Fincery (I), Walsh (S), Clancy (S)

REFEREE: Dick Jarrett

ATTENDANCE: 3,000 (estimated)

OCTOBER 25, 1912

MILLION-FAN MUNY LEAGUE LAUNCHES

A MEETING of interested teams and organizers at the St. Louis Municipal Courts Building resulted in the founding of the Municipal Soccer League. The Muny League, as it was known, was the first structured amateur soccer league in St. Louis with an executive committee and an appeals process.

The league became wildly successful, at its height drawing more than a million fans per season. The league's popularity resulted from free admission (except, in some cases, for playoff games) and a belief that the level of competition rivaled that of the professional St. Louis League, which charged admission.

While the pros often won head-to-head matches with Muny teams, many of the games were fiercely contested and close in score. One of the most memorable of those games was on March 29, 1925, when Henses, the Muny League runners-up, upset the pros' Vesper Buick, 1924 US Open Cup runners-up, 1–0.

By 1946, the Muny League had grown to 114 teams for men and boys. Citing rising costs and declining revenue, the league folded in 1957. The CYC and Khoury leagues filled the gap in St. Louis amateur soccer left by the end of the Muny League.

Henses, a team sponsored by Henses Market in Dogtown, gave one of the finest performances in the history of the amateur Muny League when the club upset the professional Vesper Buick team of the St. Louis League, 1–0, on March 29, 1925. Vesper lost in the finals of the 1924 US Open Cup. **WEBSTER UNIVERSITY**

DECEMBER 29, 1912

ST. LEO'S BEATS EAST'S BEST FOR MYTHICAL NATIONAL CHAMPIONSHIP

THE *NEW YORK TIMES* declared St. Leo's of St. Louis as the nation's soccer champion after St. Leo's defeated West Hudson (New Jersey), 4–2, in St. Louis.

This was the first victory by a St. Louis team over a powerful Eastern club. At a time before the US Open Cup, West Hudson had won the American Cup the previous season. St. Leo's was on a run of 10 city championships and was the best team in St. Louis soccer before 1920.

St. Leo's 4, West Hudson (NJ) 2

Friendly at Sportsman's Park

ST. LEO'S (first names given if known): GK Duke Sheahan; LB Bill Abstein; RB James Flynn; LHB Johnny Miller; CHB Swede Petersen; RHB McCarthy; OL Billy Monahan; IL William Tallman; CF Richard "Bull" Brannigan; IR Punky McCormack; OR James Donahue

WEST HUDSON (first names given if known): GK William Lickley; LB A. Kettles; RB J. Wilson; LHB D. Lawson; CHB Bob Lennox; RHB R. McKay; OL H. "Buck" Cooper; IL P. Adamson; CF G. Richardson; IR F.C.W. Elliott; OR J. Fachie

GOALS: Monahan (SL), Petersen (SL), Donahue (SL), Lennox (WH) 2, Kettles (WH) OG

REFEREE: Paul McSweeney

ATTENDANCE: 6,000 (estimated)

St. Leo's, 1911. Back row (L-R): Swede Petersen, Duke Sheehan, Bill Abstein, BIlly Monahan. Middle: Al Sucher, Johnny Miller, William Tallman. Front: James Donahue, Punky McCormack, Richard "Bull" Brannigan, James Flynn

LOUISA H. BOWEN UNIVERSITY ARCHIVES AND SPECIAL COLLECTIONS, SOUTHERN ILLINOIS UNIVERSITY AT EDWARDSVILLE

By virtue of their victory over West Hudson, "St. Leo . . . annexed the American soccer championship," according to the *New York Times*.

West Hudson took some solace in the fact that the match was their third in five days in St. Louis. West Hudson won and tied against other St. Louis teams.

St. Leo's manager, Billy Klosterman, transformed St. Leo's from a parish team to a professional club in 1906. He led the team to its 10 city championships and its momentous victory over West Hudson, earning St. Leo's the title of "the most famous team in the United States" by the authoritative *Spalding's Official Soccer Foot Ball Guide* of 1913.

APRIL 2, 1916

MAA'S MARATHON MEN WIN MUNY TITLE IN 212-MINUTE MATCH

THE MISSOURI Athletic Association prevailed in a marathon Municipal League championship game, 3–1, over Christian Brothers College, then a school for elementary, secondary, and college males, before 10,000 fans.

The game to crown the city's amateur soccer champions required three hours and 32 minutes to complete and is believed to be the longest soccer match played up to that point in St. Louis. The teams tied, 1–1, in a match called after 90 regulation minutes and four eight-minute overtimes on March 26. The replay on April 2 went the regulation 90.

Missouri Athletic Association 3, CBC 1

Muny League championship at Fairground Park 2

MAA: GK Charlie LaBarge; LB Herman Zeigenbalg; RB Al Oberle; LHB Al Schlesinger; CHB Frank Szepanski; RHB John King (Ed Britton); OL Jimmy DeLaney; IL Johnny Marre; CF Rube Potee; IR Granville McCormack; OR Tommy O'Toole

CBC (first names given if known): GK Mayer; LB Paul Murphy; RB G. Bentley (Danny Murphy); LHB Anse Murphy; CHB Billy Quinn; RHB Tommy O'Hanlon; OL Moran; IL Dunn; CF Miles; IR Bryne (Flavin); OR George Corrigan

GOALS: McCormack (M), Marre (M), Potee (M) (OG by D. Murphy), Corrigan (C)

REFEREE: Ollie Miller, Timers Tommy Lyster, Otto Kaiser

LINESMEN: J.J. Kelly, Frank Healy, Alex Kennedy, Phil Kavanaugh

ATTENDANCE: 10,000 (estimated)

CBC, the defending champion, was a team "of which three-fourths are schoolboys, who have plenty of time to train," while the MAA team was "made up entirely of boys who work from morning to night," according to the April 3, 1916, *St. Louis Globe-Democrat*.

Playing in the rain on "ground soft and very wet," Johnny Marre scored the winning goal 32 minutes into the match. Marre's goal put the MAA ahead, 2–0. CBC cut the lead to 2–1 about 12 minutes into the second half, but an own goal on a deflection off the head of CBC defender Danny Murphy sealed the victory for the MAA.

The *St. Louis Star-Times* describes the epic 1916 Muny League final in the newspaper's edition of April 3, 1916.
NEWSPAPERS.COM

M. A. A. SOCCER TEAM IS AMATEUR CHAMP

Amateur soccer champions of St. Louis, season of 1915-16—Missouri Athletic Association eleven.

In a brilliantly played game, through a drizzling rain, the Cherry Diamond kickers defeated the Christian Brothers' College team at Fairground Park, Sunday afternoon, 3 to 1. A crowd of about 8,000 or 10,000 watched the game.

Wonderful defensive work on the part of the M. A. A. won the match and the championship. The backfield, composed of Oberle and Ziegenbalg, fullbacks, and King, Szpanski and Schlesinger, halfbacks, played the game "safe" at all stages. The fullbacks never left their penalty area and the halves seldom passed center. These tactics beat the College. Had the M. A. A. backs played out, Dunn, Corrigan and Co. would undoubtedly have counted several times.

TEN LONG SHOTS.

Nine out of ten of the College shots were long ones from outside the penalty area. This stye of shooting should have brought good results when the ball was so slippery but Charlie LaBarge handled all of them cleanly.

Granville McCormack shot the first goal of the game. In trying to hook a boot which he should have packed up to the goal-tender, Fullback Bentley miscued and Granville put a regular Bull Brannigan shot halfback's kick, Johnny Marre close in and drove the second goal through for the M. A. A. in the latter part of the first half. The C. B. C. tally came in the second half by virtue of some beautiful passing and shooting. Corrigan was the man who toed the leather through.

COME BACK STRONG.

Seeming to like the experience of shooting goals, the Brothers came back strong and started a bombardment of the Reds' goal. Here was where the great defensive work showed to its best advantage. At last, Oberle cleared the ball, Marre got it and carried it past two College men. He passed to Potee at center and the latter crossed to Tommy O'Toole at outside right. Tom brought the ball up and then returned a beautiful cross to Potee. "Rube" fooled O'Hanlon and shifted the ball to his left foot and let 'er sail. Halfback Murphy attempted to head the shot but only succeeded in deflecting it into one corner of the net. In justice to Murphy it must be said that the ball was labeled for the upper corner before he touched it.

Undoubtedly C. B. C. would have played a better game on a dry field but neither Brother Hubert nor the players will use this argument to detract from the glory of the M. A. A. victory.

SEPTEMBER 3, 1916

DIEDRICHSEN FIRST ST. LOUISAN TO PLAY FOR UNITED STATES

MATT DIEDRICHSEN became the first of many St. Louisans to represent their country in soccer when he played in a 1–1 tie with Norway for the All-American Football Club.

The squad is considered the first US National Team. Former St. Louisan Tom Cahill organized the tour and managed the team. Cahill, a player, manager, and promoter in St. Louis, moved to New York in 1910 and helped found the US Soccer Federation in 1913.

All-American Football Club 1, Norway 1

Friendly at Frogner Stadium, Kristiania (later renamed Oslo), Norway

ALL-AMERICAN: GK George Tintle; LB Dick Spalding; RB James Robertson; LHB Clarence Smith; CHB Neil Clarke; RHB Thomas Murray; OL Thomas Swords; IL Matt Diedrichsen; CF Charles Ellis; IR John Heminsley; OR James Ford

NORWAY: GK Ingolf Pedersen; LB Yngvar Tørnros; RB Otto Aulie; LHB Gunnar Andersen; CHB Per Haraldsen; RHB Raganvald Smedvik; OL Per Helsing; IL Kaare Engebretsen; CF Halfdan Ditlev-Simonsen; IR David Andersen; OR Rolf Aas

GOALS: Ellis (A), Engebretsen (N)

REFEREE: Ernst Albihn

LINESMEN: Arne Wendelborg, Harry Cooper

ATTENDANCE: 12,000 or 25,000 (estimated)

Matt Diedrichsen (No. 14) and the All-American Football Club. Back (L-R): Charles Ellis, George Tintle, Dick Spalding, Tom Cahill, Walter Burgin, Clarence Smith. Middle: James Robertson, Thomas Murray, Neil Clarke, Albert Blakey. Front: James Ford, Thomas Swords, John Heminsley, Diedrichsen, Harry Cooper
SPALDING'S SOCCER OFFICIAL FOOT BALL GUIDE (1916–17)

Diedrichsen's appearance against Norway was his only one for the United States. Diedrichsen suffered a knee injury in the 35th minute and left the match, leaving the Americans a man short. (The Laws of the Game did not allow substitutions at that time.) The injury and World War I—Diedrichsen served as a gunners' mate on the USS *Nebraska* in 1918—kept him out of St. Louis soccer until 1919.

A reliable goal-scorer at inside left in the 2-3-5 pyramid formation, Diedrichsen played professionally for Innisfails in St. Louis before the war and for various other pro teams afterward. Most importantly, he opened the door for more than 75 St. Louis men and women who have reached the highest level of soccer: playing for their country.

SEPTEMBER 23, 1916

RATICAN ON A ROLL IN BETHLEHEM STEEL DEBUT

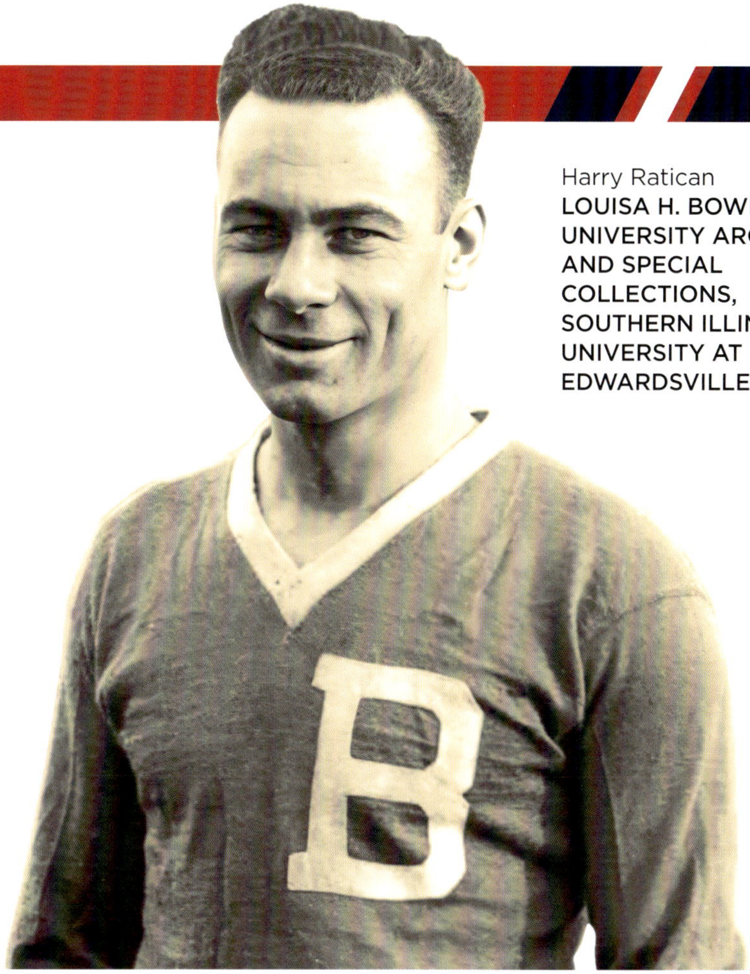

Harry Ratican
LOUISA H. BOWEN UNIVERSITY ARCHIVES AND SPECIAL COLLECTIONS, SOUTHERN ILLINOIS UNIVERSITY AT EDWARDSVILLE

HARRY RATICAN required just 45 minutes to show that St. Louisans could excel on the national stage. Playing his first game for Bethlehem (Pennsylvania) Steel, the East's best team, he scored twice in the first half and added a third in the second as Bethlehem blasted West Hudson (Harrison, New Jersey), 7–0, in the season opener. He assisted on two other goals.

Ratican, one of many players developed at Christian Brothers College, scored almost at will for St. Teresa's in 1914–15 and Ben Miller in 1915–16. Word got out about the big, fast, and hard-shooting center forward. Bethlehem Steel, a team built primarily with players from Britain and winner of the 1915 and 1916 National Challenge Cups (today's US Open Cup), enlisted Ratican for the 1916–17 season.

Ratican helped Bethlehem Steel to Cup titles in 1918 and 1919 and Robins Dry Dock to a Cup championship in 1921. He coached the soccer team at the US Military Academy in 1922. Ratican returned to St. Louis for good in 1923, where he played until 1928.

Regarded as the best American-born player of his time, Ratican was in the first class inducted into the US Soccer Hall of Fame in 1950.

Bethlehem Steel 7, West Hudson (Harrison, NJ) 0

Season opener at Bethlehem, PA

BETHLEHEM: GK William Duncan; LB Jack Ferguson; RB Sam Fletcher; LHB Bobby Morrison; CHB Dugald Campbell; RHB Willie Kirkpatrick; OL Tommy "Whitey" Fleming; IL Paddy Butler; CF Harry Ratican; IR Fred Pepper; OR George McKelvey

WEST HUDSON (first names unknown): GK Explin; LB Lennox; RB Barr; LHB Wenst; CHB Ellicot; RHB Smyth; OL Brown; IL Miller; CF Allen; IR Seegal; OR Brierly

GOALS: Ratican 3, Fleming 3 (one a PK), Butler

REFEREE: James Walters

LINESMEN: Mills, Forrest

ATTENDANCE: Unknown

DECEMBER 24–25, 1916

ST. LOUIS TEAMS TOP AND TIE BETHLEHEM STEEL

BETHLEHEM STEEL, winner of five US Open Cups from 1915 to 1926, already was a legend in the making when the team visited St. Louis for two exhibition matches.

The Pennsylvania steel giant signed the best players, typically from Great Britain, that money could buy. An exception was St. Louisan Harry Ratican, a high-scoring player considered one of the best developed in St. Louis. Steel money lured him to Bethlehem in 1916.

Bethlehem won the Open Cup (then the National Challenge Cup) in 1915 and 1916. The Cup, started in 1914 and symbolic of the US national champion, was generally out of reach for St. Louisans. The rigors and expenses of traveling to Cup games in the East kept St. Louis teams from entering.

The results thrilled St. Louisans. A team of St. Louis all-stars rallied from a 1–0 halftime deficit to defeat Bethlehem, 3–1, on December 24. The next day, the Ben Millers, 1916 champions of the professional St. Louis League, tied Bethlehem, 2–2. Further vindication of St. Louis soccer was that Ratican scored two of Bethlehem's three goals.

Ben Miller's 1916–17 team. Back (L-R): Al McHenry, Dick Fitzgibbon, Paul Murphy, Joe Lancaster, Hap Marre, Jimmy Dunn. Middle: Billy Quinn, C.F. Miller, Zarschal. Front: Ben W. Miller, Rube Potee, Honus King, Frank Shea, Pete McLaughlin, Manager Pete Ratican
SPALDING'S SOCCER OFFICIAL FOOT BALL GUIDE (1917–18)

Bethlehem Steel and Ben Miller line up for their match at Robison Field.
SPALDING'S SOCCER OFFICIAL FOOT BALL GUIDE (1917–18)

Bethlehem Steel's 1916–17 team. 1. Treasurer J. Machen, 2. Dick Spalding, 3. MacDonald, 4. George McKelvey, 5. Sam Fletcher, 6. Thomas Murray, 7. Bland, 8. Fred Pepper, 9. Manager Edgar Lewis, 10. William Duncan, 11. Dugald Campbell, 12. Neil Clarke, 13. Harry Ratican, 14. Jack Ferguson, 15. Robert Morrison, 16. Paddy Butler, 17. George Forrest, 18. Business Manager Harry Trend, 19. Willie Kirkpatrick, 20. Miles Chadwick, 21. Tommy "Whitey" Fleming **SPALDING'S SOCCER OFFICIAL FOOT BALL GUIDE (1917–18)**

December 24, 1916

St. Louis All-Stars 3, Bethlehem Steel 1

Friendly at Robison Field

ST. LOUIS: GK Duke Sheahan; LB Bill Abstein; RB Tate Brady; LHB Pete Harris; CHB Jack Callahan; RHB Johnny Miller; OL Al Maender; IL James "Dike" Brannigan; CF Allie Schwarz; IR Rich "Bull" Brannigan (Eddie Mulligan); OR Gert Kehrman

BETHLEHEM (first names given if known)**:** GK Willliam Duncan; LB Jack Ferguson; RB Sam Fletcher; LHB Willie Kirkpatrick; CHB Dugald Campbell; RHB Thomas Murray; OL Tommy "Whitey" Fleming; IL Paddy Butler; CF Harry Ratican; IR Fred Pepper; OR McDonald

GOALS: Ratican (B), Schwarz (S), Callahan (S), Kerhman (S)

REFEREE: Phil Kavanaugh

ATTENDANCE: 5,200 (estimated)

December 25, 1916

Ben Miller 2, Bethlehem Steel 2

Friendly at Robison Field

BEN MILLER: GK Honus King; LB Frank "Doc" Shea; RB Joe Lancaster; LHB Billy Quinn; CHB Len Zarschal; RHB Paul Murphy; OL Rube Potee; IL Hap Marre; CF Dick Fitzgibbon; IR Jimmy Dunn; OR Al McHenry

BETHLEHEM (first names given if known)**:** GK William Duncan (Jim Easton); LB George McKelvey; RB Sam Fletcher; LHB Thomas Murray; CHB Neil Clarke; RHB Dugald Campbell; OL Tommy "Whitey" Fleming; IL Jim Easton (MacDonald); CF Harry Ratican; IR Willie Kirkpatrick; OR Fred Pepper

GOALS: Ratican (B) 35, Potee (BM) (PK) 44, McHenry (BM) (second half), Fleming (B) (late in second half)

REFEREE: Phil Kavanaugh

ATTENDANCE: 6,000 (estimated)

MAY 9, 1920

HATS OFF TO BEN MILLER'S FIRST NATIONAL TITLE FOR ST. LOUIS

ON A banner day for US soccer, the Ben Millers defeated Fore River of Quincy, Massachusetts, 2–1 in the National Challenge Cup final in St. Louis.

The Cup was the first of more than 90 national soccer championships won by St. Louis teams. More importantly for American soccer, the all–St. Louis Ben Millers were the first team of native-born players to win the Cup, first awarded in 1914 and today called the US Open Cup. Fore River, a subsidiary of soccer giant Bethlehem Steel, was comprised completely of English and Scottish players.

Ben Miller, St. Louis's first national championship team. Back (L-R): Owner Ben Miller, Manager Pete Ratican, St. Louis League president Winton Barker, George Miller, Al McHenry, Hap Marre, Larry Riley, Tommy O'Hanlon, US Football Association president Peter Peel, St. Louis soccer official Phil Riley. Front: USFA executive secretary Tom Cahill, Johnny Redden, Joe Lancaster, Rube Potee, Billy Quinn, Jimmy Johnston, Jimmy Dunn, Charley McGarry
DUNN FAMILY COLLECTION

Ben Miller 2, Fore River (Quincy, MA) 1

National Challenge (today's US Open) Cup final at High School Field, also called Federal League Park and Federal Field, located at Grand and Laclede

BEN MILLER: GK Charley McGarry; LB Jimmy Johnston; RB Joe Lancaster; LHB Tommy O'Hanlon; CHB Billy Quinn; RHB Johnny Redden; OL Rube Potee; IL Hap Marre; CF Jimmy Dunn; IR Larry Reilly; OR Al McHenry

FORE RIVER: GK Jimmy Lambie; LB Tommy Littlejohn; RB William Parkinson; LHB Joe Black; CHB George Green; RHB William Daly; OL James Daly; IL Tommy Underwood; CF Jack Kershaw; IR David Page; OR Jimmy Farquhar

GOALS: Marre (B) 22, Kershaw (F) 35, Dunn (B) 63

SAVES: McGarry (B) 3, Lambie (F) 8

REFEREE: Alex McKenzie

LINESMEN: Phil Kavanaugh, Paul McSweeney

ATTENDANCE: 10,000–12,000 (estimated)

Fans saw Jimmy Dunn earn his place in St. Louis soccer history with the score tied 1–1 midway through the second half. A Ben Miller player saw Dunn centered in front of the goal and fed him the ball. Dunn one-timed it into the net.

The goal stood up and Dunn was on his way to the US Soccer Hall of Fame. The "Hatters," as they were called because of their sponsorship by locally owned Ben Miller Hat Co., were the nation's soccer champions.

The 1919–20 season was the first in which St. Louis teams entered the Cup. They reached the finals 13 times in 18 seasons starting in 1920.

MARCH 19, 1922

SCULLIN STEEL OVERCOMES 2-0 DEFICIT TO WIN US TITLE

IN A rematch of the 1921 final, Scullin Steel topped Todd Shipyards of Brooklyn, New York, 3–2, on Allie Schwarz's 86th-minute goal in the National Challenge Cup title match in St. Louis.

Local players filled Scullin Steel's roster, led by coach, captain, and starting fullback Tate Brady. He guided Scullin to the 1921 Cup final, losing, 4–2, to Robins Dry Dock. Robins changed names to Todd Shipyards the next season.

Robins/Todd fielded almost all foreign players. St. Louisan and US Soccer Hall of Famer Harry Ratican was an exception. He assisted on Todd's first goal in the 17th minute of the 1922 final. Todd struck again just two minutes later. Tate Brady's brother, Cliff, made it 2–1. Schwarz tied it with his first of two goals in the 71st minute.

But fate tricked Scullin on April Fool's Day 1923. Scullin reached the final for the third consecutive year and fought the Paterson (New Jersey) Silk Sox to a 2–2 draw in Harrison, New Jersey, on April 1. The replay was scheduled a week later in Harrison. But four Scullin players, who also played pro baseball, were off to spring training. With several others injured, Scullin forfeited the replay.

Scullin Steel 3, Todd Shipyards 2

National Challenge (today's US Open) Cup final at High School Field

SCULLIN: GK Harry Oellerman; LB Tate Brady; RB George Bentley; LHB Joe Nolan; CHB Len Zarschal; RHB Joe Hennessey; OL Emmet Mulvey; IL Jim Brannigan; CF Allie Schwarz; IR Cliff Brady; OR Charles Bechtold

TODD: GK Pete Renzulli; LB William Whitehead; RB Adam Smith; LHB Joseph Irvine; CHB James Campbell; RHB Bill Fryer; OL Peter Sweeney; IL Frank McKenna; CF Harry Ratican; IR Jack McGuire; OR George McKelvey

GOALS: McGuire (T) (Ratican) 17, McGuire (T) 19, Brady (S) (Bechtold) 37, Schwarz (S) (Hennessey) 71, Schwarz (S) 86

SAVES: Oellerman (S) 13, Renzulli (T) 7

REFEREE: George Young

LINESMEN: Phil Kavanaugh, Paul McSweeney

ATTENDANCE: 8,568

Scullin Steel's national champions. Back (L-R): Al Oberle, Dan Murphy, George Bentley, Tate Brady, Harry Oellermann, Len Zarschal, Emmet Mulvey, Jim Nolan, Tom O'Hanlon, Leo Diel. Front: Charles Bechtold, Cliff Brady, Allie Schwarz, Joe Hennessey, Jim "Dike" Brannigan
SPALDING'S OFFICIAL SOCCER FOOT BALL GUIDE (1922–23)

DECEMBER 17, 1929

ST. LOUIS SOCCER MOVES INDOORS

A CROWD of 6,200 watched what was believed to be a first in St. Louis: indoor soccer. The Arena, which opened on September 23, 1929, played host to the match, the featured game of a doubleheader that opened with a high school football contest. Proceeds benefited disabled veterans.

Following East St. Louis High's 6–0 victory over a group of St. Louis all-stars in football, all-stars from the professional St. Louis League defeated an aggregation of foreign-born players from southern Illinois mining companies, 1–0.

St. Louis Arena
MISSOURI HISTORICAL SOCIETY

St. Louis Professionals 1, Southern Illinois All-Stars 0

Indoor friendly at the Arena

ST. LOUIS: GK Charlie LaBarge; LB Joe Hand; RB George Bentley or Tommy Erbe; LHB Erbe or George Schweppe; CHB Eddie Burke; RHB Bill Lehman; OL Tal Mulroy; IL Eddie Hart; CF John "Dinty" Moore; IR Lou Ahrens; OR Harry Bochnicek

SOUTHERN ILLINOIS: GK Bernard "Brownie" Witunski; LB Walter Patterson; RB Bob Smith; LHB Jimmy Slack; CHB Matt Robinson; RHB Posey McClintick; OL John Witunski; IL Leslie Ward; CF Walter Smillie; IR Peggy Barlow; OR Jimmy Coulson

GOAL: Moore (Lehman) 30:30

TIME OF HALVES: 30 minutes

REFEREE: Oscar Mossman

ATTENDANCE: 6,200

Reports highlighted the biggest issue: too many men on the field. The full outdoor complement of 11 players was on the floor for each team trying to replicate outdoor soccer on a smaller indoor field.

The home team broke through on a goal by John "Dinty" Moore off a well-placed cross from Bill Lehman. One account of the game ended prophetically: "If nothing else, the test showed that indoor soccer, with probably seven men on a team, could be played to advantage during inclement weather." Almost exactly 50 years later, the St. Louis Steamers of the Major Indoor Soccer League played their first-ever home game at the same facility, playing six-aside soccer before a sellout crowd of 18,005.

APRIL 23, 1933

STIX STARTS THREE-YEAR STREAK OF NATIONAL CHAMPIONSHIPS

BOLSTERED BY players who had been their nemeses a year before, Stix, Baer & Fuller returned St. Louis to American soccer's pinnacle by clinching the National Challenge Cup with a 2–1 triumph over the New York Americans.

Stix won the best-of-three series two games to none. Stix won the opener, 1–0, at Sportsman's Park on April 16.

Willie McLean opened the scoring in game two on a pass from Ollie Bohlman in the 15th minute, then delivered a corner kick that Werner Nilsen headed into the net with seven minutes to play. The Cup clincher was St. Louis's first since Scullin Steel had won in 1922.

Stix reached the Cup final for the second consecutive year, thanks especially to players from the American Soccer League's (ASL's) New Bedford Whalers, who had defeated Stix in 1932. The ASL collapsed the next season. Four Whalers—Bill McPherson and future US Soccer Hall of Famers Nilsen, Billy Gonsalves, and Alex McNab—joined Stix over the course of the 1932–33 season.

SOCCER SCRIMMAGES WHEN STIX WON TITLE. INTERESTING ACTION PLAYS ARE SHOWN HERE AS NEW YORK TEAM LOST IN FINALS

The *St. Louis Star and Times* edition of April 24, 1933, shows some of the action in the second game of the National Challenge Cup finals.
NEWSPAPERS.COM

New York Americans goalkeeper Stan Chesney leaps for the ball over a Stix player in the first game of the National Challenge Cup finals at Sportsman's Park on April 16, 1933.
MISSOURI HISTORICAL SOCIETY

Stix, Baer & Fuller 2, New York Americans 1

Game two, National Challenge (today's US Open) Cup best-of-three series at Starlight Park, New York. Stix won series, two games to none.

NEW YORK: GK Stan Chesney; LB George Moorhouse; RB Teddy Glover; LHB Willie Ballantyne; CHB Bob Fleming; RHB James Hendren; OL George Milne; IL Shamus O'Brien; CF George Michaels (Auerbach); IR Moritz Hausler; OR Erno Schwarcz

STIX: GK Charley LaBarge; LB Jimmy Nolan; RB Bill Lehman; LHB Ollie Bohlman; CHB Bill Watson; RHB Bill McPherson; OL Willie McLean; IL Jimmy Roe; CF Werner Nilsen; IR Billy Gonsalves; OR Alex McNab

GOALS: McLean (S) (Bohlman) 15, Michaels (N) 29, Nilsen (S) (McLean) 83

REFEREE: Patrick Howley

LINESMEN: Ed Donaghy, William Murray

ATTENDANCE: 4,200

APRIL 16, 1934

STIX ROUTS RANGERS FOR SECOND CUP CHAMPIONSHIP

A DAY late, Stix, Baer & Fuller of St. Louis retained the National Challenge Cup by beating the Pawtucket (Rhode Island) Rangers, 5–0, in the third and deciding game of the series.

Rain postponed the game originally scheduled for the afternoon of Sunday, April 15, at Walsh Memorial Stadium in St. Louis. The game was moved to Monday night at Walsh, making it the first National Challenge Cup final played under the lights.

Referee Tom Crompton halted play early in the first half when Stix captain Alex McNab complained that flashbulbs from photographers' cameras were blinding his team. "The arbiter obliged the St. Louis captain and had the cameramen chased," according to the *St. Louis Globe-Democrat*'s Harry Mitauer.

Stix won the opener, 4–2, at Walsh Stadium April 1 and Pawtucket prevailed, 3–2, at Pawtucket April 8. US Soccer Hall of Famer Billy Gonsalves, considered one of the best players in American soccer history, "uncorked his finest effort of the season" in game three. Gonsalves opened the scoring on a header in the 41st minute. Stix broke open the game with four second-half goals, one by Gonsalves, two by US Soccer Hall of Famer Werner Nilsen, and one by Willie McLean.

Above: Artist's concept of Walsh Memorial Stadium
NATIONAL BUILDING ARTS CENTER, NATIONALBUILDINGARTS.ORG
Left: Billy Gonsalves
LOUISA H. BOWEN UNIVERSITY ARCHIVES AND SPECIAL COLLECTIONS, SOUTHERN ILLINOIS UNIVERSITY AT EDWARDSVILLE

Stix, Baer & Fuller 5, Pawtucket (RI) Rangers 0

Game three of best-of-three National Challenge Cup finals at Walsh Memorial Stadium

STIX: GK James McGowan; LB Jimmy Nolan; RB Bill Lehman; LH Harry Hebberger; CH Billy Watson; RH Bill McPherson; OL Willie McLean; IL Jimmy Roe, CF Werner Nilsen; IR Billy Gonsalves; OR Alex McNab

PAWTUCKET: GK Johnny Conroy; LB Donald Ferrie; RB Ed Czerkiewicz; LH Andy Auld; CH Antone Raposa; RH Joe Martinelli; OL Tom Florie; IL Jimmy McAuley (Sandy Park); CF Bob McIntyre; IR Walter Dick; OR Johnny Harvey (Stewart)

GOALS: Gonsalves (McNab) 41, Gonsalves (Roe) 55, Nilsen (McLean) 70, McLean (McNab) 80, Nilsen (McLean) 81

REFEREE: Thomas Crompton

LINESMEN: Robert Murphy, Jimmy Dunn

ATTENDANCE: 8,000 (7,657 paid)

Stix, Baer & Fuller vs. Ben Miller at Sportsman's Park in the early 1930s
LOUISA H. BOWEN UNIVERSITY ARCHIVES AND SPECIAL COLLECTIONS, SOUTHERN ILLINOIS UNIVERSITY AT EDWARDSVILLE

MAY 12, 1935

CUP THREE-PEAT FOR ST. LOUIS

SPORTING A new name, the same team won its third consecutive National Challenge Cup on aggregate goals over the Pawtucket (Rhode Island) Rangers.

Central Breweries of East St. Louis, Illinois, assumed sponsorship of two-time defending Cup winner Stix, Baer & Fuller following the 1933–34 season.

The newly named Central Brewers added a key ingredient in November 1933: Bert Patenaude. The US Soccer Hall of Famer from Fall River, Massachusetts, had scored the first hat trick in World Cup history in 1930. Joining US Soccer Hall of Famers Billy Gonsalves, Alex McNab, and Jimmy Roe on the forward line, Patenaude scored two goals in the Cup opener in St. Louis as Central breezed to a 5–2 victory on April 28.

The teams tied, 1–1, in Pawtucket on May 5 in what was scheduled as a best-of-three series, prompting a ruling that the Cup would be decided on goal differential after game three in Newark on May 12. The Rangers won, 3–1, but Central Brewers captured the Cup with seven total goals to the Rangers' six.

The team lost in the next two Cup finals as the St. Louis Shamrocks. The 1935 Cup was the last for a St. Louis side until 1948.

Central Brewers, 1934–35 National Challenge Cup champions. Back (L-R): Johnny Hamm, Frank Pastor, Ed Kane, Bill Lehman, Maury Kramer, Jimmy Nolan, Ollie Bohlman, Harry Hebberger, Bob Gregg, Trainer Lou "Mouse" Dietrich, Manager Andy Frederick. Front: Alex McNab, Billy Gonsalves, Bert Patenaude, Jimmy Roe, Willie McLean
ROE FAMILY COLLECTION

Pawtucket Rangers 3, Central Brewers 1

Game three, National Challenge (today's US Open) Cup, at Newark School Stadium, New Jersey. Central Brewers won series 7–6 on aggregate goals.

PAWTUCKET: GK Johnny Conroy or Sandy Park (accounts differ); LB Joe Bowden; RB Ed Czerkiecwicz; LHB Joe Martinelli; CHB Antone Raposa; RHB Bill McPherson; OL Frank Moniz; IL Jimmy McAuley; CF Bob McIntyre; IR Walter Dick; OR Johnny Harvey (Smith)

CENTRAL BREWERIES: GK Johnny Hamm; LB Jimmy Nolan; RB Maurice Kramer (Bob Gregg); LHB Harry Hebberger (Ollie Bohlman); CHB Bill Lehman; RHB Eddie Kane; OL Willie McLean; IL Jimmy Roe; CF Bert Patenaude; IR Billy Gonsalves; OR Alex McNab

GOALS: McLean (C) 20; McIntyre (P) 52; Dick (P) 54, 80

REFEREE: Andrew Tehel

LINESMEN: Fred Coggins, J.A. Cation

ATTENDANCE: 2,000 or 3,000 (accounts differ)

JUNE 23, 1946

SCHUMACHER WINS FIRST JUNIOR CUP FOR ST. LOUIS

ST. LOUIS teams, dominant in the men's National Challenge Cup since 1920, began a long run of success in the under-19 boys' US Junior Cup in 1946.

Schumacher of St. Louis won the 1946 US Junior Cup for the second consecutive year on the field. Schumacher, which had to forfeit its 1945 Cup, kept the title in 1946 after beating Prague of New York, 2–0, in the championship game.

Schumacher forfeited the title in 1945 when it was discovered that three Schumacher players had appeared in games with senior teams earlier that season.

Schumacher 2, Prague (New York) 0

US Junior Cup championship game at Throggs Neck Stadium, New York

PRAGUE (first names unavailable): GK Romano; LB Matejov; RB Cividanes; LHB Kriezek; CHB Zacek; RHB Cruz; OL Caputi; IL Helenek; CF Baran; IR Prochazka; OR Johnston

SCHUMACHER (first names given if known): GK Albert Pidgeon; LB Bob Annis; RB Ralph Stocker; LHB Holmes; CHB Henry Lincks; RHB Tucker; OL Warren Smith; IL Paul Douglas; CF Bill Brady; IR Bellers; OR Farina

GOALS: Brady (Smith) 12, Douglas 65

REFEREE: Sam Galin

LINESMEN: J. Zirbes, E. Sotzek

TIME OF HALVES: 35 minutes

ATTENDANCE: 1,000 (estimated)

In 1946, Schumacher scored just 12 minutes into the final when Bill Brady drove home a pass from Warren Smith. The teams battled fiercely the rest of the way. Schumacher's tough defense, led by right fullback Ralph Stocker, US Soccer Hall of Famer Bob Annis, and goalkeeper Albert Pidgeon, stymied the home team. Paul Douglas sealed the victory with an insurance goal with five minutes remaining.

The boys' Junior Cup (today's McGuire Boys U-19 Cup) began in 1935. The 1946 Junior Cup was the first of 22 won by St. Louis teams. See soccerhistoryusa.org/asha/juniorcups.html for a list of all winners.

Schumachers Win National Title; Pragues Protest

By a Special Correspondent.

NEW YORK, June 24.—The National Junior Soccer Cup championship of the United States was won by the Schumachers of St. Louis at Throggs Neck Stadium yesterday by handing Prague of New York, unbeaten this season, a 2 to 0 defeat after leading at half time 1 to 0 in the grand finale of the annual competition. One thousand fans looked on.

The snappy Schumacher squad defeated Pompei of Baltimore in the big final a year ago, 4 to 1, which was nullified when the Marylanders successfully protested that the St. Louisans had used ineligible players during the game. The same kind of trouble loomed up after yesterday's contest when George S. Biscoll, president of the Prague club, announced that he would file a protest with the United States Football Association today on the grounds that some of the Schumacher players were more than 18 years old, the age limit to participate in cup games of the junior competition.

The Schumachers netted their first goal with only 12 minutes gone in the opening period and it was Center Forward Brady who did the trick from a fine set up by Smith. His low curling shot, with plenty of "english" on it, was fired in at Goal Keeper George Rotano from 10 yards out and it was too hot to hold.

The second tally came only five minutes from the final whistle and it was Douglass who tore through to brush aside all opposition and smack the ball into the net after picking up another great pass by Smith.

Lineup and summary:

SCHUMACHERS (2).		PRAGUE (0).
Pigeon	G.	Romano
Stocker	R.B	Cividanes
Annis	L.B	Matejov
Tucker	R.H	Cruz
Lincks	C.H	Zacek
Holmes	L.H	Kriezek
Farini	O.R	Johnston
Bellers	I.R	Prochazka
Brady	C.	Baran
Douglass	I.L	Helenek
Smith	O.L	Caputi

Referee—Sam Galine.
Linesmen—J. Zirbes and E. Sotzek.
Goals—Brady and Douglass.
Time of halves—35 minutes.

The *St. Louis Star and Times* edition of June 24, 1946, reports on Schumacher's US Junior Cup championship.
NEWSPAPERS.COM

OCTOBER 26, 1947

PRO SOCCER RETURNS: ST. LOUIS MAJOR SOCCER LEAGUE PREMIERS

AFTER A nine-year absence, pro soccer returned to St. Louis with the debut of the St. Louis Major Soccer League at Sportsman's Park.

The league featured four teams, including 1947–48 US Open Cup champion Simpkins Ford. The Raiders, DeAndreis Council, and the Steamfitters rounded out the league, which played Sunday doubleheaders.

Pro soccer's hiatus coincided with World War II, fought by the United States from 1941 to 1945. The war drew many players into military service. The time seemed ripe to restart high-level soccer with players back after the war ended.

The league kicked off October 26 in rain and mud, holding attendance to 1,010. Many war veterans played, including Simpkins goalkeeper Frank Borghi and forward Frank "Pee Wee" Wallace, and Raiders forward Bill Keough, older brother of US Soccer Hall of Famer Harry Keough.

DeAndreis and the Steamfitters drew, 1–1, in the opener. The Raiders won the nightcap, 3–1.

The league moved from Sportsman's Park after the 1951–52 season to the North Side Sports Arena. That facility closed after the 1952–53 season, and the league went out of business. The St. Louis Major teams moved to the amateur Muny League.

RICH MEISEMANN COLLECTION

DeAndreis Council 1, Steamfitters 1

DEANDREIS: GK Glenn Schaeffer; FB Bob Fuchs (Harry Desmuke); FB Nick Osterholt; HB Joe Randazzo; HB Bill Cohan; HB John Finn; OL Joe Stratmann; IL Ray Beckman; CF Dick Lodderhose (Ed Leahy); IR Willy Welsher; OR Ray Snyder

STEAMFITTERS: GK Ray Galvin; FB Jim Lanigan; FB Bauer (V. Murphy); HB Ray Marsek; HB Edward Dueker; HB Joe Lanigan; OL Ed Marsek (Ed Linehan); IL Emil Gerth; CF Harold "Whitey" Gunning; IR Jim Sheldon (John Dooley, Larry Kickham); OR John "Buzzy" Randazzo

GOALS: Gerth (S), Stratmann (D) PK

REFEREES: Howard Blaisdell, Tom Erbe

TIME OF HALVES: 35 minutes

Raiders 3, Simpkins 1

SIMPKINS: GK Frank Borghi; FB Bob Annis; FB Matt Mugavero; HB Henry Merlo; HB Charley Colombo; HB Jack Galimberti (John Barrale); OL Frank "Pee Wee" Wallace; IL Edwin Dueker (Cesar Perez); CF Bill Bertani; IR Gino Pariani; OR Herman Mugavero (Garcia)

RAIDERS: GK Manuel Muniz; FB Leo Puttin; FB Tom Kavanaugh; HB Gus Alberici; HB Ollie Bohlman; HB Mike Montani; OL Amiel Muniz; IL Bob Fitzgerald; CF Bob Corbett (Harry Keough); IR Joe Spica; OR Bill Keough (Willy Murphy)

GOALS: Bertani (S), A. Muniz (R) 2, Fitzgerald (R)

REFEREES: Tom Erbe, Howard Blaisdell

TIME OF HALVES: 35 minutes

ATTENDANCE: 1,010 (889 paid)

OCTOBER 17, 1948

MERLO STRIKES LATE TO LIFT SIMPKINS TO US CHAMPIONSHIP

AN 89TH-MINUTE goal by Henry Merlo propelled all–St. Louis Simpkins Ford to a 3–2 victory over the New York Brookhattans in the National Challenge Cup finals.

Leo Lange crossed to Merlo for the winner. Bill Bertani and Frank "Pee Wee" Wallace scored Simpkins's other goals. New York's first goal came from Joe Gaetjens, who went down in history by scoring in the USA's 1–0 upset of England in the 1950 World Cup.

Simpkins Ford 3, New York Brookhattans 2

National Challenge (today's US Open) Cup championship game at Sportsman's Park

SIMPKINS: GK Frank Borghi; LB Bob Annis; RB John Galimberti; LH Leo Lange; CH Charley Colombo; RH Matt Mugavero; OL Frank "Pee Wee" Wallace; IL Ed Dueker (John Barrale); CF Bill Bertani; IR Gino Pariani; OR Herman Mugavero (Cesar Perez) (Henry Merlo)

NEW YORK: GK Paddy Barnes; LB Ed Ruddy; RB Wally Bassett; LH Jesus Dios (Louis Burges); CH Armando Granados; RH Rodolfo Llana; OL Alfredo Carro; IL Al Jennette; CF Joe Gaetjens (Florenzo Brandaris); IR Jesus Villanon; OR Robert Roure

GOALS: Bertani (S) (M. Mugavero) 6, Gaetjens (N) (Granados) 35, Wallace (S) (time unknown; accounts put it "several minutes" after Gaetjens' goal), Llana (N) (Dios) 68, Merlo (S) (Lange) 89. Saves: Borghi (S) 14, Barnes (N) 14

REFEREE: Jack Maher

LINESMEN: Sam Dueker, Justin Keenoy

ATTENDANCE: 2,226

Joe Simpkins Ford tried to drum up attendance for the 1948 National Challenge Cup championship game with this ad in the St. Louis newspapers. **NEWSPAPERS.COM**

Simpkins's victory ended a 13-year drought of Challenge Cup titles for St. Louis. Tactically innovative, highly physical, and fiercely competitive, Simpkins was a dominant team in US soccer for the next decade and a legendary rival of Kutis, the best in the nation during the 1950s.

Simpkins is thought to be the first prominent St. Louis team to ditch the decades-old pyramid formation of two fullbacks, three halfbacks, and five forwards in favor of the WM formation. The bruising Charley Colombo excelled at center fullback in the WM.

Drawing mostly from the Italian Hill neighborhood, Simpkins fielded five US Soccer Hall of Famers: Colombo, Wallace, goalkeeper Frank Borghi, defender Bob Annis, and forward Gino Pariani. All made the 1950 World Cup team, and all but Annis started against England.

MAY 7, 1950

SIMPKINS COPS SECOND CUP IN THREE YEARS

SIMPKINS FORD won its second National Challenge Cup in three years by gaining a 1–1 tie with 1947 champion Ponta Delgada of Fall River, Massachusetts. The title was decided on goal differential over a two-game series. Simpkins won the opener, 2–0, in St. Louis on April 22.

Ponta Delgada's goal in game two came on a penalty kick by US Soccer Hall of Famer Ed Souza after John Galimberti was called for handling the ball in the penalty area midway through the first half.

Ponta Delgada pressured Simpkins throughout the game. But US Soccer Hall of Famer Frank Borghi, fronted by a stout defense, was up to the task in goal. Galimberti, Harry Desmuke, and US Soccer Hall of Famers Bob Annis and Charley Colombo played especially strong games. Buddy Marshak, a substitute at forward, clinched the title when he slammed in a rebound with three minutes left.

Rivals in this game were teammates a month later for the USA in the World Cup: Simpkins's Borghi, Annis, Colombo, Gino Pariani, and Frank "Pee Wee" Wallace, and Ponta Delgada's John and Ed Souza and Frank Moniz.

Five members of Simpkins's 1950 National Challenge Cup champions made the US World Cup team later that year (L-R): Bob Annis, Charley Colombo, Frank Borghi, Frank "Pee Wee" Wallace, and Gino Pariani. **HILL 2000 NEIGHBORHOOD ASSOCIATION**

Simpkins Ford 1, Ponta Delgada (Fall River, MA) 1

Game two of two-game National Challenge (today's Lamar Hunt US Open) Cup finals at Ponta Delgada Stadium (Tiverton, RI). Simpkins won series 3-1 on aggregate goals.

PONTA DELGADA: GK John Kitchen; FB Joe Rego, Gordon Andrews; HB: Jesse Braga, Joe Ferreira (Joe Medeiros), George Denardo; OL John Millington; IL John Souza; CF Frank Moniz; IR Ed Souza; OR John Travis (Aldo Gianotti)

SIMPKINS: GK Frank Borghi; FB John Galimberti, Bob Annis; HB Leo Lange (Matt Mugavero, Ebby McHugh), Charley Colombo, Harry Desmuke; OL Frank "Pee Wee" Wallace; IL John Barrale; CF John Stier (Buddy Marshak); IR Gino Pariani; OR John "Buzzy" Randazzo

GOALS: E. Sousa (P) PK 20, Marshak (S) (Pariani) 85

REFEREE: Sam Galin

LINESMEN: Manuel Texeira, Joseph Amaral

ATTENDANCE: 3,130

Simpkins 1950 National Challenge Cup champions. Back (L-R): Manager Joe Numi, Leo Lange, Charley Colombo, Glen Schaeffer, Frank Borghi, John Stier, Trainer Louis "Nola" Marnati, Tom Kennedy, Business Manager Caesar Sorrentino. Middle: Trainer Vince Costello, Ebby McHugh, Harry Desmuke, John Galimberti, Matt Mugavero, Bob Annis. Front: Bobby Lawton (mascot), John "Buzzy" Randazzo, Charlie DuBois, Gino Pariani, Bill Bertani, John Barrale, Frank "Pee Wee" Wallace, Ronnie Colombo

FRANK BORGHI COLLECTION

JUNE 29, 1950

PETE GARCIA FIRST US REFEREE AT WORLD CUP

ST. LOUISAN Prudencio "Pete" Garcia became the first US referee to officiate a World Cup game when he served as a linesman in Paraguay's 2–2 draw with Sweden at the Durival de Brito, Curitiba, Brazil.

Named to FIFA's 26-man referee pool for the World Cup, he worked two group-stage matches, the semifinal between Sweden and Brazil before nearly 139,000 fans, and the third-place game. Only two other referees officiated in as many games at the 1950 World Cup.

Garcia's family was among the many immigrants from the zinc mining and smelting province of Asturias in Spain who moved to St. Louis to work at Edgar Zinc Company. Garcia, who came to St. Louis as a child, became a bookkeeper at Mercantile Commerce Bank and Trust Co. But his real passions were his community and, especially, soccer. Garcia and Ben "Chic" Fernandez cofounded the St. Louis Spanish Society in 1927. In soccer, Garcia helped start the Missouri Referees Association and helped organize teams and leagues. He refereed in the Muny League for 20 years and officiated international matches played in St. Louis.

Garcia was enshrined in the US Soccer Hall of Fame in 1964.

Pete Garcia
NATIONAL SOCCER HALL OF FAME

JUNE 29, 1950

FIVE ST. LOUISANS HELP USA UPEND ENGLAND

IN PERHAPS the biggest upset in the Men's World Cup, the United States stunned England, 1–0, in a group stage match with five St. Louisans in the lineup: goalkeeper Frank Borghi, backs Charley Colombo and Harry Keough, and forwards Gino Pariani and Frank "Pee Wee" Wallace. St. Louisan Bob Annis was on the bench.

Forward Stanley Matthews, England's most famous player, did not appear in England's first two Cup matches, including game two against the USA. His absence seemed unimportant with England heavily favored to beat the Americans.

Joe Gaetjens scored the game's only goal in the 38th minute. One of the match's other key plays happened as England pressed forward with eight minutes left. Stanley Mortensen broke behind the US defense just outside the penalty area and was about to go one-on-one against Borghi. Colombo tackled Mortensen from behind. Referee Generoso Dattilo called a foul but did not issue a red card that would have ejected Colombo.

On the resulting free kick, Jimmy Mullen headed the ball past Borghi. Borghi reached behind and knocked the ball away just before it crossed the goal line completely. Sixty years later, Keough called it the greatest save he had ever seen.

United States 1, England 0

Group two stage match, World Cup, Estádio Independência, Belo Horizonte, Brazil

ENGLAND: GK Bert Williams, Alf Ramsey, John Aston, Billy Wright, Laurie Hughes, Jimmy Dickinson, Tom Finney, Wilf Mannion, Roy Bentley, Stan Mortensen, Jimmy Mullen

USA: GK Frank Borghi; LB Harry Keough; RB Joe Macca; LH Walter Bahr; CH Charley Colombo; RH Ed McIlvenny; OL Ed Souza; IL John Souza; CF Joe Gaetjens; IR Gino Pariani; OR Frank "Pee Wee" Wallace

GOAL: Gaetjens 38

REFEREE: Generoso Dattilo

LINESMEN: Charles De La Salle, Giovanni Galeatl

ATTENDANCE: 10,151

Members of the US team at the 1950 World Cup in Brazil pause while sightseeing at the *Christ the Redeemer* statue in Rio de Janeiro. St. Louis players are Harry Keough, Frank Borghi, and Gino Pariani (front, L-R); Frank "Pee Wee" Wallace (middle, left), and Charley Colombo (back, right). The player to the left of Colombo is believed to be St. Louis player Bob Annis. Coach Bill Jeffrey is seated third from the left.
PARIANI FAMILY COLLECTION

NOVEMBER 5, 1950

"FUN WHILE IT LASTED": FIRST WOMEN'S LEAGUE BEGINS

THE FIRST women's soccer league in St. Louis kicked off with its four teams playing a doubleheader.

The Craig Club Girls Soccer League, named for Rev. Walter Craig of St. Matthews Catholic parish, drew 70 players ages 16 to 22 from St. Teresa's and St. Matthews in north St. Louis. The league staged its first games on a vacant lot at Spring and Market Streets. The next day's *St. Louis Post-Dispatch* reported the scores but no players' names. The opener saw the Co-Eds defeat the Bobby Soccers, 3–2. The Bombers edged the Flyers, 1–0, in the second game.

Action in the Craig Club Girls Soccer League, from a photo feature in the *St. Louis Star-Times*
GILLIAM FAMILY COLLECTION

"Most of us were in high school and we had been kicking a ball around since we were little girls," recalled Dorothy Gilliam, a Bobby Soccer, almost 60 years later. "We didn't want to be treated differently. We wanted to play the game the way it was supposed to be played."

The league folded after two seasons. "Some girls went off to college, some got married and got pregnant, things like that," Gillliam said. "There wasn't any interest in anyone behind us coming up in school who wanted to carry on. It was over, but it was fun while it lasted."

Dorothy Gilliam (wearing Craig Club jersey) and teammates
GILLIAM FAMILY COLLECTION

JUNE 15, 1952

FINK'S BRACE HELPS BRING FIRST AMATEUR CUP TO ST. LOUIS

THE RAIDERS began a decade of dominance by winning the first US Amateur Cup by a St. Louis team.

Al Fink's two goals powered the Raiders to a 3–1 victory over the Ludlow Lusitanos. A few months later, Kutis Funeral Home sponsored the club. Kutis won six consecutive Amateur Cups from 1956 to 1961 and the Open Cup in 1957. Kutis is the last club to win both cups in one season. The team also defeated major German clubs such as Eintracht Frankfurt and FC Nurnberg in friendlies in St. Louis.

Val Pelizzaro heads the ball for the Raiders as teammate Herman Wecke watches during a St. Louis Major Soccer League match in 1952. LOUISA H. BOWEN UNIVERSITY ARCHIVES AND SPECIAL COLLECTIONS, SOUTHERN ILLINOIS UNIVERSITY AT EDWARDSVILLE

Raiders 3, Ludlow (MA) Lusitanos 1

US Amateur Cup championship game, Franklin Field, Ludlow, MA

LUDLOW (first names given if known): GK Mac Vaz, LF Gil Bello, RF D. Francisco, LH Garcia, CH Teixera, RH A. Francisco, OL Moraes, IL Lefty Costa, CF Fonte, IR Bales Costa, OR Perreira. Subs: J. Francisco, A. Silva, Pal Nascimento, Silva, Ferguson

RAIDERS: GK Bob Burkard, LF Joe Lanigan, RF Herman Wecke, LH Val Pelizzaro or Bob Whitehead (accounts differ), CH Harry Keough, RH Russ Murphy, OL Tom Schultz, IL Ruben Mendoza, CF Hal Weigel, IR Al Fink (Ed Cody), OR Oscar Corona (Danny McVey)

GOALS: Schultz (R) 15; Bello (L) 35 PK; Fink (R) 50, 62

REFEREE: Rose

LINESMEN: Watling, Feicha

ATTENDANCE: 3,000

Formed by Nick Jost and Gene Thumm in 1947, the team experienced numerous name changes before becoming Kutis. As Zenthoefer's, the club lost in the 1949 Amateur Cup finals.

The team boasted a bevy of stars, led by US Soccer Hall of Famer Harry Keough. Joining him for part or most of the 1950s were US Soccer Hall of Famers Joe Carenza Sr. and Bill Looby.

A key to their success was Hans Stranadl, an Austrian player/coach who trained the team in the early 1950s. He emphasized ball skills, turned fullback Herman Wecke into an attacking defender, and taught forwards to come back and defend, trends new to St. Louis soccer.

JUNE 17, 1956

FIRST OF SIX CONSECUTIVE AMATEUR CUPS FOR KUTIS

FOR THE first time in the 33-year history of the US Amateur Cup, the US Soccer Football Association awarded the championship on a forfeit. For Kutis, the champion, the title began a streak of six consecutive Amateur Cups.

Kutis 1, Philadelphia Ukrainians 0

Game one of scheduled two-game US Amateur Cup championship series, Public Schools Stadium. Game ended by referee in 88th minute after Ukrainians refused to permit Kutis to take a penalty kick. Championship awarded to Kutis on June 18 because the Ukrainians refused to complete game one.

KUTIS (accounts differ on left and right fullbacks): GK Bob Burkard; LF Russ Murphy or Herman Wecke; LF Herman Wecke or Russ Murphy; LH Bill Eppy; CH Harry Keough; RH Val Pelizzaro; OL Butch Cook; IL Ruben Mendoza; CF Clem Niewoehner; IR Jim Murphy; OR Fred Vasquez. Subs: Bill Looby, Oscar Corona, Joe Carenza Sr.

UKRAINIANS (first names given if known): GK Bohdan Anniuk; LF Kudenko; RF Korolyk; LH Gene Chyzowych; CH Wolodymyr Harasym; RH Marchuk; OL Pawlichka; IL Cherniwasky; CF Ihor Chyzowych; IR Walt Chyzowych; OR Senyk. Subs: Lucenko, Switenko, Kozak, Ollynyk

GOAL: Vazsquez (J. Murphy) 85

REFEREE: Julius Riepze or Rietzke (accounts differ)

LINESMEN: Harold Maher or Mayer (accounts differ), Ray Krumm

ATTENDANCE: 1,100 paid

Celebrating after Kutis defeated FC Nurnberg of West Germany, 3–2, in 1955 are (L-R) Bob Burkard, Harry Keough, Rich Meisemann, and Ruben Mendoza.
RICH MEISEMANN COLLECTION

Kutis was declared champion the day after Kutis defeated the Philadelphia Ukrainians, 1–0, in game one of a home-and-home series. Kutis led on a goal by Fred Vasquez when Jim Murphy had a breakaway in the 88th minute and was fouled in Philadelphia's penalty area. The referee awarded Kutis a penalty kick. The Ukrainians and their manager surrounded the referee. He ended the match after the Ukrainians refused to clear the penalty area.

Given that the penalty kick likely would have made the score 2-0 in a series decided on goal differential, Missouri Amateur Cup commissioner Harry Luecke contended that the Ukrainians had forfeited their right to continue the series in Philadelphia. The USSFA agreed and awarded the title to Kutis.

Footnotes to the series are that Ukrainians' forward Walt Chyzowych was head coach of the US Men's National Team from 1976 to 1980 and was inducted into the US Soccer Hall of Fame in 1997.

JUNE 9, 1957

KUTIS CROWNED KING OF US PRO AND AMATEUR SOCCER

KUTIS REACHED heights scaled by only two other teams in US soccer history when it defeated the Rochester (New York) Ukrainian-Americans, 1–0, in the US Amateur Cup final. Coupled with its US Open Cup victory on April 14, Kutis became the third and last team to win both cups in the same season.

Kutis captured the Open Cup by dispatching New York Hakoah 3–0 on March 31 and 3–1 on April 14 in a two-game series decided on aggregate goals. The Amateur Cup final was a far different story. The Ukrainian-Americans, all born in Europe and miffed that the final was a single game in St. Louis rather than a home-and-home series, outplayed Kutis. But the visitors were thwarted by spectacular goalkeeping from Leroy Franks. Due to report for military service on July 15, Franks "produced his finest effort," US Soccer Hall of Fame journalist Dent McSkimming wrote in the *St. Louis Post-Dispatch*.

Battling in humid 85-degree temperatures, both teams played "to the point of complete exhaustion," yet gave "a great show," McSkimming wrote.

Butch Cook scored about 30 minutes into the match. Cook's goal came on a pass from Ruben Mendoza that put the ball at Cook's feet at the penalty spot.

Kutis 1, Rochester (NY) Ukrainians 0

US Amateur Cup championship game, Public Schools Stadium. Accounts differ on several names and time of the goal.

KUTIS: GK Leroy Franks; LF Tom Julius; RF Herman Wecke; LH Val Pelizzaro; CH Harry Keough; RH Russ Murphy; OL Butch Cook; IL Ruben Mendoza; CF Bill Looby; IR Jim Murphy; OR Fred Vasquez. Subs: Bill Eppy, Bob Whitehead, Bob Rooney, Tom Murphy

UKRAINIANS (first names given if known): GK Wolodymyr or Walter Drewntkyj; LF Olyjnyk; RF Walter Kamad; LH Zenon Snylyk; CH Anton Shapka; RH Steckiw; OL Myron Bereza; IL Walter Zakaluznyj; CF Vitas Grybauskas; IR Lev Dyzkiwiwskj or Daniel Zawadiwskyj; OR Nick Shewchyshyn. Subs: Janchuk, Grevon or Greven, Garbowski or Garbosld, Zawadiwskyj or Dyzkiwiwskj

GOAL: Cook (Mendoza) 32 or 34

REFEREE: Nels Dahlquist

LINESMEN: Harold Blaisdell, Harold Maher

ATTENDANCE: 1,000 or 1,500 (estimated)

Kutis, 1957 US Amateur and Open Cup champions. Back (L-R): Manager Nick Jost, Herman Wecke, Rich Meisemann, Bill Eppy, Bob Burkard, Jim Krull, Tom Julius, Val Pelizzaro, Harry Keough, Russ Murphy, Trainer Tony Mercurio. Front: Joe Carenza, Oscar Corona, James Murphy, Fred Vasquez, Bill Looby, Bob Rooney, Ruben Mendoza, Butch Cook
RICH MEISEMANN COLLECTION

JUNE 15, 1958

KUTIS CAPTURES AMATEUR CUP AGAIN

Butch Cook set up both of the goals for Kutis in the 1958 Amateur Cup final.
RICH MEISEMANN COLLECTION

KUTIS LEFT it late as it gained its third consecutive US Amateur Cup by defeating the Beadling Terriers of Pittsburgh 2–1 on an 88th-minute goal by Bob Whitehead.

Played on a field with no stands and "not a blade of grass," according to *St. Louis Post-Dispatch* sportswriter Dent McSkimming, the game drew an estimated 1,500 Beadling fans who paid $2 apiece to stand just out of bounds and watch. They saw the defending champs rally from a 1–0 deficit in great measure because of forward Butch Cook and because of Kutis's legendary fitness.

The Terriers, big and athletically gifted but not as skillful or physically fit as Kutis, tired as the second half wound down. Cook, who had a first-half goal nullified for offsides, set up Kutis's second-half goals in the game's final 17 minutes. He relayed a pass from Bill Looby to Bob Rooney, who ripped a 15-yard shot into the net in the 73rd minute. With time winding down, Cook controlled a Beadling clear at midfield and immediately redirected the ball to Whitehead 18 yards from goal. Whitehead picked Cook's pass out of the air and fired the ball just inside the left goalpost for the winner.

Kutis 2, Beadling (Pittsburgh) 1

US Amateur Cup championship game, Hillside Field, Pittsburgh

BEADLING (first names given if known): GK Wassil Klemash, LF Ted Hustava, RF Jim Bressanelli, LH Vanzin, CH Chappel, RH DeLach, OL Ken Ball, IL Jerry Bressanelli, CF George Watson, IR Frank Pollack, OR Al Lorenzato. Subs: Don Cherry, Zak, E. Lorenzato, Kkorensky, Cleveland

KUTIS: GK Leroy Franks; LF Tom Julius, RF Herman Wecke, LH Val Pelizzaro, CH Harry Keough, RH Bill Eppy, OL Butch Cook, IL Bill Looby, CF Bob Rooney, IR Tom Murphy, OR Bob Whitehead. Subs**:** Jim Murphy, Rich Meisemann, Russ Murphy

GOALS: Cherry (B) second half (time unknown), Rooney (K) 73, Whitehead (K) 88

REFEREE: Dan or Al (accounts differ) Liebermann

LINESMEN: John Cherokee, Al Crompton

ATTENDANCE: 1,500 (estimated)

AUGUST 1, 1959

LOOBY HELPS KUTIS LIFT FOURTH STRAIGHT AMATEUR CUP

KUTIS FORWARD and US Soccer Hall of Famer Bill Looby enjoyed a fabulous year in 1959.

Believed to have scored the most single-season goals in St. Louis history in the 1958–59 season, Looby helped Kutis to its fourth consecutive US Amateur Cup. Kutis captured it by tying Detroit's St. Andrews Scots 2–2 August 1 in the finale of a two-game series decided on total goals. Kutis had overwhelmed the Scots 5–0 on July 25.

Looby's final tally is unknown, but he had 54 by early April 1959 and certainly exceeded 60 by season's end on August 1. He had three in the Amateur Cup Western semifinals on July 11. He scored in each of the Amateur Cup finals and assisted on Kutis's other goal in its 2–2 title-clinching tie against a team called "Detroit's finest squad in years."

Kutis finished 30–4–2 and outscored opponents 187–32. Looby was one of Kutis's three US Soccer Hall of Famers that season, along with Bob Kehoe and Harry Keough. Later in August, Looby starred for the USA in the Pan American Games, scoring six goals in six games for the bronze medalists. Kutis's Val Pelizzaro, John Traina, and Herman Wecke also played at the Games.

Bill Looby rises for the ball ahead of teammate Ruben Mendoza against Simpkins Ford.
LOOBY FAMILY COLLECTION

Kutis 2, St. Andrews Scots (Detroit) 2

Second game of two-game US Amateur Cup finals at McCabe Field, Detroit. Kutis won title 7–2 on total goals.

ST. ANDREWS: GK Norm Clements, LF Owen Tague, RF George Gardinar, LH Bill Clelland, CH Ron McManus, RH Sandy Hepburn, OL Bob Rennie, IL Bob Burnett, CF Alec Phillip, IR Bob Harrison, OR Matt Brown. Subs: Jim McKimmon, John Pyper, Jim Craig

KUTIS: GK Bob Burkard; LF Tom Julius, RF Herman Wecke, LH Val Pelizzaro, CH Harry Keough, RH Bill Eppy, OL Butch Cook, IL Bill Looby, CF Bob Rooney, IR Fred Vasquez, OR Ruben Mendoza. Subs: John Traina, Pete Traina, Bob Whitehead, Rich Meisemann

GOALS: Looby (K) 31, Vasquez (K) 44, Brown (S) PK 60, Harrison (S) 89

REFEREE: Nels Dahlquist

LINESMEN: Tom Syme, Dave Collins

ATTENDANCE: 1,000 (estimated)

NOVEMBER 28, 1959

BILLIKENS GIVE BIRTH TO A SOCCER DYNASTY

SAINT LOUIS University's Billikens battled through rain, mud, and wind to win their first of an NCAA-record 10 men's soccer championships, defeating Bridgeport (Connecticut), 5–2.

Jack Dueker, filling in for injured 24-goal-scorer George Endler, scored three times as the Bills overcame John Majesko's goal for Bridgeport two minutes into the match. Future Blues chairman Mike Shanahan scored the winning goal, breaking a 2–2 tie.

Saint Louis University 5, Bridgeport (CT) 2

NCAA men's soccer championship game at Memorial Stadium, Storrs, Connecticut

SLU: GK Gene Block, LF John Fuchs, RF John Michalski, LH Tom Richmond, CH Jerry Knobbe, RH John Klein, OL Tom Trost, IL Bob Malone, CF Jack Dueker, IR Don Range, OR Mike Shanahan. Subs: Bill Mueller, Pat Griffard, Tom Barry, Terry Malone, Lee Manna

BRIDGEPORT (first names given if known): GK Nick Wirth, LF Brew, RF Tasso Chirogians, LH Hatzis, CH Jim Kuhlman, RH Ev Hart, OL Bob Dikranian, IL John Majesko, CF Jack Coogan, IR Hans Zucker, OR Merritt. Subs: Bogli, McCullagh, Landers, Jon Olsen

GOALS: Dueker (S) 3, Shannahan (S), Richmond (S), Majesko (B), Olsen (B)

REFEREES: Ralph Carlsen, Albert Loeffler

ATTENDANCE: Less than 500 (estimated)

Saint Louis University's 1959 NCAA champions. Front (L-R): Gene Block, Bob Kaufman, Bill Mueller. Second row: Bob Malone, Terry Malone, Tom Richmond, Pat Griffard. Third row: Tom Trost, John Fuchs, Bob Pisoni, John Michalski, Jerry Knobbe, Coach Bob Guelker. Back: John Klein, Bob Endler, George Endler, Jack Dueker, Tom Barry, Don Range
SAINT LOUIS UNIVERSITY

Playing "under almost impossible weather conditions," according to the *St. Louis Post-Dispatch*, the Bills pulled away from their exhausted opponents with two unanswered goals from Tom Richmond and Dueker in the final 20 minutes. Bridgeport had prevailed in eight overtimes to defeat West Chester, 2–1, in the semifinals.

Although college soccer had been played under the auspices of the Intercollegiate Soccer Football Association since 1905, the 1959 season was the first sanctioned by the NCAA. Seeing the 1959 season as an opportunity for SLU, US Soccer Hall of Famer Bob Guelker started soccer as a club sport at SLU in 1958. He continued as head coach when soccer became an official sport at SLU the following season.

Using all homegrown players, Guelker coached the 1959 Bills to an 11–1–0 record. The Bills outscored opponents, 71–10.

MAY 28, 1960

KUTIS CATCHES FIRE IN FINAL 45 OF AMATEUR CUP

KUTIS OVERCAME an injury and a slow start to collect a record fifth consecutive US Amateur Cup with a 4–0 triumph over Patchogue of New York.

The champs juggled their lineup when starting right halfback Bill Eppy left the match after colliding heads with an opponent in the 30th minute. Kutis inserted three subs, brothers John and Pete Traina and forward Ruben Mendoza.

"There was an immediate improvement in the attack," noted the *St. Louis Post-Dispatch*. Kutis peppered goalkeeper Dieter Backhaus with shots. Fullback Herman Wecke finally connected just before halftime. Mendoza made it 2–0 early in the second half. "A sensational 30-yard shot from Butch Cook," according to the *Post-Dispatch*, gave Kutis a 3–0 lead. Fred Vasquez finished the scoring in the 77th minute.

Patchogue infrequently tested Kutis keeper Leroy Franks, who benefited from a rugged defensive line led by US Soccer Hall of Famer Harry Keough. On one rare attack from the New Yorkers, "Keough won a 40-yard race with center forward Konrad Englert," wrote the *Post-Dispatch*. "Just when Englert cocked his leg for a close-in shot, Keough stuck his big foot in front, saving the situation."

Kutis 4, Patchogue SC (New York) 0

US Amateur Cup championship game at Public Schools Stadium

KUTIS: GK Leroy Franks, LF Bob Whitehead, RF Herman Wecke, LH Val Pelizzaro, CH Harry Keough, RH Bill Eppy, OL Butch Cook, IL Larry Hausmann, CF Bob Rooney, IR Bill Looby, OR Fred Vasquez. Subs: John Traina, Pete Traina, Ruben Mendoza

PATCHOGUE (first names given if known): GK Dieter Backhaus, LF Fred Glueckert, RF Richard DeBruyn, LH Douglas Johnson, CH H.A. Themann, RH Hans Ratje, OL Tony DeBruyn, IL Fritz Gruenheid, CF Konrad Englert, IR Tom Lawn, OR Art Leseberg. Subs: Unknown

GOALS: Wecke 44, Mendoza (early second half, time unknown), Cook 59, Vasquez 77

REFEREE: Jerry Ditter

LINESMEN: Harry Crawford, Larry Sucher

ATTENDANCE: Unknown

Herman Wecke of Kutis and St. Ambrose's Paul Pisani race for the ball as St. Ambrose goalkeeper Nick Riggio prepares to stop the shot.
ST. LOUIS SOCCER HALL OF FAME

NOVEMBER 26, 1960

TWO-FOR-TWO FOR SLU

THE SECOND men's NCAA soccer season ended exactly as the first in 1959: Saint Louis University's Billikens brought home the national championship.

As in the 1959 final, the Bills battled back from a 1–0 deficit. Maryland's Juan Martin scored just five minutes into the match. SLU's comeback came courtesy of Don Range, who tied the match on a penalty kick in the 12th minute and scored what proved to be the winning goal later in the first half. Range's tallies sandwiched Gerry Balassi's goal in the 15th minute. Balassi caught Maryland by surprise with a 30-yard shot, "not especially well hit," according to the *St. Louis Post-Dispatch*, that found the near corner untouched by Terrapins goalkeeper Ronald Williamson.

Maryland made it close on a misplay by Bills backup keeper Mike Quinn. Starting in place of the injured Bill Mueller, Quinn failed to push a shot over the crossbar 20 minutes into the second half. The ball fell to Cliff Krug, who capitalized for his 26th goal of the season.

The Bills, who opened the season falling 3–2 to Fairleigh Dickinson, never lost over their last 14 games. They outscored their 15 opponents 73–10.

Saint Louis University 3, Maryland 2

NCAA men's soccer championship game at Brooklyn College, Brooklyn, New York

SLU: GK Mike Quinn, LF Mike Shanahan, RF Tom Hennessy, LH Tom Richmond, CH John Michalski, RH John Klein, OL Tom Barry, IL Bob Malone, CF Bob Trigg, IR Don Range, OR Gerry Balassi. Subs: Pat Griffard, Tom Klein, John Winecoff

MARYLAND (first names given if known): GK Ron Williamson, LF John Zarubaiko, RF Robert Vosswinkel, LH Robert Cummings, CH Richard Romano, RH Anthony Greene, OL Franco Triolo, IL Nick Limer, CF Juan Martin, IR Cliff Krug, OR Harry Sanders. Subs: Calvert, John Korz, Howard Krs

GOALS: Range (S) 2 (including one on PK), Balassi (S), Martin (M), Krug (M)

REFEREE: McLean, Callahan

ATTENDANCE: 1,000 (estimated)

Bobby Malone dribbles down the field.
SAINT LOUIS UNIVERSITY

JULY 23, 1961

KUTIS CAPS AMATEUR CUP RUN WITH SIXTH IN ROW

KUTIS, THE dominant team in US soccer for a decade, coasted to its sixth consecutive US Amateur Cup championship by tying the Hartford (Connecticut) Italian-American Stars, 3–3, in the second of a two-game series decided on total goals.

Kutis won the first game in St. Louis, 11–0, on July 15 behind five goals from US Soccer Hall of Famer Bill Looby, two apiece from Butch Cook and US Soccer Hall of Famer Bobby Kehoe, and one each from Fred Vasquez and Bill Eppy.

The 1961 national title was the last of eight for the core group of Kutis players who had won the previous five Amateur Cups and the 1957 US Open Cup, as well as the 1952 Amateur Cup when known as the Raiders. US Soccer Hall of Famer Harry Keough was the heart of the team from start to finish, playing at center back/center half, making game substitutions and running training sessions.

In addition to its eight national titles, Kutis also won three of five games against some of the best teams from then–West Germany in friendlies, beating Eintracht Frankfurt in 1951, Nuernburg in 1955, and Schwaben Augsburg in 1956.

Kutis 3, Italian-American Stars (Hartford, CT) 3

Game two of two-game US Amateur Cup finals at Dillon Field (Hartford, CT); Kutis won series 14-3 on aggregate goals.

ITALIAN-AMERICANS (first names given if known): GK Lazlo Varsegia, LF Kickham, RF Schwabe, LH Lenares, CH Lino Indomenico, RH Tony Ruddy, OL Sal Rizza, IL John Potts, CF Ralph D'Agostini, IR John McCully, OR Indomenico. Subs: Giannini, Santo Legana, Coco

KUTIS: GK Leroy Franks, LF Tom Julius, RF Herman Wecke, LH Val Pelizzaro, CH Harry Keough, RH Bill Eppy, OL Fred Vasquez, IL Larry Hausmann, CF Bob Rooney, IR Bill Looby, OR Bob Whitehead. Subs: Guenther Reinholdt

GOALS: Rizza (I) 10, D'Agostini (I) 18, McCully (I) 31 or 35 (accounts differ), Hausmann (K) 40, Vasquez (K) 44, Looby (K) 85

REFEREE: Leo Goldstein

ATTENDANCE: 1,100 (estimated)

US Soccer Hall of Famers Harry Keough (right) and Joe Carenza Sr. (middle) collect another trophy for Kutis. **JOE CLARKE COLLECTION**

NOVEMBER 24, 1962

BILLS WIN NCAA ON BALASSI'S BIG DAY

SAINT LOUIS University's Billikens, winners of the NCAA's first two national tournaments in 1959 and 1960 and runners-up in 1961, returned to the throne by beating Maryland, 4–3.

The game featured two subplots. The first: Mike Quinn, the Bills' goalkeeper in the 1960 championship game, also against Maryland, had died the week before in a car accident. The second: Gerry Balassi, the only foreign-born Billiken, played the game of his life in his last appearance for SLU. The Italian forward scored three times and set up the game winner.

Saint Louis University 4, Maryland 3

NCAA men's soccer championship game at Francis Field

SLU: GK Roger Rupp, LF Al Toczylowski, RF Joe Hennessy, LH Bill Vieth, CH Don Ceresia, RH Ed Oswald, OL Tom McDonnell, IL Tom Mataya, CF Bob Trigg, IR Tom Klein, OR Gerry Balassi

MARYLAND: GK Ron Williamson, LF John Zarubaiko, RF Henry Oustecky, LH Ersim Bacinogu, CH Daniel Kupchyk, RH John Kanarchuk, OL John Ruhs, IL Oyten Tertemiz, CF Dick Roe, IR Eberhard Klein, OR Frank Marasco

GOALS: Balassi (S) 3 (including one on PK), Hennessy (S), Roe (M), Ruhs (M), E. Klein (M)

REFEREES: Nels Dahlquist, Ray Bernebel

ATTENDANCE: 6,149

Gerry Balassi scored three goals and assisted on another in the 1962 NCAA championship game.
SAINT LOUIS UNIVERSITY

Balassi was a proven scorer with 36 goals in his first two seasons. In his third and final season—freshmen did not play on the varsity at that time—he had 13 goals coming into the NCAA final. Balassi needed only four minutes to score against Maryland. He made it 2–0 on a penalty kick. The Terps took the lead with three unanswered goals. Balassi evened the score when he headed in his own rebound midway through the fourth quarter. Three minutes later, he put a corner kick on the head of Joe Hennessy, who nodded in the winner.

The NCAA title capped the first undefeated season for the Bills, who finished 12–0–1.

DECEMBER 7, 1963

BILLS' BIG GUNS BLAST NAVY

THE 1963 season marked the debut of one of the most powerful offensive pairings in NCAA soccer history: Carl Gentile and US Soccer Hall of Famer Pat McBride. Saint Louis University's sensational sophomores combined for 48 goals, 30 from Gentile (a still-standing school record) and 18 (along with 17 assists) from McBride.

McBride amassed two of those assists, as well as a goal, as the Billikens battered Navy, 3–0, to win their fourth NCAA championship. Gentile generated a goal and an assist.

McBride converted a pass from Gentile for the opening goal in the fourth minute. The pair reversed roles in the third quarter, when McBride fed Gentile for a goal. McBride set up Terry Knox for the game's final goal.

Saint Louis University 3, Navy 0

NCAA men's soccer championship game at Rutgers University

SUMMARY: Full recap unavailable

GOALS: McBride (Gentile) 3:43, first period; Gentile (McBride) 9:14, third period; Knox (McBride) 11:56, third period. (College soccer games at that time were played in four quarters.)

ATTENDANCE: 5,000 (estimated)

Carl Gentile (left) and Pat McBride demolished defenses in their three seasons as Billikens.
SAINT LOUIS UNIVERISTY

Navy suffered its first defeat of the season. "We were outrun from the start and the way St. Louis sped those forward-moving passes, we didn't have a chance," Navy coach Glenn Warner said.

The Billikens finished the season with a school-record 94 goals and a 13–1–0 record. Their only loss came against Michigan State, 4–3, on November 9. SLU blanked the Spartans, 2–0, 13 days later in the first round of the NCAA playoffs on goals from Gentile and McBride.

MAY 13, 1964

CYC ALL-STARS STYMIE LIVERPOOL

THE CYC All-Stars nearly notched an upset of global proportions before yielding late to tie English First-Division champion Liverpool, 1–1.

The local amateurs faced one of the world's best clubs. Liverpool, missing three players with the national team and captain Ronnie Yeats out with a gimpy knee, scored with four minutes left.

The underdogs created dangerous chances in the second half. Bob Renaud redirected a pass just wide. Pete Traina rattled a drive off the crossbar. John "Bootie" Calcaterra hit the bar again 30 seconds later. St. Louis went ahead on an own goal six minutes from time. Liverpool halfback Phil Ferns stopped John Vitale's shot but inadvertently knocked the ball into the net.

Liverpool's Willie Stevenson scored two minutes later. "You'd like to say it was a fluke goal, but there was nothing flukey about it," US Soccer Hall of Famer Bob Kehoe said. "This guy hit a BB from just outside the penalty box."

Although in his mid-30s, Kehoe blanketed Liverpool's Ian St. John, who scored 21 goals during the 1963–64 First Division season. "Kehoe's performance was probably the finest of his long career," US Soccer Hall of Fame journalist Dent McSkimming wrote in the *St. Louis Post-Dispatch*.

The CYC's Sammy Davis (top) battles Liverpool's Alan A'Court.
CYC SPORTS

Bob Kehoe (right on the program) played perhaps his best game against Liverpool.
CYC SPORTS

St. Louis CYC All-Stars 1, Liverpool 1

International friendly at Public Schools Stadium

ST. LOUIS: GK Tommy Lyons, LF Dolph Kraus, RF Sammy Davis, LH Jim Murphy, CH Bob Kehoe, RH John Traina, OL Pete Traina, IL Pat McBride, CF Bob Renaud, IR Don Range, OR John "Bootie" Calcaterra. Subs: Tom Layton, Don Ceresia, John "Sonny" Vitale, Bill O'Brien, Roger Rupp, Paul Pisani

LIVERPOOL: GK Tommy Lawrence, LF Ronnie Moran, RF Gerry Byrne, LH Willie Stevenson, CH Chris Lawler, RH Tommy Smith, OL Alan A'Court, IL Gordon Wallace, CF Alf Arrowsmith, IR Ian St. John, OR Ian Callaghan. Subs: Phil Ferns, Phil Chisnall

GOALS: Liverpool OG 84 (off Ferns), Stevenson (L) 86

REFEREE: Gene Meyer

LINESMEN: Vince Forst, Llacks

ATTENDANCE: 5,721

DECEMBER 4, 1965

SLU FIGHTS FOR FIFTH NCAA TITLE

AMID PUSHES, shoves, and fisticuffs, Saint Louis University prevailed, 1–0, over Michigan State in a bitterly fought NCAA championship game.

The longtime rivals waged soccer warfare before an overflow crowd of 10,500. In a game marred by what the *St. Louis Post-Dispatch* called "vicious body contact," tempers boiled over in the last 30 seconds. SLU's Dave Schlitt and MSU's Rich Nelke, one of four St. Louisans playing for the Spartans, were ejected after both benches emptied following Schlitt receiving a stomach punch from MSU's Bert Jacobsen.

Saint Louis University 1, Michigan State 0

NCAA men's soccer championship game at Francis Field

SLU: GK Don Brennan; Backs: Joe Westhus, Gene Baker, Jack Gilsinn, Jim Murphy, Jim McAuliffe; Forwards: Jay Moore, Wally Werner, Jack Kinealy, Pat McBride, Carl Gentile. Subs: Dave Schlitt, Steve Rick

MICHIGAN STATE: GK George Janes; Backs: Terry Bidiak, Bert Jacobsen, Nick Krat, Pete Hens, Maury Ruscheinski; Forwards: Gary McBrady, Payton Fuller, Guy Busch, Orhan Enuston, Rich Nelke. Subs: Turgid Eunston, Manny Ruscheinski

GOAL: Gentile PK 9:30, third quarter

REFEREE: Jerry Ditter, Rich Giebner

ATTENDANCE: 10,500 (estimated)

Saint Louis University's Joe Westhus blocks a shot in the NCAA final. Michigan State's Guy Busch (9) and SLU's Jack Gilsinn and Jim Murphy (right) watch.
SAINT LOUIS UNIVERSITY

Fittingly, the game's only goal followed a foul in the penalty area from MSU's Nick Krat on US Soccer Hall of Famer Pat McBride in the third quarter. Carl Gentile converted the PK. Gentile later missed another PK.

MSU goalkeeper George Janes was otherwise unbeatable. His SLU counterpart, Don Brennan, kept his sixth clean sheet of the season with a big assist to center halfback Jack Gilsinn. MSU, which had lost in the 1964 NCAA final to Navy, failed to win for the ninth time in 10 tries against SLU. The Spartans lost only twice in 1965, both times to the Bills.

SLU put the finishing touches on its first perfect season, finishing 14–0.

JUNE 16, 1966

HERMANN LEADS LAUNCH OF NATIONAL PRO LEAGUE AND ST. LOUIS TEAM

A GROUP including St. Louis businessman Robert R. Hermann announced the formation of the National Professional Soccer League (NPSL). Hermann and his associates slated 10 cities, including St. Louis, for teams.

The announcement marked the first of many soccer milestones that landed Hermann in the US Soccer Hall of Fame.

Credited as a key architect of the rise of pro soccer in the United States, Hermann chaired the NPSL's executive committee and served as the league's president. He also ensured that St. Louis, the nation's first soccer capital, had a place at the league's table. He was a co-owner of the NPSL's St. Louis franchise. Christened the Stars, the team played 11 seasons, 10 of them in the North American Soccer League, created by a merger of the NPSL with another league in 1968. The Stars moved to Anaheim, California, after the 1977 season.

One of Hermann's lasting soccer legacies is the Hermann Trophy, awarded to college soccer's best player annually since 1967. Another is Hermann Stadium, Saint Louis University's soccer-specific complex. The stadium was named for him in 1999 after he contributed to the $5.1 million renovation of the facility.

Robert R. Hermann (left) presents the first Hermann Trophy to Dov Markus (center) of Long Island University as college soccer's top player in 1967.
MISSOURI HISTORICAL SOCIETY

NOVEMBER 8, 1966

HOMETOWN TEAM TAKES McBRIDE AS FIRST PLAYER

THE NEW pro team in town, later christened the St. Louis Stars, made local star Pat McBride its first player, launching a long pro career for the US Soccer Hall of Famer from Saint Louis University.

McBride, considered one of the first exceptional US-born players of the modern era, manned the midfield from 1967–76 for the Stars. He thrived in the foreign-dominated North American Soccer League. He earned selection to All-NASL teams three times, a feat matched by US Soccer Hall of Famer Al Trost, another St. Louisan and McBride's mate in the Stars' midfield for four seasons.

McBride helped the Stars reach the NASL playoffs three times, a considerable achievement for a team reliant on St. Louis players.

He transitioned to full-time head coaching in 1976, leading Meramec Community College to a national championship in his first season. He coached the indoor St. Louis Steamers in their first two seasons and spent six more years as an MISL head coach. He guided Forest Park Community College for 19 years starting in 1988. There he developed players such as Steve Ralston, the only St. Louisan named one of the top 25 players in the first 25 seasons of MLS.

Pat McBride (17) rises for a header in a 1967 match for the St. Louis Stars against the Baltimore Bays' Hipolito Chilinque.
NASLJERSEYS.COM

NOVEMBER 26, 1966

ST. LOUISANS SUPERCHARGE NAIA POWERHOUSE AT QUINCY

A CONTINGENT of students and staffers from St. Louis at Quincy College proposed an idea the Illinois school wisely approved in 1964: Let's start a men's soccer team. Two years later, that decision yielded the first of a record 11 NAIA national championships, won with talent primarily from 140-miles-distant St. Louis.

The 1966 Hawks often fielded nine starters from St. Louis. They included junior Mike Villa, a Vianney High School graduate who lettered 12 times in soccer, basketball, and baseball at Quincy and finished as Quincy's all-time leading scorer with 94 goals. Fifteen of those goals came in 1966, including the game winner when the Hawks stunned defending NCAA champion Saint Louis University, 2–1, on September 29. Quincy's first goal came from Carl Schwarzen, another St. Louisan.

Quincy's Edmundo Camacho eludes two defenders in 1966.
JACK MACKENZIE COLLECTION

Quincy 6, Trenton State (NJ) 1

NAIA men's soccer championship game at Alumni Field, Belmont (NC) Abbey College

SUMMARY: Full recap unavailable

GOALS: Edmundo Camacho (Q) 3, first quarter; Gary Kovarik (Q) 3, first quarter; Tom Doyle (T) 21, first quarter; Mike Villa (Q) 13, third quarter; Camacho (Q), late third/early fourth quarter (exact time unknown); Camacho (Q) 4, fourth quarter; Fred Schmalz (Q), fourth quarter (exact time unknown)

But the goal-scoring star of the '66 Hawks was Edmundo Camacho, a Mexican by way of California. Camacho paced the Hawks with 24 goals, including three in the NAIA championship game on November 26. Quincy trounced 1964 and '65 NAIA champion Trenton State, 6–1.

That victory put an exclamation point on a 13–0–0 season and began Quincy's reign over NAIA soccer, which lasted through 1981, mostly under St. Louisan Jack Mackenzie, Hawks' head coach from 1969 to 2012.

APRIL 16, 1967

THE STARS ARE BORN

THE GRAND experiment of a nationwide pro soccer league—two, actually—kicked off in 1967. Unable to agree on a single league, warring factions started the National Professional Soccer League (NPSL) and the United Soccer Association (USA).

The NPSL's St. Louis Stars lost their inaugural game, 2–1, to the Chicago Spurs. In a match fielding almost all foreign-born players, Chicago native and US Soccer Hall of Famer Willy Roy netted both goals for the winners.

Chicago Spurs 2, St. Louis Stars 1

NPSL season opener at Soldier Field, Chicago

CHICAGO: GK Manuel Comacho, LF George Caragiannides, RF Heinz Banschewitz, LH Luigi DeRobertis, CH Milos Grbic, RH Nick Krat, OL Joe Haverty, IL Gerd Ziemann, CF Willy Roy, IR Horst Szymaniak, OR Wolfgang Glock. Sub: Marcel Nowak

ST. LOUIS: GK Branko Topalovic, LF Joe Fuhrmann, RF Ilija Tojagic, LH Mike Kalicanin, CH Joe Puls, RH Ratislav Matic, OL Rudi Kolbl, IL Tomis Basic, CF Norb Pogrzeba, IR Bora Kostic, OR Casey Frankiewicz. Subs: Tim Markovic, Harry Smits

GOALS: Roy (C) 13, Kostic (S) 40, Roy (C) (second half, time unknown)

REFEREE: Walter Crosley

LINESMEN: Jack Huszpigiel, Tony Halavac

ATTENDANCE: 4,720

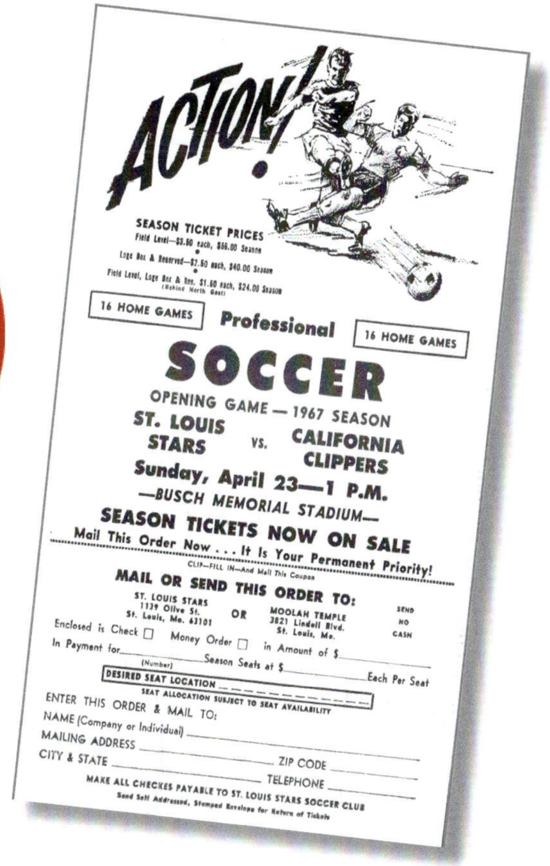

The St. Louis Stars made their debut in 1967, offering a 16-game season ticket for as low as $24. NEWSPAPERS.COM

Rain in the morning and a tornado alert throughout the game held the crowd to only 4,720 at Soldier Field, which seated about 74,000 at the time.

Based in a city loaded with homegrown talent, the Stars did not play a single St. Louisan. One who might have seen minutes, US Soccer Hall of Famer Pat McBride, had left the Stars almost two weeks earlier in a dispute with Stars head coach Rudy Gutendorf.

They reconciled in time for McBride to play in the Stars' next game. He scored one goal and had one assist in 21 matches in 1967.

NOVEMBER 18, 1967

FIRST OF 10 TITLES FOR FLO VALLEY

PETE SORBER made a memorable debut as soccer coach at Florissant Valley Community College in 1967. Sorber, who played many years in St. Louis senior soccer, replaced Harry Keough when Keough moved to Saint Louis University. Sorber expertly directed the Norsemen to the first-ever national junior college soccer championship for a St. Louis team. Nine more, along with 415 victories, followed during Sorber's 30 seasons at Flo Valley.

But the first title might have been the hardest. Although the Norsemen's 4–3 triumph over Monroe County concluded a 15–0–0 season, Flo Valley survived three overtimes in the semifinals against New York City Community College, then won the championship on a slush-and-snow-covered field against Monroe late in regulation.

Jack Blake played a leading role. His overtime goal had beaten NYC, 5–4, in the semifinals. He scored Flo's third goal just before halftime in the final, then took the shot that resulted in the winner. Blake's shot deflected off Monroe defender Jimmy Pascheerer into the net with 1:45 remaining.

Tom Ferguson scored twice, and Bob Meyer and Joe Patrico had one each to go with Blake's winner in the semifinals. Mike Lowrey had two goals for Flo in the first quarter of the final.

Jack Blake, shown later in his career at SIU-Edwardsville, scored the goal that won the first-ever national junior college championship for Florissant Valley.
SOUTHERN ILLINOIS UNIVERISTY-EDWARDSVILLE

Florissant Valley 4, Monroe County (Rochester, NY) 3

NJCAA men's soccer championship game at Erie County Technical Institute, Williamsville, New York

SUMMARY: Full recap unavailable

GOALS: Mike Lowery (F) 3:53 and 12:04, first quarter; Andre Sluk (M) 16:13, second quarter; Jack Blake (F) 22:23, second quarter; Sluk (M) 6:53 and 16:29, fourth quarter; Blake (F) 21:15, fourth quarter

NOVEMBER 25, 1967

ST. LOUIS BEATS ST. LOUIS IN NAIA FINAL

THE NAIA championship game pitted Quincy against Rockhurst. But the final could have been billed "St. Louis versus St. Louis." Twenty of the game's 22 starters were St. Louisans. The teams shared two pairs of brothers, Mike (Rockhurst)/Jerry (Quincy) Tucker and Mike (Rockhurst)/Tim (Quincy) Morrell.

In a battle of Hawks versus Hawks—both teams have the same nickname—St. Louisan Mike Villa ended a spectacular college soccer career with two goals that broke a 1–1 tie to give Quincy's Hawks their second consecutive NAIA championship. Villa amassed 44 goals during the 1967 season, including seven against Blackburn and an NAIA-record 10 against Notre Dame. He had three more in the NAIA semifinal, a 7–1 triumph over Alderson-Broaddus. His career total of 94 still tops Quincy's all-time leaders.

Rockhurst, however, stunned Quincy on Quincy's own field just one minute into the final. St. Louisan Geof Melchior scored off a corner kick. Quincy quickly leveled the score when Villa set up a goal by St. Louisan Rich Manna. Villa broke the tie with a goal on a penalty kick early in the second half, then hit a long-range bomb for the insurance goal with 10 minutes left.

Tom DiMaria stops a shot for Quincy in 1967.
JACK MACKENZIE COLLECTION

Quincy 3, Rockhurst 1

NAIA men's soccer championship game at Quincy

SUMMARY: Full recap unavailable

GOALS: Geof Melchior (R) 1, first quarter; Rich Manna (Q) 3, first quarter; Mike Villa (Q) 2 (PK), third quarter, Villa 12, fourth quarter

ATTENDANCE: 2,000 (estimated)

DECEMBER 2, 1967

BILLS AND SPARTANS SHARE NCAA SPOILS

TWO OF college soccer's fiercest rivals, Saint Louis University and Michigan State, met for the NCAA championship.

Frustrated in 1963 when MSU lost only two games—both to SLU—the Spartans recruited St. Louis players. There were plenty capable of raising the soccer bar at MSU.

The Spartan team that faced the Bills at Francis Field in 1967 included 10 St. Louisans. Among them were Joe Baum in goal, Barry Tiemann (defender), Tom Kreft and Gary McBrady (forwards), and Rich Nelke and Guy Busch (substitutes).

Guy Busch, one of many St. Louisans at Michigan State, unwittingly played a central role in the 1967 NCAA final. **MICHIGAN STATE UNIVERSITY**

Saint Louis University 0, Michigan State 0

NCAA men's soccer championship game at Francis Field

Game called with 2:15 remaining in the first half because of unplayable conditions; cochampions declared.

SLU: GK Jim Conley; Backs: Tom Rich, Brad Melchior, Steve Frank, Gary Rensing, Bill McDermott; Forwards: Gene Geimer, Paul Pisani, Wally Werner, Dave Schlitt, Tom Bokern. Sub: Jack Galmiche

MICHIGAN STATE: GK Joe Baum; Backs: Kenneth Hamann, Terry Sanders, Peter Hens, Bert Jacobsen, Barry Tiemann; Forwards: Tim Kreft, Alex Skotarek, Trevor Harris, Ernie Tuchsherer, Gary McBrady. Subs: Rich Nelke, Guy Busch, Edward Skotarek

REFEREES: Harry Rogers, Pat Smith, Kettering (first name unknown)

ATTENDANCE: 3,000 (estimated)

Busch, who finished the 1967 season as MSU's all-time leading scorer, unwittingly played the game's leading role on a field turned by rain into a swamp. Players frequently lost their footing, and the ball often stopped in standing water. The final straw came when Busch slid headfirst into the Billikens' goalpost just before halftime. He remembered nothing after the collision until boarding a plane back to MSU several hours later. Officials called the game and declared cochampions.

The title was the first of five for the Billikens under new head coach and US Soccer Hall of Famer Harry Keough. He succeeded another Hall of Famer, Bob Guelker, who became head coach at brand-new Southern Illinois University–Edwardsville.

JUNE 30, 1968

PELÉ PLEASES 20,000 WITH WINNING GOAL

PELÉ, THE world's greatest player, pleased the 20,116 fans who endured 95-degree temperatures at Busch Memorial Stadium by scoring the winning goal in the 63rd minute to lead heavily favored Santos of Brazil to a 3–2 victory over the NASL's St. Louis Stars.

The Stars stunned Santos with two goals by Casey Frankiewicz in the game's first eight minutes. Pepe, who scored 405 goals in 750

A $2 ticket admitted a fan to see Pelé at Busch Stadium in 1968. **PAT McBRIDE COLLECTION**

appearances for Santos from 1954 to 1969, drew Santos level with two goals, both on free kicks, in the 35th and 39th minutes.

While the 32-year-old Pepe was near the end of his career, Pelé was in his prime at age 27. He already was a veteran of three World Cups, including Brazil's 1958 and 1962 championships. Pelé scored the winner in St. Louis when he slipped behind defender Mike Kalicanin for a long pass from Amaury Silva. "Pelé instantly controlled the ball and flipped a short shot over the onrushing (goalkeeper Barney) Vidinic," the *St. Louis Post-Dispatch* reported.

The furious Stars argued that Pelé was offside. Afterward, Pelé said diplomatically: "I don't think I was offside. That is my opinion. But I'm not saying I wasn't offside."

Santos 3, St. Louis Stars 2

International friendly at Busch Memorial Stadium

ST. LOUIS: GK Barney Vidnic, LF Carl Gentile, RF Joe Fuhrmann, LH Mike Kalicanin, CH Joe Puls, RH Nick Krat, OL Casey Frankiewicz, IL Norb Pogrzeba, CF Rudi Kolbl, IR Willi Wrenger, OR Eli Durante. Subs: Pat McBride, Milenko Rus, Eddie Clear, Oscar Black, Jack Kinealy, Don Ceresia

SANTOS: GK Laércio, LF José Ramos Delgado, RF Turcão, LH Orlando Peçanha, CH Mengálvio, RH Oberdan Vilaín, OL Pepe, IL Pelé, CF Tonihno Guerreiro, IR Lima, OR Amaury Silva. Subs: Geraldino, Abel Verônico, Douglas, Eliseu, Manoel Maria

GOALS: Frankiewicz (StL) 5, 8; Pepe (Santos) 35, 39; Pelé (Santos) 63

REFEREE: Menachem Ashkenazi

LINESMEN: Harry Keough, Ray Puricelli

ATTENDANCE: 20,116

NOVEMBER 29, 1969

NORSEMEN MAUL MIAMI DADE-NORTH IN NJCAA FINAL

FLORISSANT VALLEY'S all–St. Louis team emphatically demonstrated its mastery of junior college soccer with a 6–2 demolition of Miami Dade–North. The Norsemen outshot their opponents 47–6. Tom Knapp, who enrolled at Flo Valley after serving in the Vietnam War, connected for three goals in Flo's fourth consecutive appearance in the NJCAA championship game.

Carlos Ojeda, a 50-goal scorer in 1969, tallied the losers' goals.

Flo Valley defeated Canton, New York, 2–1 in the quarterfinals and Loraine, Ohio, 5–2 in the semifinals. "I think we set some of the Eastern teams on their ears," Norsemen coach Pete Sorber told the *St. Louis Post-Dispatch*. "Some of them, who rely heavily on foreign-born players, apparently didn't believe a team made up entirely of Americans could play the caliber of soccer we showed."

Sorber's squad played high-caliber soccer throughout the season. The Norsemen finished with a 13–1–0 record, the only loss by a 2–0 score to undefeated 1969 NCAA champion Saint Louis University. Sorber, who coached the Norseman to their only previous title in 1967, guided Flo to a total of 10 NJCAA titles, five of them over seven seasons from 1969 to 1975.

The 1969 national champion Florissant Valley Norsemen. Front (L-R): Henry Amann, Bill Renaud, Steve Lucido, Phil Thomann, Johnnie Meyer. Middle: Tim Rooney, Gary Geise, Bobby Lemp, Bob O'Leary, Mike Margulis, Rich Neitzert. Back: Dave Fitzler, Dale Harmon, Tom Knapp, Joe Right, Jim Milner, Steve Buckley, Coach Pete Sorber

PETE SORBER COLLECTION

Florissant Valley 6, Miami Dade-North 2

NJCAA men's championship game at Miami Dade-North

SUMMARY: Full recap unavailable

GOALS: Tim Rooney (F) 4:30, first quarter; Tom Knapp (F) 13:45, first quarter; Knapp (F) 9:20, second quarter; Carlos Ojeda (M) 17:05, second quarter; Knapp (F) 1:00, third quarter; Bob O'Leary (F) 4:45, third quarter; Ojeda (M) :55, fourth quarter; Mike Margulis (F) 21:22, fourth quarter

DECEMBER 6, 1969

BILLS FLOWER WITH FOUR IN SECOND HALF OF NCAA FINAL

AFTER WHAT head coach Harry Keough called "a little get-together at the half," Saint Louis University scored four times to defeat San Francisco, 4–0, for the Billikens' seventh NCAA soccer championship.

The Bills' four goals were bookended by penalty kicks converted by US Soccer Hall of Famer Al Trost two minutes into the second half and by Gary Rensing five minutes from the final whistle. In between, Jim Leeker and John Pisani scored from short range.

Tempers ran short, especially after the awarding of the first penalty kick. USF's John Camacho stopped Trost's attempt, but officials ruled that Camacho had moved too soon. Trost successfully converted his second try.

Saint Louis University 4, San Francisco 0

NCAA men's championship game at Spartan Field, San Jose (Calif.) State College

SUMMARY: Full recap unavailable

GOALS: Al Trost (PK) 2, third quarter; Jim Leeker 2, fourth quarter; Pisani 8, fourth quarter; Gary Rensing (PK) 17, fourth quarter

REFEREES: Derrick Lewis, Derk Zylker

ATTENDANCE: 8,000

Saint Louis University's Jim Leeker challenges Florissant Valley goalkeeper Joe Right in 1969. Joe Leeker is at left. The undefeated Bills handed Flo Valley its only loss of the season, 2-0.
SAINT LOUIS UNIVERSITY

Punches were exchanged after Pisani's goal, and three USF players were ejected. The referees required a police escort after the game.

The Bills had played inspired soccer two days before to defeat previously unbeaten and untied Harvard, 2–1, in the semifinals, thanks to Trost's goal on a rebound from Gene Geimer's shot with just two minutes left in regulation.

SLU finished the season with a 13–0–0 record, the second perfect season in Billikens' history. The Bills outscored their 13 opponents, 48–7.

MAY 31, 1970

"MR. SOCCER" BEGINS 50-PLUS YEARS OF SOCCER BROADCASTING

A YOUNG St. Louisan realized a dream as the World Cup began in Mexico. Bill McDermott vowed as a teenager that his life's goal was to broadcast at the World Cup. That came to pass when the just-graduated Saint Louis University student athlete, who traveled to Mexico with a CYC group, called KMOX radio in St. Louis with daily reports on the World Cup.

He's been calling soccer locally, nationally, and internationally ever since. Dubbed "Mr. Soccer" by lifelong friend and National Baseball Hall of Fame broadcaster Bob Costas, McDermott has called soccer for Saint Louis University, St. Louis pro teams, local radio and TV, and national networks such as ESPN.

McDermott played midfield for national championship teams at St. Philip Neri and SLU. But he decided his true ambition was to man a microphone at a World Cup game after watching a documentary on the 1966 Cup with his St. Philip Neri teammates. His telephoned reports to KMOX were a start. His career fully blossomed when he served as an ESPN analyst at the 1994 World Cup.

Several World Cups and many pro and college games later, McDermott is the longest-tenured soccer announcer in the United States.

Bill McDermott, the longest-tenured soccer announcer in the United States, with Pelé, the sport's greatest player.
BILL McDERMOTT COLLECTION

NOVEMBER 28, 1970

FLO VALLEY'S MARATHON MEN MASTER NJCAA

FLORISSANT VALLEY won its second consecutive national title, and third in four years, the hard way.

The Norsemen required 11 overtimes to overcome Lorain College, 2–1, at Flo Valley. Tim Rooney, who later became the winningest women's soccer coach in junior college history at Lewis & Clark, rescued Flo when he converted a cross from Jim Lemp for the winner.

The teams played two regular five-minute overtimes and nine five-minute sudden-death extra periods. Rooney ended it in the third minute of the ninth sudden-death overtime.

Marty Stellar put the Norsemen ahead at 12:43 of the first period after receiving a pass from Tim Smith. Lorain drew even on John Gonsalves's goal in the 75th minute.

The Norseman had also prevailed by a 2–1 score in the quarterfinals, thanks to Lemp's goal on a breakaway with three minutes left. Flo then topped Nassau County, 3–0, in the semifinals.

The victory over Lorain put an exclamation point on a 13–0–0 season for Flo and ran its record over three seasons to 58–2–0.

Tim Rooney (left) scores in the 11th overtime (above) to give Florissant Valley its third national championship.
PETE SORBER COLLECTION

Florissant Valley 2, Lorain (Ellyra, OH) 1 (11 overtimes)

NJCAA men's championship game at Florissant Valley

SUMMARY: Full recap unavailable

GOALS: Marty Stellar (F) 12:48, John Gonsalves (L) 74:20, Tim Rooney (F) 140:41

DECEMBER 5, 1970

"BEST BILLIKEN TEAM" BULLDOZES ANOTHER NCAA TITLE

THE 1970 Bills excelled under pressure. Consider: Quarterfinals—With 10 seconds to go against archrival SIU–Edwardsville, Mike Seerey's header redirected Pat Leahy's shot into the net for a 2–1 victory.

Semifinals—Seerey struck nine minutes into the fourth quarter, to lift the Bills past previously unbeaten Hartwick, 1–0.

Final—Against undefeated UCLA, a team dominated by foreign-born players, the homegrown Billikens got the game winner from Denny Hadican, a freshman reserve forward, who headed in Seerey's cross in the third quarter.

This superior SLU team fielded three winners of the Hermann Trophy, emblematic of the best player in men's college soccer: US Soccer Hall of Famer Al Trost (1969 and 1970), Seerey (1971 and 1972), and Dan Counce (1973). SLU's victory over UCLA capped a 14–0–1 season, with the only tie against NAIA power and St. Louisan–loaded Quincy College. The Bills ran their unbeaten streak to 28 games.

Saint Louis University 1, UCLA 0

NCAA men's championship game at Cougar Field, SIU–Edwardsville

SLU: GK Don Copple; Backs: Denny Werner, Mark Demling, Bob Matteson, Ed Neusel, Joe Hamm; Forwards: Al Trost, Joe Leeker, Dan Counce, Mike Seerey, Jim Draude. Subs: Denny Hadican, Jim Bokern, Pat Leahy

UCLA: GK Steve Burnside; Backs: Berhanie Snderberhan, Jose Lopez, Dieter Schulte, Art Szylewicz, Bob Thrussell; Forwards: Fesseha Wolde-Emanuel, Terry Scott, Bernardo Ortiz, Solomon Terfa, Shoa Agonafer. Subs: David Chu, Girma Belay, Ruben Gonzales, Salvador Baez

GOAL: Hadican 55:36

REFEREE: Larry King, Dick Giebner

ATTENDANCE: 8,000 (estimated)

US Soccer Hall of Famer Al Trost (right) embraces Denny Hadican, who scored the only goal in the 1970 NCAA final.
SAINT LOUIS UNIVERSITY

JUNE 6, 1971

KUTIS BACK ON TOP IN AMATEUR CUP

KUTIS, WINNERS of a record six consecutive US Amateur Cups from 1956 to 1961, captured their seventh on its third try in five years by defeating Cleveland Inter-Italian, 4–1.

Losers in the 1967 and 1969 finals, Kutis controlled the 1971 match after Inter-Italian's best player, Luciano Taccone, left with a knee injury. Using a mix of veteran and new players, all but one from St. Louis, Kutis rolled to a 4–0 lead. All the goals came from Saint Louis University players: Jim Bokern had two, and Gene Geimer and Bob Matteson had one apiece. Inter-Italian, fielding mostly foreign-born players, scored a late consolation goal.

Kutis, 26–5–3, was coached by Friedel Geissert, a World War II German U-boat crewman captured after his sub was sunk. He immigrated to St. Louis in 1954. "We started as a team and we finished as a team," Geissert said of Kutis in 1971. "All season long this is what I teach: teamwork, teamwork, teamwork."

Kutis practiced what Geissert preached, especially on the goal that put them ahead 3–0. Bokern passed back to John Klein, who sent the ball diagonally to Wally Werner. Werner passed to Gene Geimer, who spotted Matteson for a pass that Matteson put into the net.

Denny Vaninger (left) and Gene Geimer of Kutis battle Hamm's Joe Hamm in the 1971 Missouri Amateur Cup final. Geimer scored in the final minute to tie the match. Vaninger won it with an overtime goal.
JOE HAMM COLLECTION

Kutis 4, Inter-Italians (Cleveland) 1

US Amateur Cup championship game at Brooklyn High School, Cleveland

SUMMARY: Full recap unavailable

GOALS (accounts vary on times of all goals)**:** Jim Bokern (K) 27, 31, or 36; Gene Geimer (K) 37 or "late in first half"; Bob Matteson (K) 55 or 64; Bokern (K) 63 or 72; Vito Colonna (I) 78 or 80

ATTENDANCE: 2,000 (estimated)

NOVEMBER 11, 1971

FIRST CLASS INDUCTED INTO ST. LOUIS SOCCER HALL OF FAME

THE 1920 Ben Millers, the first St. Louis team to win a national soccer championship, proposed a grand idea at their 50-year reunion in 1970: a local soccer Hall of Fame. The idea came to fruition when the Old Time Soccer Players' Hall of Fame inducted its first class on November 11, 1971.

An induction dinner has been held almost every year since. The shrine, renamed the St. Louis Soccer Hall of Fame in 2005, has inducted more than 900 local players, coaches, and administrators. The dinner is one of the highlights of the St. Louis soccer calendar. The event attracts as many as 1,000 attendees. They gather to witness the induction of the newest class, regale each other (again) with tales from the past, and contribute significantly to Anheuser-Busch's bottom line.

The inaugural class of 22 included four already in the US Soccer Hall of Fame: forwards Jimmy Dunn (Ben Miller) and Harry Ratican (Bethlehem Steel and other powerful Eastern and St. Louis teams), 1950 US World Cup team architect Walter Gieseler, and longtime *St. Louis Post-Dispatch* soccer writer Dent McSkimming. The complete list of the 900-plus inductees can be found at stlsoccerhalloffame.com.

First Inductee Class, St. Louis Soccer Hall of Fame

PLAYERS: Dave Bartnett, goalkeeper, 1924–35; Ed Begley, halfback, 1937–47; Richard "Bull" Brannigan, forward, 1908–17; Jimmy Dunn, forward, 1915–27; William "Dutch" Gockel, halfback, 1920–38; James Hagerty, forward, 1907–17; Msgr. Jimmy Johnston, fullback, 1916–21; Charlie LaBarge, goalkeeper, 1920–34; Charles McGarry, goalkeeper, 1917–22; John "Dinty" Moore, forward, 1928–40; Robert "Ribby" Murphy, halfback, 1910–25; Tommy O'Hanlon, halfback, 1915–25; Allan "Swede" Petersen, halfback, 1919–29; Billy Quinn, halfback, 1915–25; Harry Ratican, forward, 1912–27; John "Bucky" Reddan, halfback, 1917–23; Larry Reilly, forward, 1918–25; John "Duke" Sheahan, goalkeeper, 1910–20; Irv Wimer, forward, 1919–29

BUILDERS: Dent McSkimming, *St. Louis Post-Dispatch* soccer writer; Walter Giesler, president, US Soccer Football Association (today's US Soccer Federation); Bob Burnes, *St. Louis Globe-Democrat* executive sports editor

The St. Louis Soccer Hall of Fame has been recognizing St. Louis's best players since its first induction ceremony in 1971.

NOVEMBER 27, 1971

FLO VALLEY VANQUISHES 17-0 MONROE

ANOTHER YEAR, another national junior college championship for Florissant Valley . . . but its third consecutive title and fourth in five years didn't come easy.

Monroe took a 1–0 lead when Ferdinand Treusacher converted a penalty kick four minutes after kickoff.

But lightning struck Monroe twice just before halftime. Flo's Denny Vaninger, a future pro and US National Team player considered one of the best in St. Louis soccer history in scoring on headers, struck for the tying goal with one of his trademark head balls on a pass from Mike Caraffa. Less than a minute later, Vaninger unleashed a long pass to spring Tim Smith on a breakaway. Smith converted, and just like that, Flo led, 2–1. Smith doubled the lead on a pass from Bill McCabe early in the fourth quarter.

"We have nothing to be ashamed of," Monroe coach Joe Mancarella said. "Florissant has a clean, highly skilled team."

The victory gave the all–St. Louis Norsemen a 12–0–1 record for the season and ran their three-year unbeaten streak to 38 games. Flo outscored their 1971 opponents, 76–8.

Florissant Valley 3, Monroe (Rochester, NY) 2

NJCAA men's championship game at Miami (FL) Dade-South

SUMMARY: Full recap unavailable

GOALS: Ferdinand Treusacher (M) PK 4:05, first quarter; Denny Vaninger (F) 18:40, second quarter; Tim Smith (F) 18:53, second quarter, Smith :43, fourth quarter; Nelson Cupello (M) 8:25, fourth quarter

Denny Vaninger (with towel) and goalkeeper Frank Tusinski hold Flo Valley's 1971 national championship trophy. Others in the photo include Robin Geisz (with ball) and Tim Kersting (glasses).
PETE SORBER COLLECTION

DECEMBER 4, 1971

QUINCY PULLS SNOW JOB IN NAIA FINAL

NEWS REACHED Quincy College on Thursday night, December 2, that Quincy had won its NAIA soccer semifinal. On a whim, several students drove to Dunn, North Carolina, to cheer the Hawks at Saturday night's championship game. A snowstorm made the trip a 40-hour marathon. Still, the dedicated fans pulled into Dunn two hours before game time.

Unknown to them, the game had been moved up five hours because of the snow. The match had ended an hour before they arrived.

They missed a tightly played match that ended with the Hawks, loaded as usual with St. Louisans, winning, 1–0, on a snow-blanketed field that became a muddy mess. They defeated the team that had beaten them, 2–0, in the 1970 final. St. Louisan Tom Pollihan scored on a play begun with a throw-in by another St. Louisan, Rich Zeidler.

The Hawks finished the season with a 17–2–0 record and their third NAIA title. Meanwhile, the QC students late for the game toasted the team with a beer and headed home, intent on beating the team plane to Quincy on Sunday. "The last thing I heard was, 'See ya at the airport,'" Quincy coach and St. Louis native Jack Mackenzie wrote years later.

St. Louisan Dan Rothery plays the ball past SIU-Edwardsville's Chris Carenza during Quincy's 1-0 regular-season loss to the Cougars. The Hawks lost only one other game in 1971, 2-0 to Saint Louis University. **JACK MACKENZIE COLLECTION**

Quincy 1, Davis & Elkins (Elkins, WV) 0

NAIA men's championship game at Dunn (NC) High School

SUMMARY: Full recap unavailable

GOAL: Tom Pollihan 9, second quarter

MAY 14, 1972

LOCAL LADS HELP BOOK OLYMPIC BERTH AT BUSCH

THE UNITED States qualified for the 1972 Olympics by beating Jamaica, 2–1, in St. Louis, hometown of many of the USA's players and its head coach.

Four locals—Buzz Demling, Joe Hamm, Mike Seerey, and John Carenza—started for Bob Guelker, a US Soccer Hall of Famer and SIU–Edwardsville's head coach.

The clincher ended a yearlong marathon of 11 qualifiers to land one of two berths from Concacaf. St. Louisans' influence extended from Guelker's coaching to midfield play by Demling, Hamm, and US Soccer Hall of Famer Al Trost and goal-scoring prowess by forwards Carenza and Seerey.

Hamm replaced the injured Trost against Jamaica. Hamm and Demling "were tireless workers in midfield," according to an account of the match.

Carenza and Seerey provided firepower. Mani Hernandez opened the scoring when he knocked in the rebound of Carenza's drive off the crossbar. Carenza extended the lead to 2–0 on a pass from Seerey. Seerey was defended closely after scoring all the USA's goals in their previous two qualifiers, 2–2 with Mexico and 2–1 over Guatemala.

The USA did not survive Olympic group play. But qualifying was a boost for soccer in the United States, which had not kicked in the Olympics since 1956.

United States 2, Jamaica 1

Olympic qualifier at Busch Stadium

USA: GK Mike Ivanow; Backs: Casey Bahr, Horst Stemke, Neil Stam, John Bocwinski; Midfielders: Joe Hamm, Buzz Demling; Forwards: John Carenza, Mike Seerey, Mani Hernandez, Archie Roboostoff. Subs: None

JAMAICA: GK Bruce Black; Backs: Ken Campbell, Carl Brown, Desmond Smith, Keith Tulloch; Midfielders: Leonard Mason, Dave Bernard; Forwards: Clarence Prendes, Milverton Brooks, Calvin Stewart, Errol Barrett. Subs: Vester Constantine (GK), Owen Stewart

GOALS: Hernandez (Carenza) USA 22, Carenza (Seerey) USA 35, Leonard Mason (UA) Jamaica

REFEREE: Werner Winsman

LINESMEN: Mike Wuertz, Larry King

ATTENDANCE: 7,196

The 1972 US Olympic Team, taken in Germany during the Games, included eight St. Louisans and one former East St. Louisan. Front (L-R): Hugo Salcedo, St. Louisan Joe Hamm, Jim Zylker, St. Louisan Buzz Demling, Archie Roboostoff, John Bocwinski, Mani Hernandez, Wally Ziaja, St. Louisan Mike Margulis, Casey Bahr. Back: Head coach and St. Louisan Bob Guelker, assistant coach and East St. Louis native Julie Menendez, Mike Flater, Neil Stam, Horst Stemke, Mike Ivanow, St. Louisans John Carenza and Al Trost, Steve Gay, St. Louisan Mike Seerey, Shep Messing, trainer and St. Louisan Bud Buddell, US Soccer Federation manager Gene Edwards
BUZZ DEMLING COLLECTION

JUNE 18, 1972

MISSEY DOESN'T MISS IN AMATEUR CUP FINAL

BUSCH BATTERED the New Bedford Portugese-Americans with 30 shots in the US Amateur Cup championship game, but only Kevin Missey didn't miss. His goal was all Busch needed to become the second St. Louis team in two years to win the Cup.

Busch goalkeeper Frank Tusinski tries to punch the ball away from Kutis forward Denny Vaninger during a 1972 match.
DENNY VANINGER COLLECTION

Missey, a midfielder from Meramec Community College, hit a shot out of a crowd from 10 yards out in the 39th minute.

Busch's young, fast, and well-conditioned club dominated New Bedford, a team of older players mixed with three teenagers. Busch kept goalkeeper Joao Miguel busy, hitting the post or crossbar seven times and forcing 12 saves. But failure to score more than once almost bit Busch 90 seconds from the end, when Alfredo Rodriguez ripped a hard shot that goalkeeper Frank Tusinski tipped over the crossbar.

Busch fielded a mixture of players, such as Tusinski from the University of Missouri–St. Louis and Meramec's Missey, with others mostly from national junior college champion Florissant Valley. Busch also featured forward Mike Villa, the all-time leading scorer at Quincy College, where he played from 1964 to 1967.

Busch lost its first three games but caught fire after the fall college season and finished with a 22–5–6 record.

Busch 1, New Bedford (MA) Portugese-Americans 0

US Amateur Cup championship game at Florissant Valley Community College

BUSCH: GK Frank Tusinski; Backs: Nolan Reimnitz, Steve Buckley, Tim Fitzsimmons, Robin Geisz; Midfielders: Kevin Missey, Mark Mathis; Forwards: Mike Villa, Greg Geisz, John Garland, Bob Lemp. Subs: Jim Milner

NEW BEDFORD: GK Joao Miguel; Backs: Jose Almeider, Pinto Herminio, Gil Coimbra, Antonio Borges, Nuno Moniz; Forwards: Jose Santos, Neylor Santos, Fernando Meio, Alfredo Rodriguez, Manuel Franca. Subs: Nelson Cardosa, Thompson Nascimento

GOAL: Missey 39

REFEREE: Mike Wuertz

LINESMEN: Larry King, Bob Fitzgerald

ATTENDANCE: 1,500 (estimated)

AUGUST 26, 1972

QUESTIONABLE CALLS MAR STARS' LOSS IN NASL FINAL

THINGS WENT badly before the game even started between the St. Louis Stars and the New York Cosmos. Rain puddled the field. Lightning briefly killed the lights.

Thirty-nine fouls, an ejection, and a nullified tying goal later, the Stars lost, 2–1.

New York Cosmos 2, St. Louis Stars 1

NASL championship game at Hofstra Stadium, Uniondale, NY

NEW YORK: GK Richard Blackmore; Backs: Karol Kapcinski, Werner Roth, Dieter Zajdel, Barry Mahy; Midfielders: Johnny Kerr, Sigi Stritzl, Josef Jelinek; Forwards: Randy Horton, Willie Mfum, Roby Young. Subs: Everald Cummings, Gordon Bradley

ST. LOUIS: GK Mike Winter; Backs: John Sewell, Wilf Tranter, Steve Frank, Joe Puls; Midfielders: Pat McBride, Gary Rensing, Larry Hausmann; Forwards: Casey Frankiewicz, Gene Geimer, Willy Roy. Subs: Yao Kan Kam

GOALS: Horton (N) (Young) 5, Frankiewicz (S) (Sewell) 52, Jelinek (N) (PK) 86

REFEREE: Roger Schott

LINESMEN: Bill Maxwell, Bob Sumpter

ATTENDANCE: 6,102

The NASL's 1972 runners-up, the St. Louis Stars. Front (L-R): General Manager Jim Koerner, Player-Coach Casey Frankiewicz, Gene Geimer, Jim Draude, Paul Pisani, Jim Leeker, Pat McBride, Mike Winter. Back: Trainer Steve Middleman, Steve Frank, Joe Puls, Wilf Tranter, Tom Howe, Gary Rensing, Larry Hausmann, John Pisani, John Sewell. Frankiewicz, Winter, Puls, Tranter, and Sewell were the only non-St. Louis players in the photo. **JIM LEEKER COLLECTION**

Even the winners complained. "There were too many fouls in the game, and a lot had to do with the rain and the officiating," the Cosmos' Johnny Kerr said.

Kerr was fouled by Gary Rensing in the penalty area with four minutes left. Josef Jelinek converted for the apparent winner. But Werner Roth was ejected for kicking Willy Roy with two minutes remaining. The Stars swarmed the man-short Cosmos. Roy scored with 13 seconds left, but the goal was called offsides.

League-leading scorer Randy Horton struck five minutes into the match. Stars player-coach Casey Frankiewicz tied it in the 52nd minute. Offsides was called, but linesman Bill Maxwell overruled the referee.

A moral victory for the Stars: five starters were St. Louisans. A sixth, US Soccer Hall of Famer Roy, was a Chicago native. Only one US-born player started for the Cosmos.

NOVEMBER 25, 1972

MERAMEC CRASHES NJCAA PARTY

FOR THE fourth consecutive season, a St. Louis team won the national junior college soccer championship. No surprise there.

But the winner wasn't three-time defending champion and 1972 No. 1–ranked Florissant Valley. Big surprise there.

Meramec's Warriors, ranked seventh, received an at-large bid after losing to Florissant Valley, 2–0, in the Region 16 final. Given new life, the Warriors won all three of their games in the nationals, finishing with a 3–0 defeat of Miami–Dade South in the championship game.

The Warriors dispatched Mercer, 5–1, and Westchester, 2–0, to gain the final. Meanwhile, Flo Valley was upset by Queensborough in the quarterfinals.

Neither snow, nor slush, nor Miami–Dade South could stop the Warriors from winning it all. Meramec made Miami goalkeeper Mike Marquez come up with 17 saves, but three first-half shots eluded him. Mike Beck, Meramec's leading scorer with 24 goals, knocked in a rebound in the 12th minute, then passed to Len Deschler for the first of his two goals. Deschler slotted his second in the 41st minute. A 3–0 deficit under deteriorating field conditions made a comeback nearly impossible for Miami. Sure enough, Meramec held on for its first national soccer title and finished with a 16–3–1 record.

Joe Barron finished fourth in team scoring for Meramec in 1972 with 17 points on six goals and 11 assists.
ST. LOUIS COMMUNITY COLLEGE

Meramec 3, Miami–Dade South 0

NJCAA men's championship game at Florissant Valley Community College

SUMMARY: Full recap unavailable

GOALS: Mike Beck (Dan Vogler, Joe Vitale) 13, Len Deschler (Beck, Kevin Missey) 23, Deschler (Vitale) 41

ATTENDANCE: 400 (estimated)

DECEMBER 9, 1972

COUGARS CROWNED NCAA COLLEGE DIVISION CHAMPS

SAINT LOUIS University won eight of the first 13 NCAA soccer titles. Before season 14 in 1972, the NCAA split soccer into the University and College divisions.

If the NCAA hoped for a non–St. Louis winner in at least one division, then the move failed. Bob Guelker's SIU–Edwardsville Cougars and Harry Keough's SLU Billikens saw to that.

Guelker, SLU's coach when the Bills won the first NCAA soccer championship in 1959, directed the Cougars to the first College Division title. Chris Carenza, younger brother of SIUE all-time leading scorer John, had the only goal as the Cougars blanked Oneonta State in the championship game at SIUE.

SIU-Edwardsville 1, Oneonta State 0

NCAA men's College Division championship game at Cougar Field, SIU-Edwardsville

SUMMARY: Full recap unavailable

GOALS: Chris Carenza (Denny Driscoll) 52

ATTENDANCE: 3,000 (estimated)

Freezing rain and sleet led both teams to don sneakers. The Cougars let the ball do the work on the slippery grass. The goal-scoring sequence began with Tom Twellman's pass to Denny Driscoll. Driscoll fed Carenza, who drew out goalkeeper Steve Plisinski and shot into the net. Meanwhile, SIUE goalkeeper Rick Benben made 15 saves, including one on a point-blank shot by Carlos Camacho in the first half.

SIUE finished with an 11–0–3 record. Their season included a tie against SLU, which won the University championship three weeks after the Cougars copped the College crown.

Chris Carenza, who scored the only goal in the 1972 NCAA College Division final, eludes a defender. SIU-EDWARDSVILLE

DECEMBER 29, 1972

BILLS WIN BIG IN MUST-WIN SEASON

SAINT LOUIS University's Billikens lost to Howard, 3–2, in the 1971 NCAA finals, snapping a 45-game unbeaten streak. (Howard later lost the title for using ineligible players.) SLU viewed 1972 as must-win. "If we didn't win it all, our season would have been a failure," Billiken Joe Clarke said.

Saint Louis University beat or tied everyone but St. Louis in 1972, losing to the University of Missouri–St. Louis and Quincy, both by 1–0 scores, as well as tying SIU–Edwardsville, 1–1. The Bills went 15–0–2 against everyone else. They clipped Howard, 2–1, in the University Division semifinals and defeated UCLA, 4–2, in the championship game.

The 1972 club featured two-time Hermann Trophy winner Mike Seerey and 1973 Hermann winner Dan Counce. Counce opened the scoring against UCLA late in the first half. Ten minutes after Denny Hadican made it 2–0, a brawl erupted after Tekeda Alemu scored for UCLA in the 62nd minute. SLU goalkeeper Chuck Zorumski and teammate Bruce Hudson were hurt and left the game.

Seerey, although double-teamed and nursing a pulled hamstring, went to work. He scored twice in a minute with 15 minutes to go, sending the Bills on their way to their ninth NCAA title.

Saint Louis University 4, UCLA 2

NCAA men's University Division championship game at Miami Orange Bowl

SLU: GK Chuck Zorumski; Backs: Mark Demling, Bruce Hudson, Bob Matteson, Denny Werner, Bob O'Leary, Joe Hamm; Forwards: Jim Bokern, Dan Counce, Mike Seerey, Denny Hadican. Subs: Tim Logush, Joe Clarke, Tim Hoffman, Al Steck, Dale Harmon

UCLA (first names given if known)**:** GK Steve Burnside; Backs: Jose Lopez, Sigi Schmid, Yaregal Gebreyesus, Terry Lippman, Carlos Trevino, Fesseha Wolde-Emanuel; Forwards: Shoa Agonafer, Bernardo Ortiz, Solomon Terfa, Tekeda Alemu. Subs: Girma Belay, Garrick, Ruben Ochoa, Cherif Zein

GOALS: Counce (S) (Clarke, Matteson) 42, Hadican (S) (Logush) 52, Alemu (U) (Agonafer) 62, Seerey (S) (Logush) 75, Seerey (S) (Counce) 76, Alemu (U) (Ortiz) 77

REFEREES: William Rose, Arthur Wachter

ATTENDANCE: 3,037

Happy Billikens celebrate their 1972 championship (L-R): Joe Hamm, Mike Seerey, Dan Counce, Al Steck, Joe Clarke.
SAINT LOUIS UNIVERSITY

AUGUST 12, 1973

TROST'S TALLY TOPPLES POLAND

IN HIS first appearance for the US National Team, US Soccer Hall of Famer Al Trost scored on an assist from fellow St. Louisan and St. Louis Stars teammate Gene Geimer as the USA surprised 1972 Olympic champion Poland, 1–0, in a friendly in New Britain, Connecticut.

Trost's was the USA's only goal in six matches against Poland from 1973 to 1990. The Poles outscored the USA, 22–1, in those games.

At the time, the victory was considered second only to the US triumph over England in the 1950 World Cup, with five St. Louisans in the starting lineup, as the biggest upset in US soccer history.

St. Louisan Buzz Demling was in the starting 11 with Trost and Geimer against Poland, one of the world's top teams in the early 1970s. The Poles finished third in the 1974 World Cup to go along with their 1972 gold medal.

Trost's goal against Poland was one of many highlights in a career that included winning back-to-back Hermann Trophies at Saint Louis University, being named to the All-NASL Team three times, and playing on the US team that qualified for the 1972 Olympics. He captained the USA during 1974 and 1978 World Cup qualifying.

United States 1, Poland 0

International friendly at Willowbrook Park, New Britain (CT)

USA: GK Mike Ivanow. Field players: Bobby Smith, Buzz Demling, Stefan Szefer, Charlie McCully, Barry Barto, Al Trost, Frank Ivic, Fred Grgurev, Paul Child, Gene Geimer. Subs: Marko Vukovic, Tony Francillo, Jerry Panek, Kyle Rote Jr.

POLAND: GK Jan Tomaszewski. Field players: Antoni Szymanowski, Miroslaw Bulzacki, Jerzy Gorgon, Adam Musial, Leslaw Cmikiewiez, Kaz Deyna, Andrzej Drozdowski, Jan Banas, Andrzej Szarmach, Robert Gadocha. Subs: Marian Szeja, Krzysztof Rzesny, Zenon Kasztelan, Henry Kasperczak, Zenon Kasztelan, Henry Kasperczak, Jan Domarski

GOAL: Trost (Geimer) 37

ATTENDANCE: 10,000 (estimated)

Al Trost played on the 1972 US Olympic Team and later captained the US Men's National Team in addition to a long and stellar career with the NASL's St. Louis Stars.
BILL McDERMOTT COLLECTION

NOVEMBER 9, 1973

20,112 SEE SLU CLIP TOP-RANKED SIUE

WHAT A game it figured to be: The two top-ranked college teams in the nation, both from St. Louis and both defending national champions, playing at Busch Stadium for the Bronze Boot.

And what a game it was: Dan Counce's goal against previously unscored upon SIUE gave second-ranked Saint Louis University a 1–0 win over top-ranked SIUE before the then-biggest crowd in college soccer history.

As 20,112 watched, Counce pounced on a rebound off a save by goalkeeper Chester Kowalewski and scored in the 65th minute. Kowalewski's counterpart, Chuck Zorumski, made 13 saves, perhaps his best a stop on Dan O'Sullivan's header.

SIUE, the 1972 NCAA College Division champion, saw its record fall to 9–1–1. SLU's Billikens, the defending NCAA University Division champions, improved to 9–1–2 and maintained its mastery of the Bronze Boot trophy, awarded each season to the winner of the SIUE–SLU game. SLU scored its sixth victory, to go along with one tie, in seven Bronze Boot matches.

Bolstered by their big win, the Bills went unbeaten the rest of the season, including a 3–0 victory over SIUE early in the playoffs, and won their 10th NCAA championship.

Saint Louis University 1, SIU–Edwardsville 0

Bronze Boot Game at Busch Stadium

SLU: GK Chuck Zorumski; Backs: Denny Werner, Mark Demling, Bruce Hudson, Joe Clarke; Midfielders: Bob Matteson, Bruce Rudroff; Forwards: Dan Counce, Denny Hadican, Jim Bokern, Tim Logush. Subs: Kevin Handlan, John Roeslein, Len Deschler, Dan Flynn

SIUE: GK Chester Kowalewski; Backs: Mike Smallwood, Bill Renaud, Steve Elliott, Dan O'Sullivan; Midfielders; Tom Galati, Steve Cacciatore; Forwards: John Stremlau, Tom Twellman, Tim Twellman, Bob Kessen. Subs: Paul Gentile, Mark Moran

GOAL: Counce 65

REFEREES: Pat Smith, Norman Clemens

ATTENDANCE: 20,112

Dan Counce scores the game's only goal in a Bronze Boot Game that matched No. 1-ranked SIU-Edwardsville and No. 2-ranked Saint Louis University; goalkeeper Chester Kowalewski and Bill Renaud defend. **SAINT LOUIS UNIVERSITY**

NOVEMBER 24, 1973

FLO VALLEY, QUINCY FOIL "ST. LOUIS" FOES

ST. LOUISANS played St. Louisans in the NAIA and NJCAA championship games held on the same day. In the NAIA final, Quincy blanked Rockhurst—out-of-town teams but with rosters overwhelmingly made up of St. Louis players—at Koch Park in Florissant.

For the first and only time, two St. Louis teams met in the junior college soccer championship game. Florissant Valley, winner of four NJCAA titles, outlasted defending champion Meramec, 2–1, in seven overtimes in Miami. Fran Lemons put the final touch on the game with a shot from about seven yards out after 122 minutes 30 seconds. Flo seemingly had the game wrapped up in regulation time. But Rick Brinker poked the ball out of a crowd and into Flo Valley's goal three seconds before time ran out, nullifying Steve Lucido's goal 15 minutes earlier.

While Meramec and Flo played in sunny Florida, Quincy and Rockhurst tangled in fog and steady rain. Nevertheless, Quincy thoroughly dominated for a 3–0 victory. Jim Eagan, Jim Pollihan, and Bill Fann, all St. Louisans, scored the goals. Quincy posted a remarkable turnaround after going 5–5–1 in its first 11 games. The Hawks won their last nine and collected their fourth NAIA championship.

Quincy 3, Rockhurst 0

NAIA men's championship game at Koch Park

SUMMARIES: Full recaps unavailable

GOALS: Jim Eagan (Paul Geerling) 25, Jim Pollihan (Bill Fann) 52, Fann (Mark Mathis) 83

ATTENDANCE: 3,125

Florissant Valley 2, Meramec 1 (7 OTs)

NJCAA men's championship game at Miami (FL) Dade-North

GOALS: Steve Lucido (F) 84, Rick Brinker (M) 89, Fran Lemons (F) 123

ATTENDANCE: Unknown

Quincy's Jim Eagan battles the goalkeeper for the ball while Quincy's Jim Pollihan follows the play in 1973. Eagan and Pollihan were two of many St. Louisans on the 1973 NAIA championship team.
JACK MACKENZIE COLLECTION

DECEMBER 8, 1973

DIVISION II CHAMP UMSL BEST IN NATION?

THE UNIVERSITY of Missouri–St. Louis won its only national soccer championship, overwhelming California State–Fullerton, 3–0, in the Division II (formerly College Division) final. One can make a case that the Rivermen may have been the nation's best college team of 1973.

Although competing in the "small-school" division of NCAA soccer, the 11–0–3 Rivermen played the big boys on even or better terms. The Rivermen tied Division I champion Saint Louis University and 11–2–1 SIU–Edwardsville, one-two in the final national college coaches' poll, and defeated NAIA champion Quincy. UMSL finished fifth in the national rankings.

Even with key players such as leading scorer Tim Smith and defender Ken Hudson injured, UMSL overcame early threats from Cal State, coached by St. Louis native Dennis Checkett. Goalkeeper Frank Tusinski made critical saves in the 22nd and 32nd minutes. It was all UMSL after that. Kevin Missey and Mark LeGrand scored in the last five minutes of the first half, and Missey added an unassisted goal with 10 minutes left.

The Rivermen had other seasons with more victories under head coach Don Dallas, who compiled a 236–89–30 record from 1968 to 1990. But no other UMSL team made it past the NCAA semifinals.

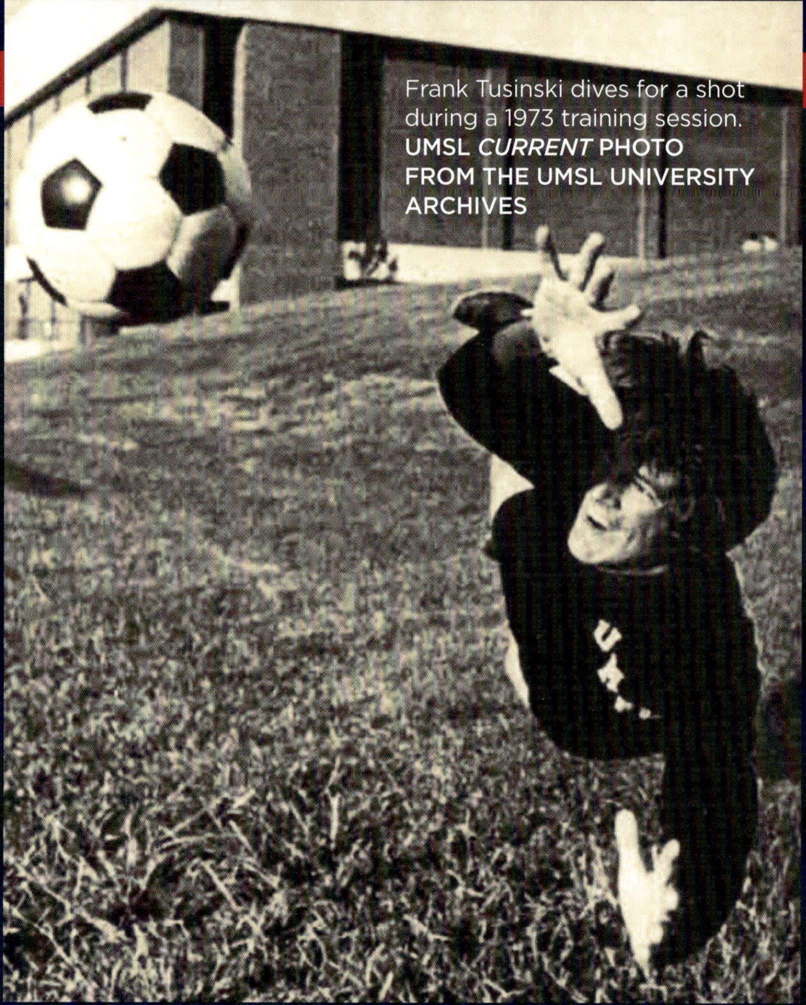

Frank Tusinski dives for a shot during a 1973 training session. UMSL *CURRENT* PHOTO FROM THE UMSL UNIVERSITY ARCHIVES

UMSL 3, California State–Fullerton 0

NCAA Division II men's championship game at Springfield (MA) College

SUMMARY: Full recap unavailable

GOALS: Kevin Missey (Ed Fleming) 41, Mark LeGrand (UA) 44, Missey (UA) 80

ATTENDANCE: 2,241

JANUARY 4, 1974

TENTH NCAA TITLE FOR SLU

DAN COUNCE put an exclamation point on the most dominant run of titles in men's NCAA soccer history when he scored at 5:43 of sudden-death overtime to lift Saint Louis University to a 2–1 victory over UCLA in the NCAA Division I championship game. The Billikens, the defending champions, won their 10th and last title over the first 15 seasons of NCAA men's soccer.

Counce also scored the Bills' first goal, tallying on a breakaway to tie the game in the 55th minute. UCLA had gone ahead when Firooz Fowzi pounced on a miskick when the Bills' defense tried to clear the ball. The Billikens took control of the game in the second half. Only the outstanding saves of goalkeeper Fred Decker kept the game tied. SLU outshot UCLA, 32–10, and had a 10–4 advantage in corner kicks.

The game winner ended a spectacular career for Counce and other Billiken seniors. Counce was selected the tournament's most valuable player and later won the Hermann Trophy for the 1973 season. Counce and his senior teammates played in four consecutive national championship games, winning three (all against UCLA), and compiling an overall 61–5–7 record.

Saint Louis University 2, UCLA 1 (OT)

NCAA men's Division I championship game at Miami Orange Bowl

SLU: GK Chuck Zorumski. Backs: Joe Clarke, Bruce Hudson, Mark Demling, Denny Werner, Bob Matteson, Bruce Rudroff. Forwards: Tim Logush, Denny Hadican, Dan Counce, Jim Bokern. Subs: Kevin Handlan, John Roeslein, Dan Flynn

UCLA: GK Fred Decker. Backs: Mark Otsea, Jose Lopez, Girma Belay, Carlos Trevino, Sigi Schmid, Terry Lippman. Forwards: Tekeda Alemu, Sergio Velasquez, Firooz Fowzi, Efrén Herrera. Subs: Hector Salcedo, Cherif Zein, Ruben Ochoa

GOALS: Fowzi (U) (UA) 5, Counce (S) (Hadican) 55, Counce (S) (Hadican) 96

REFEREES: Ray Kraft, Harold Chappel

ATTENDANCE: 5,861

Saint Louis University head coach Harry Keough poses with the Billikens' treasure trove of championship trophies.
SAINT LOUIS UNIVERSITY

NOVEMBER 30, 1974

FANN FIRES QUINCY TO ANOTHER NAIA TITLE

COLLEGE SOCCER focused on St. Louis, site of three of four national tournaments: NCAA Division 1 at Busch Stadium and Division II at the University of Missouri–St. Louis, and the NAIA at Koch Park in Florissant. Division III, which made its debut for NCAA small schools, played in Wheaton, Illinois.

After the final ball was kicked, Quincy emerged as the only school with strong St. Louis ties to prevail. Fielding an almost entirely St. Louis roster, the Hawks blasted Davis & Elkins, 6–0, with the first three goals from Florissant native Bill Fann. UMSL, the defending Division II champion, fell in the regional semifinals. In the Division I final, Howard University, as it had in 1971, denied Saint Louis University its third consecutive title, prevailing, 2–1, in four overtimes.

Quincy concluded one of its finest seasons in the snow at Koch Park. The Hawks' 17–2–1 record included victories over UMSL and nationally third-ranked SIU–Edwardsville, along with a scoreless tie with Saint Louis University The Hawks smashed their three opponents in the national tournament by a combined 20–2. All six goals in the final came from St. Louisans. Their coach, St. Louis native Jack Mackenzie, was named national coach of the year.

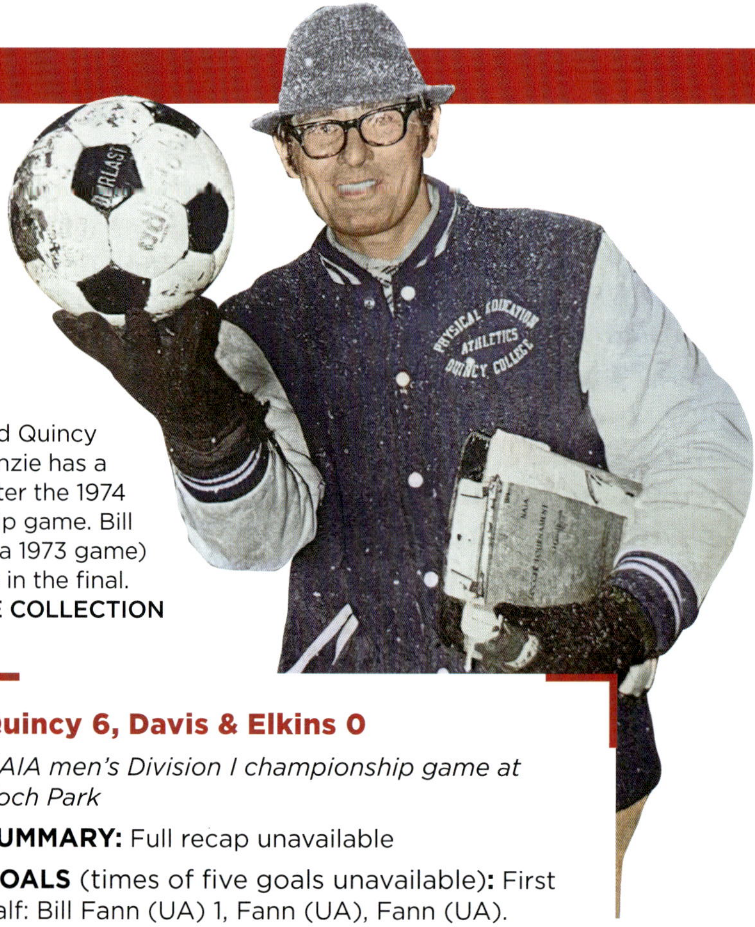

St. Louis native and Quincy coach Jack Mackenzie has a ball in the snow after the 1974 NAIA championship game. Bill Fann (below from a 1973 game) scored three goals in the final. **JACK MACKENZIE COLLECTION**

Quincy 6, Davis & Elkins 0

NAIA men's Division I championship game at Koch Park

SUMMARY: Full recap unavailable

GOALS (times of five goals unavailable)**:** First half: Bill Fann (UA) 1, Fann (UA), Fann (UA). Second half: Jim Eagan (Paul Geerling), Frank Vinciguerra, Fran Slay

ATTENDANCE: 2,813

Quincy players and coaches, almost all from St. Louis, won the 1973 and 1974 NAIA tournaments at Koch Park in Florissant. Back (L-R): Andy Probst, Larry Franzoi, Coach Jack Mackenzie, Rich Zeidler, Ed "Butch" Renaud, Neil Frederickson, Frank Camacho, Mark Mathis, Jim Pollihan, John Green, Larry Carron, Frank Vinciguerra. Kneeling: Paul Geerling, Sam Bick, Jim Eagan (son of Florissant mayor James J. Eagan), Matt Weiss, Steve Brightman, Bill Fann. The 1973 and 1974 Quincy teams also included future City of St. Louis mayor Francis Slay.
JACK MACKENZIE COLLECTION

AUGUST 17, 1975

BONETTI BACKSTOPS STARS TO NASL SEMIFINALS

PLAYING THROUGH an injury, goalkeeper Peter Bonetti gave up only one goal, but the St. Louis Stars lost to the Portland Timbers.

Portland Timbers 1, St. Louis Stars 0

NASL semifinals at Civic Stadium, Portland, OR

PORTLAND: GK Graham Brown; D Ray Martin, Barry Lynch, Graham Day; M Brian Godfrey, Tom McLaren (Tony Betts 80), Barry Powell, Chris Dangerfield; F Peter Withe, Jimmy Kelly, Willy Anderson

ST. LOUIS: GK Peter Bonetti; D Larry Hausmann (Bob Matteson 65), Steve Frank, Gary Rensing, Roger Verdi; M Bob O'Leary, Dennis Burnett, Pat McBride; F Jim Bokern (John Carenza 62), Mike Seerey (Gene Geimer 80), John Hawley

GOAL: Peter Withe (Graham Day, Barry Powell) 55:45

SAVES: Brown (P) 11, Bonetti (S) 15

REFEREE: John Davies

ATTENDANCE: 33,503

Bonetti was up to the task despite injuring his left leg on a first-half save that left him limping the rest of the match.

The Timbers tallied in the 56th minute, when Peter Withe deflected Graham Day's header into the net. The Stars' best chance came with 4:30 remaining. Goalkeeper Graham Brown dove and pushed a shot by US Soccer Hall of Famer Pat McBride just wide.

Bonetti, maligned for his performance with England in its 1970 World Cup quarterfinal loss to West Germany, had an otherwise notable career with Chelsea. He came to

the Stars on a free transfer and was widely credited for the Stars' transformation from a 4–15–1 team in 1974 to a club that won the Central Division with a 13–9 record in 1975.

The Stars won their playoff opener on penalty kicks on August 13 before facing the Timbers. The Stars played both matches without injured US Soccer Hall of Famer Al Trost. Bonetti returned to Chelsea in 1976. The Stars made one more playoff appearance, in 1977, before moving to Anaheim, California.

The 1975 St. Louis Stars, NASL semifinalists. Back (L-R): Trainer Bill Hopfinger, Steve Frank, Gary Rensing, Al Trost, Denny Vaninger, Dave Jokerst, John Carenza, Dennis Burnett, John Hawley, Mike Seerey, Gene Geimer, General Manager Jack Galmiche. Front: Bob O'Leary, John Pisani, Pat McBride, Larry Hausmann, Peter Bonetti, Jim Bokern, Roger Verdi, Bob Matteson, Player-Coach John Sewell. The only non–St. Louisans in the picture are Bonetti, Burnett, Hawley, Verdi, and Sewell. **DENNY VANINGER COLLECTION**

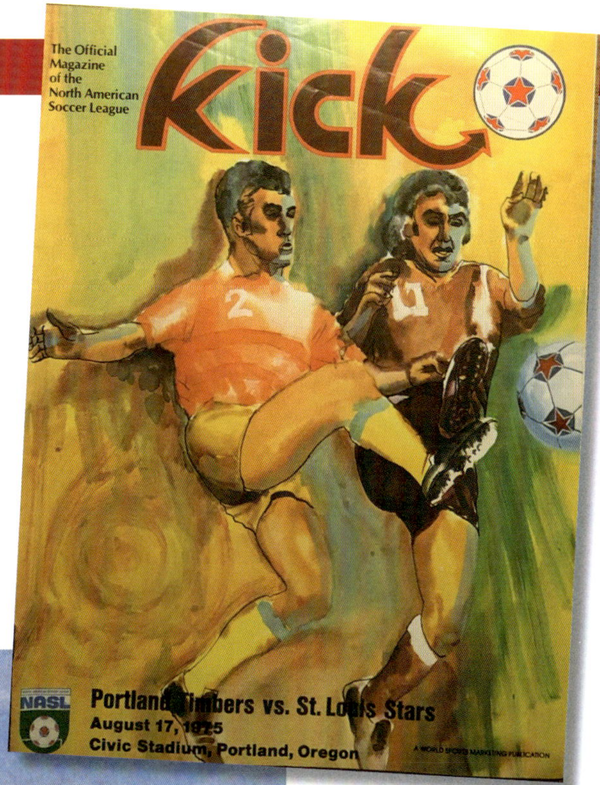

The game program for the NASL 1975 semifinal between the St. Louis Stars and the Portland Timbers **DAVE LANGE COLLECTION**

NOVEMBER 29, 1975

QUINCY, FLO VALLEY VICTORIOUS IN NATIONAL FINALS

QUINCY'S HAWKS and Florissant Valley's Norsemen expanded their impressive collections of national championships. Flo Valley captured its sixth junior college title by defeating State University of New York–Morrisville, 3–0. Quincy became the first soccer team to win three consecutive national championships in the NCAA or NAIA when the Hawks edged Simon Fraser, 1–0, in the NAIA final.

Quincy 1, Simon Fraser 0

NAIA men's championship game at Len Bauer Field, Raleigh, NC

SUMMARY: Full recap unavailable

GOAL: Emilo John (Frank Vinciguerra) 89:30

ATTENDANCE: 1,700 (estimated)

Florissant Valley 3, SUNY-Morrisville 0

NJCAA men's championship game at Essex Community College, Baltimore

GOALS: Mark Darrow :35, Matt Krankeola 44:16, 89:19

ATTENDANCE: 1,200 (estimated)

Emilio John (checked shirt) scored with 30 seconds left to lift Quincy to the 1975 NAIA title. JACK MACKENZIE COLLECTION

It wasn't easy for the Hawks. They finally went ahead on Emilio John's goal with 30 seconds left. Simon Fraser attacked from the center-off. Goalkeeper Eric Delabar, down after blocking a shot, quick-crawled to cover up the ball and robbed Simon Fraser of an easy tap-in. The last-minute heroics capped a 19–1–1 season for Quincy.

Flo Valley won behind a fast start from Mark Darrow and late goals from Matt Krankeola. Darrow scored his 20th goal of the season just 35 seconds into the game. Krankeola's two goals came in the last minute of each half. The Norsemen ended a 20–0–1 season. Flo posted 13 shutouts behind a tough defense led by 1974 All-Americans Steve Pecher and Joe Harris.

Belleville Area, which reached the NJCAA tournament for the second consecutive season, lost in its opening tournament game and the consolation semifinals.

Flo Valley's 1975 national champions. Front (L-R): Mark Darrow, Terry Barnett, Bob Hammond, Dennis Dougherty, Billy Geerling, Steve Pecher. Middle: Marty Clarke, Mike Galkowski, Kevin Magee, Matt McVey, Gary LeGrand, Don Walsh, Jim Putnam. Back: Pete Sorber, Kevin Kluge, Matt Krankeola, Jim Roth, Joe Harris, Pat Turner, Danny Geerling, Mike Thornton, Richard Twibill, Bob O'Leary, Dale Harmon **PETE SORBER COLLECTION**

NOVEMBER 27, 1976

MERCER GETS THE PUBLICITY, MERAMEC GETS THE CHAMPIONSHIP

THIS WAS the year that Pat McBride, player, retired and became Pat McBride, coach. Success in his new career came quickly as the US Soccer Hall of Famer guided Meramec to a stunning upset of previously unbeaten Mercer County, 3–2, in the NJCAA championship game.

Mercer carried a 23–0 record and the NJCAA's No. 1 ranking into the final. Meramec had lost to Mercer, 6–3, during the regular season.

Meramec turned the tables quickly. Steve Gliedt scored in the second minute off a pass from Mike Kelley. Mercer tied the score three minutes later when Meramec keeper Paul Turin deflected a corner kick into the net while trying to punch it clear. Turin stopped a penalty kick later in the first half. Gliedt made it 2–1 on another pass from Kelley in the 71st minute. Kelley converted a penalty kick for what proved to be the winning goal in the 85th minute.

"Nobody gave us much of a chance," McBride said. "They (Mercer) got the publicity, and we got the championship." McBride, a three-time all-NASL player, retired after 10 seasons with the St. Louis Stars. He went on to a successful career coaching pro indoor and junior college soccer.

Meramec 3, Mercer County (Trenton, NJ) 2

NJCAA men's championship game at Community College Stadium, Miami (FL)–Dade North

SUMMARY: Full recap unavailable

GOALS: Steve Gliedt (Meramec) 2, OG (Mercer) 8, Gliedt 71, Mike Kelley (Meramec) PK 85, Frank DiMatteo (UA) 90

ATTENDANCE: 1,647

Pat McBride (in warmup pants) leads a Meramec practice in 1976.
ST. LOUIS COMMUNITY COLLEGE

NOVEMBER 27, 1977

QUINCY "MUD-DLES" BACK TO NAIA TITLE

A YEAR after losing to Simon Fraser in 14 overtimes in the 1976 NAIA semifinals, Quincy's Hawks regained the NAIA championship with a 3–0 mudder over Keene State.

Quincy, which had a string of three straight NAIA titles broken by Simon Fraser, played the 1977 final on a muddy, slippery field swamped by three inches of rain in the previous 24 hours.

The Hawks went ahead after Emilio John, one of the team's few non–St. Louisans, was fouled in the penalty area. He converted the penalty kick for his 57th and last career goal at Quincy. St. Louisans connected for Quincy's other goals: Bob Radice stuck the dagger into Keene when he scored just seven seconds before halftime off a pass from Mike DiRaimondo, and Steve Melsheimer iced the game on an assist from Radice with five minutes remaining.

Quincy 3, Keene State (NH) 0

NAIA men's championship game at Charger Field, Huntsville, AL

SUMMARY: Full recap unavailable

GOALS: Emilio John PK 25:25, Bob Radice (Mike DiRaimondo) 44:53, Steve Melsheimer (Radice) 84:36

ATTENDANCE: Unknown

Emilio John converts a penalty kick for one of his team-leading 16 goals for Quincy in 1977. He opened the scoring in the NAIA final with another goal on a PK. **JACK MACKENZIE COLLECTION**

The NAIA title was Quincy's seventh in 12 years. The 19–3–0 Hawks outscored their opponents, 69–13, in 1977. Two of Quincy's three losses came by one goal to NCAA Division I semifinalist SIU–Edwardsville, and in overtime to Saint Louis University St. Louisan Eric Delabar posted shutouts in Quincy's last six games and had 14 for the season.

NOVEMBER 25, 1978

TIP FROM TOP HELPS TAKE QUINCY TO TITLE

QUINCY WON its eighth NAIA national championship, thanks in part to coach Jack Mackenzie's scouting of the Hawks' opponent in the final, Alabama–Huntsville.

Mackenzie told his Hawks that Huntsville was slow to organize its defense against free kicks near its goal. Sure enough, the Hawks opened the scoring in the 16th minute when two St. Louisans connected on a rapid restart. Mike DiRaimondo served a quick kick to Pat Howley, whose low shot was fumbled into the Huntsville net by the goalkeeper. Another of the Hawks' St. Louis players, Steve Melsheimer, notched the insurance goal 32 minutes into the second half. Quincy's goalkeeper, St. Louisan Eric Delabar, posted his 12th shutout of the season. The match's St. Louis flavor extended to Alabama–Huntsville, which started four St. Louisans.

Quincy's Delabar, defender Tim Werner, and forward Bob Radice—all St. Louisans—were named to the all-tournament team. Radice, a senior who didn't record a goal or an assist in the tournament, was nevertheless named its most valuable player.

Rockhurst, another team loaded with St. Louis players, won the tournament's third-place game, 1–0, over Davis & Elkins. St. Louisan Mark Scott scored the goal.

Quincy 2, Alabama-Huntsville 0

NAIA men's championship game at Charger Field, Huntsville, AL

SUMMARY: Full recap unavailable

GOALS: Pat Howley (Mike DiRaimondo) 16, Steve Melsheimer 77

ATTENDANCE: Unknown

St. Louisan Bob Radice (left) takes on a Sangamon State opponent. Radice was the most valuable player of the 1978 NAIA Tournament for national champion Quincy.
JACK MACKENZIE COLLECTION

NOVEMBER 24, 1979

ST. LOUIS EL CLASSICO GOES TO QUINCY

Quincy 1, Rockhurst 0

SUMMARY: Full recap unavailable

GOAL: John Gallo PK 25:15

ATTENDANCE: 1,752

ST. LOUIS coaches—Rockhurst's Tony Tocco and Quincy's Jack Mackenzie—led the teams in the championship game. Thirty-four of 36 players came from St. Louis. Only a disputed penalty kick separated the two teams. Quincy prevailed, 1–0, for its ninth NAIA title. Rockhurst lost for the fourth time—three against Quincy—in four NAIA finals.

The game turned on one play midway through the first half. Chris MacArthur was called for a handball in the Rockhurst penalty area. John Gallo, a freshman from Vianney High School, blasted his penalty kick into the side netting for the game's only goal.

Rockhurst protested the foul vehemently. "The ball hit Chris MacArthur in the chest," Tocco said. "It didn't hit his arm."

But the call stood, and so did Quincy's defense. Playing with the wind in the second half, Rockhurst attacked relentlessly, outshooting Quincy, 6–1. Goalkeeper Jim Harte saved five shots. Gary Hempel blocked another with a sliding save with about 16 minutes left.

Rockhurst, the tournament's top seed, finished with an 18–4–1 record. Quincy concluded its season 16–5–3.

St. Louisan John Gallo beats Rockhurst goalkeeper Jim Halaz on a penalty kick for the only goal of the 1979 NAIA championship game.
JACK MACKENZIE COLLECTION

DECEMBER 9, 1979

COUGARS WIN ONE LAST TITLE FOR GUELKER

Bob Guelker holds his NCAA-record seventh men's national championship trophy after SIU-Edwardsville defeated Clemson, 3–2. From left: Pat Malloy, Tim Guelker, Bob Bozada, Bob Guelker, and Mark Downar. **SIU-EDWARDSVILLE**

"THE WORLD lost, 3–2."

So began the *St. Louis Globe-Democrat*'s report on the NCAA Division I final between Clemson and SIU-Edwardsville. The Cougars, with a St. Louis coaching staff and an almost all–St. Louis roster, defeated Clemson's international aggregation of Canadians, Lebanese, Englishmen, Nigerians, and Americans.

The victory ended a dramatic season that began with head coach and US Soccer Hall of Famer Bob Guelker undergoing triple bypass surgery. It ended when Tim Guelker, the coach's son, set up the winning goal in the 87th minute. Matt Malloy knocked in Guelker's header. Malloy scored all the Cougars' goals.

Bob Guelker returned from surgery two games into the season and in a wheelchair. The Cougars lost their next two games. While assistant Rick Benben handled much of the load, Guelker regained strength and eventually resumed his duties. SIUE never lost after its fourth game.

Clemson rallied from a 2–0 deficit in the final. Barely three minutes after Clemson's second goal, Matt Malloy's brother, Pat, sent a free kick from midfield into the Clemson goal mouth. Tim Guelker redirected the ball out of a crowd to Matt Malloy for the winner.

The title gave Bob Guelker seven, a still-standing NCAA men's soccer coaching record.

SIU-Edwardsville 3, Clemson 2

NCAA Division I men's championship game at Tampa (FL) Stadium

SUMMARY: Full recap unavailable

GOALS: Matt Malloy (S) (Guelker) 5:56, M. Malloy (S) (Bob Bozada) 25:49, Obed Ariri (C) (Joseph Awesu) 70:57, Nnamdi Nwokocha (C) (Ariri) 83:00, M. Malloy (S) (Guelker) 86:19

ATTENDANCE: 4,000 (estimated)

DECEMBER 14, 1979

NEW TEAM IN TOWN PACKS THE HOUSE

THE NEWEST team in town, the indoor-soccer Steamers, stole the St. Louis sports spotlight with a standing-room crowd of 18,005 for their first home game. Nobody—least of all the Steamers—expected it.

Overwhelmed by a wave of unexpected walk-up fans, the Steamers began the game late. When it finally started, the sellout crowd settled in for something completely different: over-the-top player introductions, pulsating music, power plays, quick line changes, wall passes, and shots at goal by teams playing 6v6. . . lots of shots, 108 of them by game's end.

Harford Hellions 5, St. Louis Steamers 4

MISL regular-season home opener at the Checkerdome

FIRST PERIOD: Scoring—1. Yilmaz Orhan (H) (Peter Lechermann) 1:56, 2. Emilio Romero (S) (Tony Graham) 6:39, 3. Orhan (H) (UA) 12:18. Penalties—Hartford (too many players on floor) 13:37

SECOND PERIOD: Scoring—None. Penalties—None

THIRD PERIOD: Scoring—4. Steve Pecher (S) (UA) PPG 5:03, 5. Dan Counce (S) (UA) 6:33, 6. Romero (S) (UA) 7:41, 7. Mike Stojanovic (H) (Vincent Julius) 10:35. Penalties—Orhan (H, holding) 4:24, Charlie McCully (H, holding) 13:16, Carl Rose (S, holding) 13:32

FOURTH PERIOD: Scoring—8. Orhan (H) (UA) 1:03, 9. Jose Neto (H) (Telmo Pires) 14:49. Penalties—Julius (H, tripping) 5:30, Rose (S, ungentlemanly conduct) 9:05

SHOTS: Hartford 41, Steamers 67

SAVES: Roy Messing (H) 18, Paul Turin (S) 7

ATTENDANCE: 18,005

Steamers captain Steve Pecher follows a shot in a game at the Checkerdome.
RICK STANKOVEN

Almost lost in the hoopla was the final score: Hartford Hellions 5, Steamers 4.

Indoor soccer had come to St. Louis with all the subtlety of a Kiss concert.

An expansion club in the year-old Major Indoor Soccer League, the Steamers carried on a tradition of St. Louis soccer teams loaded with St. Louis players. That's where the comparison with outdoor soccer ended. Energized by the excitement of that first home game, the crowds kept coming. The Steamers averaged 14,060 in their first year and 15,219 in season two. They attracted an average crowd of 17,104 in year three.

JUNE 15, 1980

SULLIVAN'S GAME WINNER RECAPTURES AMATEUR CUP

BUSCH'S STEVE Sullivan was not supposed to play in the Amateur Cup final against defending champion Datagraphic of Atlanta.

A 20-goal scorer at Saint Louis University in 1979, Sullivan was healing from a torn ankle muscle and a possible stress fracture. He ran without pain on the morning of the final and called Busch manager Bob Brunette with the good news. Busch coach Tim Rooney inserted Sulllivan in the 50th minute of a 2–2 tie with the words, "Go in there and get us a goal."

Sullivan did just that in the 83rd minute, taking a long pass as his defender fell, leaping over the goalkeeper, and scoring the winner. SLU's John Hayes and SIU–Edwardsville's Tim Guelker had Busch's other goals.

Two weeks earlier, Hayes had amassed four goals to pace Busch to a 7–0 victory over the San Francisco Glens in the semifinals. That victory avenged Busch's 1–0 loss to the Glens in the 1979 semifinals.

Busch ran up a 32–1–1 record in winning the 10th Amateur Cup by a St. Louis team. Busch won the ninth cup for St. Louis in 1972.

Busch's Steve Sullivan leaps over Datagraphic goalkeeper Peter Murray to score the winning goal in the 1980 Amateur Cup final.
MARK SANDERBECK

Busch 3, Datagraphic (Atlanta) 2

US Amateur Cup championship game at Cougar Field, SIU–Edwardsville

SUMMARY: Full recap unavailable

GOALS (assists not available)**:** John Hayes (B) 27, Paul Newman (D) 34, John Staniforth (D) 47, Tim Guelker (B) 48, Steve Sullivan (B) 83

ATTENDANCE: 1,500 (estimated)

OCTOBER 30, 1980

BRONZE BOOT SETS COLLEGE ATTENDANCE MARK

THE ANNUAL Bronze Boot match between Gateway Arch-rivals Saint Louis University and SIU–Edwardsville attracted a still-standing record crowd for a college soccer match—22,512.

Promoters also booked popular music act Air Supply for a pregame concert. The music may have been the highlight for SIUE fans as Saint Louis University humbled the defending NCAA Division I champions, 5–1.

The Billikens ran up a 4–0 lead with two goals from John Hayes and single tallies from Steve Sullivan and Joe Olwig. Tom Groark finally put the Cougars on the board in the 82nd minute, but Sullivan struck again four minutes later. Bills' defender Dan Kustura may have made the game's biggest play when he blocked a shot by SIUE's Matt Malloy that had beaten goalkeeper Dale Smith with the game scoreless in the 21st minute.

Saint Louis University 5, SIU-Edwardsville 1

Bronze Boot game at Busch Stadium

SUMMARY: Full recap unavailable

GOALS: Steve Sullivan (SLU) (Joe Filla) 27, John Hayes (SLU) (Mike O'Mara) 40, Hayes (SLU) (O'Mara) 61, Joe Olwig (SLU) (Matt McKeon) (time unknown), Tom Groark (SIU) (Tim Guelker) 82, Sullivan (SLU) (assist unknown) 86

ATTENDANCE: 22,512 (college soccer record)

The Busch Stadium scoreboard flashes the game's final goal in Saint Louis University's 5–1 Bronze Boot win over defending NCAA D1 champion SIU-Edwardsville before a record crowd of 22,512.
SAINT LOUIS UNIVERSITY

The Bills' big win broke a 4–4–1 standoff in the previous nine Bronze Boot matches. SLU, holder of a record 10 NCAA titles, improved to 12–4–2 while SIUE dropped to 9–7–2. SLU's season ended in the second round of the playoffs with a 3–2 loss to eventual Division I champion San Francisco. SIUE lost, 2–0, in the first round to Southern Methodist University.

NOVEMBER 15, 1980

FIFTH STRAIGHT STATE TITLE TAKEN FOR GRANITE

THERE HAS never been a St. Louis–area high school soccer dynasty like Gene Baker's Granite City boys' teams. They won nine Illinois championships from 1976 to 1990. They peaked in 1980, when Granite City South won a still-standing state-record fifth consecutive title, defeating Hinsdale South, 5–1.

The Warriors said their title wasn't the biggest accomplishment of 1980. Nor was beating Missouri state champion Vianney. The Warriors savored winning the annual St. Louis Catholic Youth Council tournament, which drew teams from throughout soccer-crazy St. Louis. "Winning the CYC was a much bigger accomplishment than this one," Warriors' forward David Fernandez said.

Fernandez, a high school All-American as a junior, scored 27 goals as a senior in 1980.

Granite City South 5, Hinsdale South 1

Illinois boys' state high school championship game at Fremd High School, Palatine, IL

SUMMARY: Full recap unavailable

GOALS: David Paz (G) PK :23 left first quarter, Don Cook (G) 17:26 left second quarter, Frank Espinoza (H) 29:01, Rich Moore (G) 17:48 left fourth quarter, Cook (G) time unknown, Tony Segobiano (G) 3:19 left fourth quarter

ATTENDANCE: Unknown

Granite City South coach Gene Baker talks to his team during the 1980 season.
RICK STANKOVEN

But the Warriors were more than just Fernandez. He didn't score in the final, but David Cook scored two and David Paz, Rich Moore, and Tony Segobiano added one apiece.

More championships would come for Baker, who played at Saint Louis University and had a career high school record of 526–120–50 over 30 seasons. For example, the 1982 state champion team set Illinois records with 30 victories and 23 shutouts.

But 1980 was a very good year.

Robbie Mann advances the ball for Granite City in 1980.
RICK STANKOVEN

NOVEMBER 23, 1980

MOYERS HELPS USA MASTER MEXICO IN MAJOR UPSET

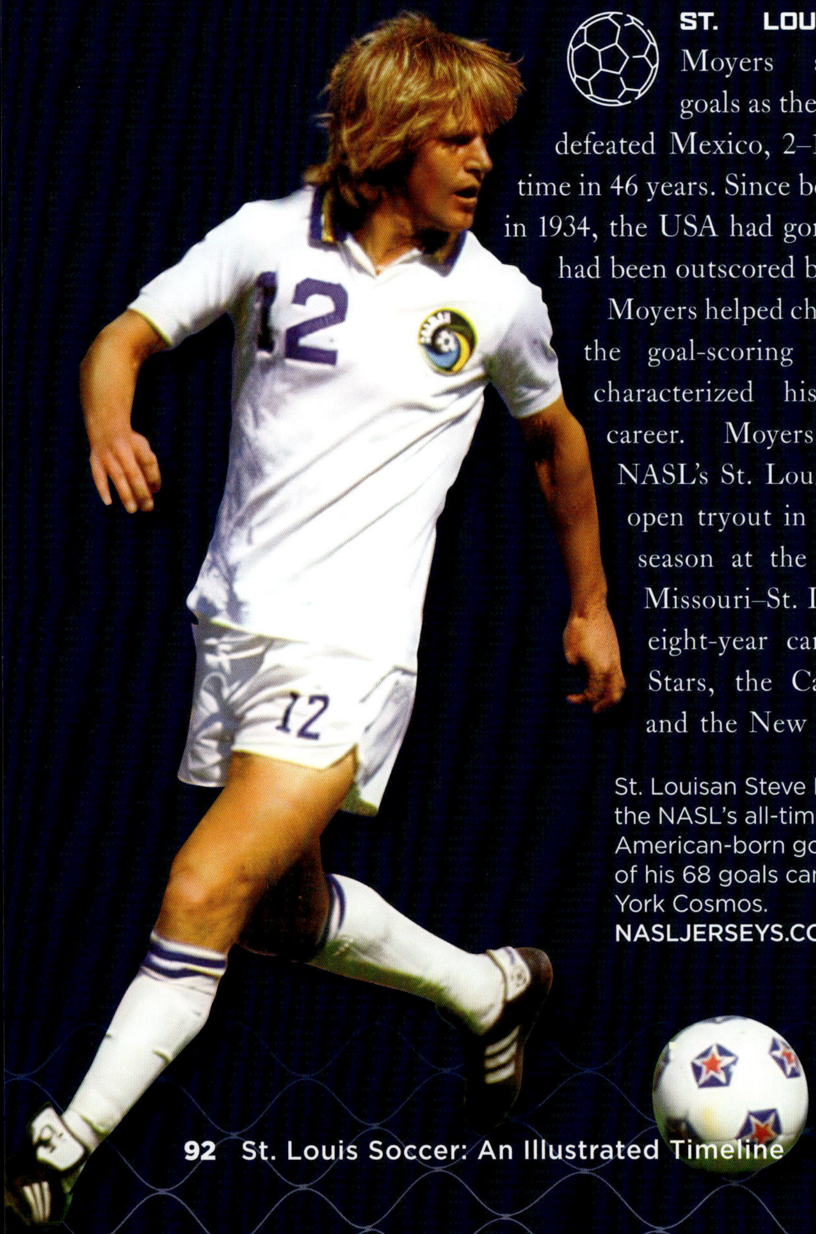

ST. LOUISAN Steve Moyers scored both goals as the United States defeated Mexico, 2–1, for the first time in 46 years. Since beating Mexico in 1934, the USA had gone 0–21–3 and had been outscored by 70 goals.

Moyers helped change that with the goal-scoring prowess that characterized his professional career. Moyers made the NASL's St. Louis Stars via an open tryout in 1977 after one season at the University of Missouri–St. Louis. Over an eight-year career with the Stars, the California Surf, and the New York Cosmos, he amassed 68 goals, most by an American-born player in the 17-year history of the NASL.

He joined the US National Team in 1980 for qualification for the 1982 World Cup along with St. Louisans Larry Hulcer, Ty Keough, Greg Makowski, Steve Pecher, and Perry Van Der Beck. Moyers played off the bench in the first two qualifiers and was not used in the third match. Already eliminated from qualifying with only a tie in the first three games, the US started Moyers in the return match with Mexico, the final qualifier. He demonstrated what might have been with his two-goal game. That made him the USA's leading scorer in 1980's qualifiers.

St. Louisan Steve Moyers was the NASL's all-time leading American-born goalscorer. Thirty of his 68 goals came for the New York Cosmos.
NASLJERSEYS.COM

United States 2, Mexico 1

World Cup qualifier at Lockart Stadium, Fort Lauderdale, FL

UNITED STATES: GK Arnie Mausser. Field players: Boris Bandov, Colin Fowles, Rick Davis, Larry Hulcer, Perry Van Der Beck (Louie Nanchoff 22), Ringo Cantillo, Angelo DiBernardo, Mark Liveric, Njego Pesa (red card 68), Steve Moyers

MEXICO: GK Ignacio Rodriguez. Field players: Mario Trejo (red card 68), Alfredo Tena, Vázquez Ayala, José Luis López, Gustavo Vargas (Ricardo Castro 73), Guillermo Mendizábal, José Luis González (Leonardo Cuéllar 67), Cristóbal Ortega, Adrián Camacho, Hugo Sánchez

GOALS: Moyers (U) (Nanchoff) 31, Sanchez (M) (Camacho) 40, Moyers (U) (UA) 65

REFEREE: M.A. Gracias Regalado

LINESMEN: Jose Luis Urena, Jorge Mario Ramirez

ATTENDANCE: 2,126

NOVEMBER 29, 1980

QUINCY CONQUERS SIMON FRASER IN OT, AGAIN

FOR THE third time, Quincy and Simon Fraser battled into overtime in an NAIA championship game. Quincy struck just 12 seconds into extra time on a goal by Tor Duner and held on for the remaining 19:48 of overtime to win, 1–0.

Quincy had topped Simon Fraser in OT in 1975 and lost a 14-overtime marathon in 1976. Their victory on their third try gave the Hawks their fourth consecutive NAIA title and 10th overall.

Title 10 may have been the toughest. The Hawks were 5–6–2 at season's midpoint. The six losses already were the most in a Quincy season. Coach Jack Mackenzie responded by switching to an attack-minded formation. The Hawks won their last 12 games, including a 1–0 overtime defeat of archrival and St. Louis–powered Rockhurst in the quarterfinals. Duner, a freshman from Sweden, meshed well with Quincy's mostly St Louis roster and led the team with 17 goals.

The play leading to Duner's OT winner began when Claes Sandstrom, another freshman from Sweden, hit a long pass from kickoff to St. Louisan Steve Lux on the left wing. Lux crossed to another St. Louisan, Mike Kossman, who laid off the ball for Duner. Duner drilled his shot into the net.

Quincy 1, Simon Fraser 0 (OT)

NAIA men's championship game at Kiwanis Stadium, Springfield, IL

SUMMARY: Full recap unavailable

GOALS: Tor Duner (Mike Kossman) :12 OT

REFEREE: John Watt

ATTENDANCE: 1,500 (estimated)

St. Louisan Pat Howley hoists Quincy's fourth consecutive NAIA championship trophy. He tied for second on the team in goalscoring with 12 in 1980. **JACK MACKENZIE COLLECTION**

MARCH 27, 1981

STEAMERS WIN "GREATEST INDOOR GAME"

SOME LATER called the Major Indoor Soccer League semifinal between the Wichita Wings and the St. Louis Steamers "the greatest indoor soccer game ever played."

Trailing 6–1 after three quarters, the Steamers tied the match, then won a shootout after a scoreless overtime before a delirious home crowd.

Ty Keough scored twice and Tony Glavin and Steve Pecher tallied to cut the score to 7–5. With three minutes remaining, goalkeeper Mike Dowler left the game after the Steamers' Don Ebert ran into Dowler's knee as Dowler cleared the ball. No penalty was called, just as no penalty was called after Steamers' all-star defender Tony Bellinger was hurt by a high kick and left in the third quarter.

Backup keeper Brad Higgs was burned less than a minute later when Yilmaz Orhan's shot deflected off a Wing. Ebert headed in the tying goal with just over a minute remaining.

A five-round shootout followed overtime. Emilio John struck the decisive blow in round four as the Steamers won the shootout, 3–1.

The Steamers fell two days later in the final. Steve Zungul scored with 30 seconds left to lift the New York Arrows to a 6–5 win and their third straight championship.

St. Louis Steamers 7, Wichita Wings 7 (OT)
Steamers win shootout, 3-1

MISL semifinals at the Checkerdome

FIRST PERIOD: Scoring—1. Brian Tinnion (W) (Helmut Dudek) 4:41, 2. Kevin Kewley (W) (Tinnion) 9:57, 3. Kewley (W) (Hank Liotart) 10:23. Penalties—None

SECOND PERIOD: Scoring—4. Andy Chapman (W) (Liotart) 5:09, 5. Kim Roentved (W) (Mike Dowler) 12:21, 6. Ty Keough (S) (Carl Rose) 14:54. Penalties—None

THIRD PERIOD: Scoring—7. Jorgen Kristensen (W) (Dudek) 13:09. Penalties—None

FOURTH PERIOD: Scoring—8. Keough (S) (Rose) :47, 9. Tony Glavin (S) (Don Ebert) 2:21, 10. Chapman (W) (Roentved) 7:04, 11. Steve Pecher (S) (Bob Bozada) 9:42, 12. Keough (S) (Yilmaz Orhan) 10:18, 13. Orhan (S) (Sam Bick) 12:16, 14. Ebert (S) (Pecher) 13:51. Penalties—Ebert (S) (unsportsmanlike conduct) 2:27, Dudek (W) (unsportsmanlike conduct) 2:27

OVERTIME: Scoring—None. Penalties: None

SHOOTOUT: Round 1—Chapman (W) score, Orhan (S) miss. Round 2—Jimmy Ryan (W) miss, Glavin (S) score. Round 3—Liotart (W) miss, Keough (S) score. Round 4—Roentved (W) miss, Emilio John (S) score. Steamers win shootout, 3-1

REFEREE: Artie Wachter. Alternate referee Anatol Popovich

ATTENDANCE: 16,236

Watching the action from the Steamers' bench during the 1981 MISL championship series are (L-R) Assistant Trainer Curt Metzger, Trainer Bill Jennings behind Tony Glavin, Coach Pat McBride, McBride's son Tim, Greg Villa, and Emilio Romero. RICK STANKOVEN

The Steamers' Emilio John attempts to redirect the ball past New York Arrows goalkeeper Shep Messing in the 1981 MISL championship game.
RICK STANKOVEN

JUNE 21, 1981

NATIONAL TITLES FOR BUSCH, SCOTT GALLAGHER

BUSCH SUCCESSFULLY defended its US Amateur Cup title with a 3–2 victory over Philadelphia Bayern, and Scott Gallagher won the US Junior Cup with a 4-2 win over the Miami Knights.

Busch rallied from a 2–0 deficit on late first-half goals from Steve Ladi and Danny O'Keefe. Ladi scored from 35 yards out. O'Keefe hit a header with less than a minute left in the half. Joe Mihaljevic netted the winner in the 70th minute.

The victory lifted Busch's record to 22–1–1 for the season and 110–4–2 over that season and the three before it.

Meanwhile, Scott Gallagher dominated the Junior Cup final, opening a 3–0 lead after 41 minutes on goals by Leo Bourneuf, Bill Stallings, and Dan Malloy. Tom Hayes accounted for Scott Gallagher's fourth goal early in the second half before 3,366 fans. The victory improved Scott Gallagher's record to 21–0–3.

The Junior Cup was the 18th in the last 26 years for a St. Louis team. Imo's Pizza won three Junior Cups, while Kutis, St. Paul, St. Philip Neri, and SECO had two each. The Florissant Celtics, Immaculate Heart of Mary, St. Engelbert, St. William, St. Bart's, Schumachers, and Scott Gallagher won the others.

Busch and Scott Gallagher brought national championships back to St. Louis on the same day in 1981.

Busch 3, Philadelphia Bayern 2

US Amateur Cup championship game, Philadelphia

SUMMARY: Full recap unavailable

GOALS: Cliff Simmons (P) (Fred Gerstenfield) time unknown, Jim Coleman (P) (Gerstenfield) time unknown, Steve Ladi (B) (assist unknown) 38, Dan O'Keefe (B) (Ladi) 44, Joe Mihaljevic (B) (O'Keefe) 70

ATTENDANCE: Unknown

Scott Gallagher 4, Miami (FL) Knights 2

US Junior Cup championship game, Camiglia Field, Omaha, NE

GOALS: Leo Bourneuf (S) (Mike Hylla) 25, Bill Stallings (S) (Tom Hayes) 30, Dan Malloy (S) (UA) 41, Kevin Connolly (M) (UA) 44, Hayes (S) (assist unknown) 46, Juan Gomez (M) (UA) 55

ATTENDANCE: 3,336

NOVEMBER 28, 1981

ERA ENDS AT QUINCY, ANOTHER CONTINUES AT FLO VALLEY

QUINCY WON its fifth consecutive and last of 11 NAIA titles, while Florissant Valley collected its seventh of an eventual 10 NJCAA crowns.

Quincy downed Alderson-Broaddus, 4–1. The Hawks soared to a 3–0 lead on a goal and two assists from Frank Bufe, one of Quincy's many St. Louisans. Quincy ended with a 21–3–1 record.

Quincy won its NAIA championships over 16 seasons with top recruits mostly from St. Louis. Quincy coach Jack Mackenzie foresaw the end when the national rankings changed in the early 1980s from one inclusive poll to separate rankings for NCAA Divisions 1, 2, and 3 and the NAIA. "The perception (among potential recruits was) that Quincy and other NAIA schools were somehow 'not in the same class' with NCAA schools," he wrote in his history of Quincy soccer.

Flo Valley won its NJCAA title by blanking Miami–Dade North, 2–0. Two freshmen, Joe Kortkamp and Marty Bixby, scored the Norsemen's goals. A sophomore, John O'Mara, set up both. The Norsemen concluded a 17–2–2 season.

Quincy 4, Alderson-Broaddus 1

NAIA men's championship game at Sangamon State University practice field, Springfield, IL

SUMMARY: Full recaps unavailable

GOALS: Jack Horas (Q) (Frank Bufe) 21:57, Tor Duner (Q) (Bufe) 39:39, Bufe (Q) (Steve Lux) 67:19, John Cole (A) (UA) 78:02, Duner (Q) (Jim Thomas) 83:21

ATTENDANCE: 1,000 (estimated)

Florissant Valley 2, Miami–Dade North 0

NJCAA men's championship game at Florissant Valley

GOALS: Joe Kortkamp (John O'Mara) 21, Marty Bixby (O'Mara) 75

ATTENDANCE: 2,000 (estimated)

Quincy's 1981 team won the Hawks' fifth consecutive, and 11th overall, NAIA championship. Front (L-R): Gary Cook, Joe Waldron, Jimmy Learned, Tor Duner, Hans Karlsson, Steve Lux, Mark Roome, John Gallo, Jim "Whitey" Thomas, Mike Mitchell, Frank Bufe, Claes Sandstrom. Middle: Rick Day, John Hirlinger, Jack Horas, Jim Stoll. Back: Coach Jack Mackenzie, Associate Coach Frank Longo, Steve Todd, Matt Derrick, Manager Farhad Valimoghaddam, Assistant Coach Elias Manassah
JACK MACKENZIE COLLECTION

MAY 26, 1982

ARROWS PIERCE STEAMERS AGAIN

THE STEAMERS began the season with a new head coach, US Soccer Hall of Famer Al Trost, and reached the MISL finals for the second consecutive season. The 1982 finals matched 1981's finalists; Slobo Ilijevski, indoors' best goalkeeper, versus Steve Zungul, indoors' greatest scorer; the Steamers, leaders in attendance and American players, versus New York's Arrows, three-time champs and leaders in everything else. The best-of-five series went the distance, including two overtime games.

Just like he had in 1981, Zungul broke Steamers fans' hearts.

Scorer of 103 goals in the regular season, Zungul—whose goal with 30 seconds left had beaten the Steamers in the 1981 final—tallied four times in 1982's fifth game. Goal number four was fatal. With the Steamers down one and on a power play, Shep Messing stopped Carl Rose's shot and found Zungul, who scored with 54 seconds remaining.

The Steamers played under protest. Between the last field check that afternoon and the start of warm-ups, "a building engineer changed the thermostat and the ice (under the playing carpet) melted," MISL commissioner Earl Foreman said. The result was playing indoors on what resembled a slippery, rain-soaked outdoor pitch. Observers agreed that conditions hurt the running-reliant Steamers more.

New York Arrows 8, St. Louis Steamers 6

Game five of best of five series, MISL finals at Nassau County Coliseum, Uniondale, NY

FIRST PERIOD: Scoring—1. Steve Zungul (N) (Paul Kitson) 1:52, 2. Ty Keough (S) (UA) PPG 8:22, 3. Kitson (N) (Val Tuksa) 9:19. Penalties—Renato Cila (N) (handball) 7:51, Redmond Lane (S) (pushing) 10:12

SECOND PERIOD: Scoring—4. Don Ebert (S) (Greg Villa) PPG 2:48, 5. Tony Glavin (S) (Jeff Sendobry) 7:57, 6. Sam Bick (S) (John Hayes) 9:18, 7. Frantz St. Lot (N) (Dragan Nikitovic) PPG 13:35. Penalties—Juan Carlos Michia (N) (boarding) 1:45, Bench (N, served by Zungul) (yellow card to Coach Don Popovic) 1:45, Villa (S) (tripping) 3:01, Stan Karasi (N) (holding) 5:32, Slobo Ilijevski (S, served by Sendobry) (handball out of penalty area) 12:24

THIRD PERIOD: Scoring—8. Zungul (Michia) :26, 9. Glavin (S) (UA) 2:23, 10. Zungul (N) (Tuksa) 3:40. Penalties—None

FOURTH PERIOD: Scoring—11. Karasi (N) (Omar Gomez) PPG 9:55, 12. St. Lot (N) (Cia) 13:15, 13. Villa (S) (Steve Pecher) 12:26, 14. Zungul (UA) SHG 14:06. Penalties—Pecher (S) (tripping) 9:48, Gene Strenicer (N) (tripping) 13:33

SHOTS: New York 53, Steamers 24

SAVES: Ilijevski (S) 27, Shep Messing (N) 12

REFEREE: Gino Dippolito. Alternate referee Bill Maxwell

ATTENDANCE: 11,023

Steve Zungul (7), shown after scoring the winning goal in the 1981 MISL championship game with 30 seconds left against the Steamers, clinched the 1982 final with a shorthanded goal with 54 seconds left in the fifth and deciding game against the Steamers. RICK STANKOVEN

OCTOBER 16, 1982

RIVERWOMEN NIP NORTH CAROLINA IN SECOND FINAL-FOUR SEASON

WOMEN'S COLLEGE soccer played its first national tournament in 1981. North Carolina won, as it did 16 more times through 2000. Just beating North Carolina was rare.

The University of Missouri–St. Louis Riverwomen, all from St. Louis, were the first to do it.

UMSL, also a national power then, defeated UNC, 2–1, on Patty Kelley's late goal. The outcome ended UNC's 29-game winning streak over two seasons.

Riverwoman goalkeeper Ruth Harker credited the win to bonding the night before. Throughout St. Louis soccer history, players from north and south St. Louis were fierce rivals. "We stayed up late and talked and got to know each other," remembered Harker, a northsider. "We meshed. The next day we beat UNC 2–1 and Patty, my old enemy from the south side, became my hero."

UMSL 2, North Carolina 1

Women's Central Florida Invitational, Orlando, FL

SUMMARY: Full recap unavailable

GOALS: Second half—Stephanie Zeh (N) (Emily Pickering) 15 minutes left, Debbie Lewis (U) (Joan Gettemeyer) 10 minutes left, Patty Kelley (U) (Joan Gettemeyer) three minutes left

UMSL's Patty Kelley, who scored the winning goal against North Carolina, dribbles in a game earlier in 1982.
UMSL *CURRENT* PHOTO BY SHARON KUBATZKY FROM THE UMSL UNIVERSITY ARCHIVES

Kelley was an unlikely hero. The tournament decided ties with penalty kicks after regulation. Kelley, one of UMSL's best, was injured. She went in with three minutes left to be available for PKs. Limping badly, she passed to Joan Gettemeyer. Gettemeyer's shot hit the crossbar. Kelley put in the rebound.

UMSL, fourth in the 1981 nationals, finished fourth again in 1982. UNC defeated unbeaten UMSL, 2–1, in the 1982 semifinals.

SEPTEMBER 10, 1983

SOCCER PARK, USA'S "FIRST SOCCER-SPECIFIC FACILITY," OPENS

FINDING A place to play has been an everlasting headache for anyone involved in St. Louis soccer. Generations of kids, collegians, and professionals kicked on bumpy, bare park fields and baseball diamonds.

Fenton's World Wide Technology Soccer Park, perhaps the nation's first soccer-specific facility, changed that.

Spurred by the field shortage, the St. Louis Youth Soccer Association sought donated land from the J.S. Alberici Construction Company. SLYSA enlisted support from Anheuser-Busch's second-in-command, Denny Long. At his behest, unions donated labor. A-B scouted European soccer facilities for ideas when planning the park.

The facility's six fields, 5,000-seat stadium, offices, and banquet facilities have been in constant use. Current headquarters of St. Louis Scott Gallagher Soccer Club, the park has held countless local, national, and international games, and even played a role in FIFA awarding the 1994 World Cup to the United States.

"We took the whole FIFA delegation to the Soccer Park and they were flabbergasted," Long said. "They said it was equal to any club facility they had ever seen. And they said if a company the size of A-B is this much interested in soccer to devote time and money to this facility, then the US was the place to hold the World Cup."

Photos of the Soccer Park under construction in the early 1980s
TIM BRASSIL COLLECTION

Above: The World Wide Technology Soccer Park as it appears today. **ST. LOUIS SCOTT-GALLAGHER SOCCER CLUB**
Inset: Anheuser-Busch executive and US Soccer Hall of Famer Denny Long (holding trophy) was instrumental in the completion of the complex in the 1980s and to soccer locally, nationally, and internationally as president of Anheuser-Busch. **DENNY LONG COLLECTION**
Also pictured is World Wide Technology cofounder Jim Kavanaugh, who, along with WWT Chief Financial Officer Tom Strunk, personally financed the purchase of the Soccer Park by St. Louis Scott Gallagher Soccer Club in 2011 and spearheaded the modernization of the facility. **DAVE LANGE COLLECTION**

JUNE 8, 1984

STEAMERS STOPPED IN MISL FINALS

THE ST. Louis Steamers lost in the MISL finals for the third time in four years as the Baltimore Blast exploded for five unanswered goals in the fourth period of game five. Baltimore won, 10–3, and clinched the best-of-seven series four games to one.

Injuries riddled the Steamers. The injured included high-scoring forward Tony Glavin (knee), Indoor Soccer Hall of Fame goalkeeper Slobo Ilijevski (shoulder), and US Soccer Hall of Famer Ricky Davis (hamstring). Team captain Steve Pecher returned shortly before the finals after a five-month absence recovering from a broken leg. Glavin missed the finals, and Ilijevski was out the first three games. Davis, the Steamers' leading scorer during the regular season, saw limited action during the series.

Nevertheless, the Steamers cruised to a 7–3 opening-game win in Baltimore.

The Blast took over from there. League-leading scorer Stan Stamenkovic came up with perhaps the series' biggest goal, an overtime winner in game four in St. Louis June 6.

The fourth quarter of game five belonged to Baltimore's Joey Fink. Fink feasted after the Steamers went to a sixth attacker midway through the final period. He scored three times in 41 seconds and notched a fourth late in the game.

The Steamers tried for the third time in four years to win in the MISL finals but took just one game in the best-of-seven series against Baltimore in 1984.

Baltimore Blast 10, St. Louis Steamers 3

MISL finals at Civic Center, Baltimore
Baltimore won best of seven series, four games to one

FIRST PERIOD: Scoring—1. Dave MacWilliams (B) (UA) 5:34, 2. Joey Fink (B) (Heinz Wirtz) 10:04. Penalties—Tim Walters (S) 5:34

SECOND PERIOD: Scoring—3. Pat Ercoli (B) (Mike Stankovic) 10:56. Penalties—None

THIRD PERIOD: Scoring—4. Njego Pesa (S) (Daryl Doran) 6:34, 5. Larry Hulcer (S) (Tony Bellinger) 7:02, 6. Stankovic (B) (Stan Stamenkovic) 9:02, 7. Paul Kitson (B) (Bob McAvan) 11:09, 8. Walters (S) (Don Ebert) 12:02. Penalties—Stankovic (B) 10:20, Stamenkovic (B) 14:42

FOURTH PERIOD: Scoring—9. MacWilliams (B) (Fink) 5:43, 10. Fink (UA) 8:53, 11. Fink (UA) 9:06, 12. Fink (B) 9:34, 13. Fink (MacWilliams) 13:52. Penalties—Stankovic (B) 14:52, Neil Cohen (S) 14:52

SHOTS: Baltimore 34, St. Louis 45. Saves: Keith Van Eron (B) 17, Slobo Ilijevski (S) 15

REFEREES: Bill Maxwell, Gino Dippolito

ATTENDANCE: 12,007 (standing room)

NOVEMBER 24, 1984

O'CONNOR HELPS CARRY FLO VALLEY TO EIGHTH TITLE

TWO GOALS and an assist from Rick O'Connor powered Florissant Valley to a 3–1 defeat of Essex in the NJCAA championship game. The national title was the first for the Norsemen since 1981 and was their eighth overall.

The 1984 champs made a strong case as one of Flo's best. They completed an 18–0–1 season and outscored opponents, 72–10. Their only tie came against another St. Louis–area school, Lewis & Clark of Godfrey, Illinois. The two teams met again in the NCAA semifinals. The Norsemen won a hard-fought match, 1–0, on a goal by O'Connor.

Lewis & Clark rebounded to defeat Mercer, 3–2, on Mark Moser's sudden-death overtime goal in the third-place game.

O'Connor continued his heroics in the championship game, opening the scoring off a cross from Dennis Kiely. O'Connor set up the second goal when he directed a long pass to Jeff Robinson, who scored on a breakaway with 34 seconds left in the first half for a 2–0 advantage. With Flo leading, 2–1, O'Connor sealed the victory when he knocked in Mike Dempster's cross with 4:50 left.

Florissant Valley 3, Essex (Baltimore) 1

NJCAA men's championship game at Mercer Community College, Trenton, NJ

SUMMARY: Full recap unavailable

GOALS: Rick O'Connor (F) (Dennis Kiely) 7:56, Jeff Robinson (F) (O'Connor) 44:26, Steve Herdecker (E) (John Shirmer) 52:48, O'Connor (F) (Mike Dempster) 85:10

Gary Amlong (17) defends for Flo Valley during a 1984 game. RICK STANKOVEN

AUGUST 23, 1985

RUTH HARKER AND FIRST USWNT "TURN THE LIGHTS ON"

ST. LOUISAN Ruth Harker took over as goalkeeper in the second half in the US Women's National Team's 3–1 loss to England in the Mundialito ("little World Cup"). Considered the unofficial World Cup for women, the tournament marked the first games for the USWNT and made Harker the first St. Louis woman to play for the USA.

The match was the USA's third of the tournament and first for Harker. She played the next day in the USA's 1–0 loss to Denmark in the third-place match. Harker played for nationally ranked University of Missouri–St. Louis teams. She earned a berth on the USWNT with her performance at the US Olympic Festival earlier in 1985.

The first FIFA World Cup for women was in 1991, after Harker's playing career ended. The USA has won the Women's World Cup four times.

"Michelle Akers probably said it best," Harker said, referring to one of her teammates on the 1985 team who made 153 appearances for the USA over 15 seasons. "She said, 'We turned the lights on.' Someone had to be the first and the road was hard and frustrating at times, but that road also shaped me. I wouldn't change a thing."

Ruth Harker (yellow) and the first US Women's National Team at the Mundialito in Italy in 1985
RUTH HARKER COLLECTION

England 3, United States 1

Mundialito Women's Tournament, Stadio Comunale Giovanni Chiggiato, Caorle, Italy

SUMMARY: Full recap unavailable

USA: GK Kim Wyant (Ruth Harker). Field players: Ann Orrison, Denise Bender, Stacey Enos, Lori Henry, Laurie Bylin, Emily Pickering (Sharon McMurtry), Tuca Healy, Denise Boyer, Cindy Gordon, Michelle Akers. USA goal: Akers, time and assist unknown

ENGLAND LINEUP AND GOAL SCORERS: Unknown

NOVEMBER 30, 1985

FLO VALLEY REPEATS AS NATIONAL CHAMPS

THREE UNUSUAL things happened to Flo Valley on the way to its second consecutive and ninth overall juco championship: Flo lost.

Undefeated in 1984, the Norsemen suffered three defeats early in the season. The defense, stung by counterattacks in the losses, resolved to stay back.

Their new tactics took the 18–3 Norsemen all the way to a 2–0 upset over No. 1-ranked, 21–0 Mercer in the final. The irony was heavy. Mercer's coach, Dave Leckie, had scored the winner when Mercer defeated Flo in the 1968 final. The Norsemen, who had grown accustomed to wet fields over the previous three weeks during a rainy spell at home, were greeted by rain in the final. "That made us feel good," Flo's Mike Dempster said.

Dempster and Mark Reiter scored on what were described as "picture strikes," the first a shot by Reiter that skipped on the wet field and deflected off Mercer's sweeper. Dempster notched the second after he blew past his defender and streaked down the left side. Flo's defense, ironclad since the three losses, came through. Fullbacks Mike Dwyer and Mike Keller each cleared Mercer shots headed for Flo's net. Flo's goalkeeper, six-foot, four-inch Tim Schulte, stopped everything else for his 15th shutout.

Goalkeeper Tim Schulte racked up 15 shutouts, including one in the NJCAA final, for Flo Valley in 1985.
PETE SORBER COLLECTION

Florissant Valley 2, Mercer 0

NJCAA men's championship game at Mercer Community College, Trenton, NJ

SUMMARY: Full recap unavailable

GOALS: Mark Reiter (Scott Eck) 14:25, Mike Dempster (assist unknown) 64:58

ATTENDANCE: 3,100 (estimated)

DECEMBER 14, 1985

VAN DER BECK NAMED US PLAYER OF THE YEAR

A PROFESSIONAL soccer journey that began in high school reached a major milestone when the US Player of the Year award went to St. Louis native Perry Van Der Beck.

In 1985, Van Der Beck made his 23rd and last appearance for the US Men's National Team in June and scored the second goal of his USMNT career in a 1–1 draw with Switzerland in February.

His first cap came in 1979, a year after the Aquinas midfielder became the first high school player drafted by an NASL team. He logged 179 games over 11 seasons with the Tampa Bay Rowdies. He captained the 1980 US Olympic team, which did not play because the US boycotted the Games.

Van Der Beck transitioned to indoor soccer while with the Rowdies. He scored 107 indoor goals with six teams through 1997. Post-playing highlights included positions as an assistant and head coach with the MLS Tampa Bay Mutiny, on the US Soccer board of directors, and as United Soccer Leagues' vice president.

Van Der Beck remains the only St. Louisan to win soccer's adult Player of the Year award. Lori Chalupny (2005) and Josh Sargent (2017) were Young Players of the Year.

St. Louisan Perry Van Der Beck appeared in 23 games for the USA, was the first player drafted out of high school by the NASL, and earned the US Player of the Year Award in 1985. **PERRY VAN DER BECK COLLECTION**

JULY 13, 1986

KUTIS BEATS THE HEAT, SAN PEDRO YUGOSLAVS IN OPEN CUP FINAL

KUTIS, RUNNER-UP in 1985, captured the US Open Cup by beating the San Pedro (California) Yugoslavs, 1–0, becoming the first St. Louis team to win the Cup since Kutis in 1957.

Playing in 94-degree heat and stifling humidity, Kutis prevailed thanks to Ted Hantak's goal with 30 minutes left. As Kutis's leading scorer, Hantak bore the brunt of the Yugoslavs' physical tactics. Among numerous hits delivered to Hantak, one saw him take an elbow in the face early in the second half. Hantak briefly left the game, then came back and converted a pass from Bob Matteson into a low shot stopped by the goalkeeper. The rebound came back to Hantak, whose header ricocheted off the post and into the net.

"They did all they could to get him out of the game, but Teddy showed a good deal of composure," Kutis coach Jim Henson said. "After they got him that last time, he really came on."

Goalkeeper Paul Dueker and defenders Matteson, Joe Clarke, Dave Bozdek, and Albert Adade combined to keep the Yugoslavs out of the scoring column. Dueker had also been the goalkeeper when Kutis lost, 2–1, to the San Francsico Greek Americans in the 1985 final.

Kutis 1, San Pedro (CA) Yugoslavs 0

US Open Cup championship game at St. Louis Soccer Park

SUMMARY: Full recap unavailable

GOAL: Ted Hantak (Bob Matteson) 60

ATTENDANCE: 2,500 (estimated)

Kutis, 1985 US Open Cup champions. Front (L-R): Steve Hunsicker, Lance Polette, Terry Brown, Albert Adade, Paul Dueker, Jim Bokern, Don Huber. Back: Coach Jim Henson, Dave Bozdeck, Bob Matteson, Ted Hantak, Steve Maurer, Ken McDonald, Joe Clarke, Joe Eppy, Manager Bill Hense. Not present: Denny Vaninger DAVE BOZDECK COLLECTION

JUNE 25, 1988

BUSCH WINS LAST OPEN CUP FOR ST. LOUIS

IN "ONE of the wildest days of my life," John Hayes deflected in what proved to be the winning goal in the 114th minute to boost Busch to a 2–1 overtime victory over the San Francisco Greek Americans in the US Open Cup final.

Hayes attended the wedding of his brother Tom at noon before playing that night. Dan Muesenfechter, who played with Denver and St. Louis in the MISL, crossed the ball from the left corner, and Hayes used his chest to redirect the pass into the net.

"Dan and I have been playing together so long that we always try this play once or twice a game," said Hayes, a former indoor and outdoor professional. "All you have to do is get the ball in the area and try and deflect it. The goalie is really at your mercy then."

Busch rallied from a 1–0 deficit. Pat Olwig tied the game in the 71st minute.

Many of the Busch players formed the core of the Busch team that won consecutive US Amateur Cups in 1981 and 1982. Busch's 1988 Open Cup title is the last of 10 US Open Cup championships won by St. Louis teams.

Busch 1988 US Open Cup champions. Back (L-R): Tom Groark, John Hayes, Bill McKeon, Dan Walters, Mike Twellman, Pat Olwig, Mike Goforth, Joe Filla, Assistant Coach Steve Ladi. Front: Tom Unger, John Johnson, Tim Loughman, Joe Koenig, Greg Makowski, Dan Muesenfechter, Gary Amlong, Head Coach Joe Olwig, Jeff Robben **JOHN HAYES COLLECTION**

Busch 2, Greek Americans (San Francisco) 1 (OT)

US Open Cup championship game at St. Louis Soccer Park

SUMMARY: Full recap unavailable

GOALS: Michael Deleroy (G) (Jan Elberse) 35, Pat Olwig (B) (UA) 71, John Hayes (B) (Dan Muesenfechter) 114. Shots: B 8, G 11. Saves: Jeff Robben (B) 3, Aram Kardazair (G) 1

NOVEMBER 20, 1988

DRURY DRIVES FLO VALLEY TO FIRST WOMEN'S TITLE FOR ST. LOUIS

FRESHMAN KELLY Drury made history for Florissant Valley and St. Louis soccer as she scored all the goals in Florissant Valley's 4–0 victory over Mercer County in the NJCAA women's final. The title marked the first women's national soccer championship for a St. Louis team.

Drury and her Norsewomen teammates mastered a muddy field and amazed even their opponents. "They played so well in that mud, I couldn't believe it," Mercer defender Kim Murawski said. "Every time we passed, it just went plop."

It didn't take long for Drury and the Norsewomen to assert themselves. Drury ripped a 15-yard drive into the net barely two minutes into the match. Drury's second put a dagger into Mercer just 40 seconds before halftime. Michele Wrozier's free kick hit the Mercer crossbar and fell into the mud. Drury beat everyone else to the ball and tapped it in.

The 1988 final was the start of something big for Flo Valley's women. They reached the next two NCJAA finals, winning in 1990. Drury finished at Flo in 1989 with 55 career goals. Drury and Karen Lombardo, Flo's coach, later were named to the NJCAA Hall of Fame.

Muddy but happy Flo Valley celebrates the first national championship for a St. Louis women's team. Front (L-R): Tricia Murphy, Julie Schob, Teri Head, Cheryl Spence. Middle: Kelly Drury, Liane Deetman, Coach Karen Lombardo, Candy Koslowski. Back: Michelle Wrozier, Michelle Powers, Chris Crawford, Angie Viviano, Nancy Gober, Kristin Kuhn, Sandy Manker, Dawn Schoenberger, Patti Moresi. Not pictured: Amy Trost, Trish Lauben, Natasha Christof, assistant coaches Pat Baker and John Schneider
KAREN LOMBARDO COLLECTION

Florissant Valley 4, Mercer County 0

NJCAA women's championship game at Mercer County Community College, Trenton, NJ

SUMMARY: Full recap unavailable

GOALS: Kelly Drury 2:01, Drury (Michelle Wrozier) 44:20, Drury (Liane Deetman) 53:31, Drury 80:08. Shots: F 10, M 9

OCTOBER 27, 1989

STORM HITS THE ARENA

A YEAR after the St. Louis Steamers folded, another pro indoor team made its debut: the St. Louis Storm.

Formed largely through the efforts of Silicon Valley businessman Milan Mandaric, the Storm were coached by Indoor Soccer Hall of Famer Don Popovic.

The Storm began their first season with seven St. Louisans: Indoor Soccer Hall of Famer Daryl Doran, former US National Team goalkeeper David Brcic, Terry Brown, John Klein, David Eise, Mark Frederickson, and Tim Walters. They were joined by US Soccer Hall of Famer Fernando Clavijo and Indoor Soccer Hall of Famers Slobo Ilijevski and Stan Terlecki. The Storm added US Soccer Hall of Famer Preki in 1990.

A St. Louisan, Kevin Hundelt, spoiled the opening-night party by scoring the winning goal in the Kansas City Comets' 3–2 victory. The Storm compiled a 24–28 regular-season record in 1989–90. The Storm lasted two more seasons and ceased operations, along with the MISL, after the 1991–92 campaign.

Kansas City Comets 3, St. Louis Storm 2

MISL regular-season opener at the Arena

FIRST PERIOD: Scoring—1. Gary Heale (S) (Thompson Usiyan) PPG 1:31, 2. Kia (K) (Jan Goosens) 11:13. Penalty—Kim Roentved (K, persistent infringement, yellow card) :33

SECOND PERIOD: Scoring—3. Godfrey Ingram (S) (Heale) 6:43, 4. Kia (K) (Goosens) PPG 12:41. Penalties— Claudio DeOliveira (S, elbowing) 3:04, Gerry Gray (K, holding) 3:29, Usiyan (S, holding) 11:35

THIRD PERIOD: Scoring—None. Penalties—Kevin Hundelt (K, tripping) 3:15, DeOliveira (S, tripping) 8:38

FOURTH PERIOD: Scoring—5. Hundelt (K) (David Doyle) :46. Penalty—Mark Frederickson (S, ungentlemanly conduct) 12:07

GOALS: Kansas City 27, Storm 25. Saves: Mike Dowler (K) 19, David Brcic (S) 17, Daryl Doran (S) 0

ATTENDANCE: 14,975

The Storm tried, but failed, to recapture the magic of the early days of the St. Louis Steamers.
DAVE LANGE COLLECTION

NOVEMBER 19, 1989

A FIRST: FLO VALLEY PUTS TWO TEAMS IN NJCAA FINALS

FLORISSANT VALLEY made history in 1989. For the first time, men's and women's teams from the same school reached the NJCAA finals, held on the same day at Mercer Community College.

Flo fell just short of a sweep.

The men won, 2–0, over Essex Community College of Baltimore. The defending champion Norsewomen couldn't break through against three-time champion Monroe of Rochester, New York, losing, 1–0.

Scott Swain scored both goals for the Norsemen, who won despite being outshot, 13–7. Kevin Gaylord posted the shutout. The Norsemen finished 19–1 and ended the most dominant era in men's junior college soccer with their 10th championship over 23 seasons. All of the Norseman's titles came with Pete Sorber as head coach.

Monroe thwarted the Norsewomen from continuing a dynasty of their own. In a tale of two halves, Monroe won the first 45 minutes, scoring on Holly Rich's header with seven minutes left. The Norsewomen opened the throttle in the second half with 10 shots to none for Monroe.

The loss was a temporary setback for the Norsewomen, who won their second title in three years in 1990.

Florissant Valley 2, Essex 0

NJCAA men's championship game at Mercer Community College, West Windsor, NJ

SUMMARY: Full recap unavailable

GOALS: Scott Swain (Brian Kelleher) 49:28, Swain (Chris Hahs) 81:03

SHOTS: FV 7, E 17. Saves: Kevin Gaylord (FV) 13, Jayson Layfield (E) 4

ATTENDANCE: Unknown

Monroe 1, Florissant Valley 0

NJCAA women's championship game at Mercer Community College, West Windsor, NJ

GOAL: Holly Rich (Jennifer DePrez) 37:60

SHOTS: FV 15, M 9. Saves: Angie Viviano (FV) 5, Nicki Bernard 14

ATTENDANCE: Unknown

The Norsemen won their 10th and last national championship in 1989. Back (L-R): Coach Pete Sorber, Mike Dey, Joe Marcinkiewicz, Bill Stefen, Kevin Gaylord, Rob Brown, Pat Galkowski, Mike LaPosha, Rick Carpenter, Assistant Coach Steve Lucido. Middle: Scott Swain, Matt Nemnich, Jay Wilkinson, Brian Kelleher, Ed Begley, Chris Boelhauf. Front: Steve Abbott, Mike Mebally, Chris Hahs, Tom Goforth, Mike Bobbitt. **PETE SORBER COLLECTION**

SEPTEMBER 19, 1990

TRITTSCHUH FIRST AMERICAN IN CHAMPIONS LEAGUE

IN A year of international firsts for Steve Trittschuh, the Granite City defender became the first American to play in the European Cup, today's UEFA Champions League.

He logged the first half for Sparta Prague, 2–0 losers to Spartak Moscow. Three months earlier, Trittschuh had played in the United States' first World Cup match in 40 years, a 5–1 loss to Czechoslovakia.

The first event led to the second. Trittschuh's play in the World Cup game and in earlier matches in 1990 caught the eye of Czechoslovakia's assistant coach, Václav Ježek. Ježek also was head coach of Sparta Prague. Trittschuh signed with Sparta Prague and helped Sparta win its league title in 1990–91.

Trittschuh's international career also included appearing in 37 games for the US Men's National Team from 1987 to 1995.

With no major US pro outdoor league from 1984 to 1996, Trittschuh performed for the indoor Steamers and helped the Ambush win the 1995 NPSL championship. With the coming of MLS in 1996, the 30-year-old Trittschuh signed with the Colorado Rapids and played in 153 games over five seasons with Colorado and Tampa Bay. He later was head coach with Colorado Springs and St. Louis FC in the United Soccer Leagues.

Spartak Moscow 2, Sparta Prague 0

European Cup (later the UEFA Champions League) first round, first leg, Stadion Letná, Prague

SPARTA PRAGUE: GK Jan Stejskal. Field players: Július Bielik, Miroslav Mlejnek, Timothy Mwitwa, Steve Trittschuh (Horst Siegl 46), Michal Bílek, Petr Vrabec, Jiří Novotný, Roman Kukleta, Pavel Černý (Petr Podany 78), Jiří Němec

SPARTAK MOSCOW: GK Stanislav Cherchesov. Field players: Sergey Bazulev, Vasily Kulkov, Dmitri Popov, Boris Pozdnyakov, Valeriy Karpin, Gennadiy Perepadenko (Dmitriy Gradilenko 84), Igor Shalimov, Valeriy Shmarov, Valeria Popovich, (Evgeniy Bushmanov 68) Aleksandr Mostovoy

GOALS: Shalimov 25, Shmarov 57

REFEREE: Serge Muhmenthaler

ATTENDANCE: 7,800

Granite City's Steve Trittschuh (white) tackles an oppenent in an exhibition match between the USA and Iceland at the Soccer Park in 1990.
RICK STANKOVEN

Steve Trittschuh (2) is mobbed by his US teammates after scoring the first goal of the game in a friendly with Iceland at the Soccer Park in 1990. The USA won, 4–1.
RICK STANKOVEN

NOVEMBER 18, 1990

NORSEWOMEN MAKE IT TWO OUT OF THREE

FLORISSANT VALLEY'S Norsewomen bounced back from a 1–0 loss in the 1989 NJCAA finals to win their second championship in three years.

Kris Kaczmarek's goal early in the second half was all the Norsewomen needed as they downed State University of New York–Farmingdale, 1–0. Kaczmarek caught the end of Mary Moynihan's long free kick with her thigh and one-timed her shot into the net.

Otherwise, the game's goalkeepers were unbeatable. The best save from Farmingdale's Tracy Donnan came a few minutes before Kaczmarek's goal, after she slipped and recovered in time to stop a bouncing shot from Debbie Hadley. Julie Murphy, named the national tournament's outstanding goalkeeper, made her best effort for Flo when she charged through a crowd to save Shannon Sepe's shot 10 minutes into the game.

Flo Valley's toughest test of a 15–1–3 season may have come in just advancing past local opposition. The Norsewomen and St. Louis rival Meramec battled through four overtimes in the regional playoff championship game before Flo won, 3–2. That game previewed what was to come as Meramec captured NJCAA titles in 1991 and 1992.

Florissant Valley 1, SUNY-Farmingdale 0

NJCAA women's championship game at Mercer Community College, West Windsor, NJ

SUMMARY: Full recap unavailable

GOAL: Kris Kaczmarek (Mary Moynihan) 55:55

SHOTS: FV 6, SUNY 7. Saves: Julie Murphy (FV) 5, Tracy Donnan (SUNY) 5

ATTENDANCE: Unknown

The 1990 national champion Norsewomen. Front (L-R): Annie Noonan, Chris McIntosh, Bridget Brisco, Kelly Donahue, Laura Goeke, Lori Corbett. Middle: Mary Reynolds, Marla Boland, Jenny Grzyb, Kim Beaman, Tina Renda, Mary Moynihan. Back: Head Coach Karen Lombardo, Cindy Frederiksen, Angie Frederiksen, Dena Hecht, Julie Murphy, Sarah Breeden, Kris Kaczmarek, Assistant Coaches John Schneider and Pat Baker. Not pictured: Debbie Hadley
KAREN LOMBARDO COLLECTION

JULY 28, 1991

J.B. MARINE KEEPS COOL, WINS GIRLS' JUNIOR CUP

IT DIDN'T look good for J.B. Marine.

The St. Louisans were less than three minutes from losing in overtime to Police Youth Express from Fairfax, Virginia, in the Girls' Junior Cup championship game. No St. Louis team had won the Girls' Junior Cup in its 12-year history, a trend that seemed certain to continue.

Then, J.B. Marine's Michelle McCarthy sent a shot into the corner of the net. The second and last 15-minute overtime ended 2:49 later, sending the match to a shootout. J.B. Marine made three of its first four PKs while Fairfax made two of four. Sally Meek began the fifth round with a shot into the corner to win the game.

The St. Louisans trailed twice in the match. Fairfax's Kimberly Smith opened the scoring. Kori Steifvater tied it for J.B. Marine. But Smith struck again 10 minutes into the first overtime for a 2–1 Fairfax lead. "We didn't get rattled, and we just kept our cool," said J.B. Marine coach Mike Gauvain.

The 1991 J.B. Marine team remains the only St. Louis club to win the Girls' Junior Cup, known then as the Athena Cup and today as the Girls' 19U US Youth Soccer Cup.

J.B. Marine lifts the US Girls' Junior Cup.
URSULA KITTNER COLLECTION

J.B. Marine 2, Fairfax (VA) Police Youth Club Express 2 (OT plus shootout) J.B. Marine wins shootout, 4-2

Women's Junior Cup championship game at Tranquility Park, Omaha, NE

SUMMARY: Full recap unavailable

GOALS: Kimberly Smith (F) 67:33, Kori Steifvater (JB) 75:34; Smith (F) 100:23, Michelle McCarthy (JB) 117:11. Shootout goals: JB—Ann Cook, McCarthy, Beth Ernst, Sally Meek. F—Paula Wilkins, Sue Saunders

SHOTS: J.B. Marine 18, Fairfax 11

NOVEMBER 24, 1991

MERAMEC LIVES THE DREAM IN NJCAA TOURNAMENT

"A DREAM season": That's how Meramec women's coach Jeff Karl described the 1991 campaign.

How pleasant the dream was. Other than two regular-season losses, the Lady Warriors dominated many opponents, capped by a comprehensive 4–0 victory over Catonsville (Maryland) in the NJCAA finals. Meramec amassed a 23–4 edge in shots. With the outcome decided by the midpoint of the second half, Karl got every player into the game.

It was that kind of season. The Lady Warriors gained the nation's No. 1 ranking in mid-October and never relinquished it. Meramec survived a two-overtime thriller against defending national champion Florissant Valley in the regional final. After that, the rout was on. The Lady Warriors won the national quarterfinal, 3–0, and disposed of unbeaten Anderson (South Carolina), 4–1, in the semifinals.

Jamie Casillas scored four goals for Meramec in the national semifinal.
ST. LOUIS COMMUNITY COLLEGE

Meramec's Kelly Watson dribbles upfield.
ST. LOUIS COMMUNITY COLLEGE

Meramec's top threat was Jamie Casillas. She scored all four Meramec goals in the semifinal match. Goalkeeper Kelly Hearne posted 20 shutouts and a 0.40 goals-against average. She stopped a penalty kick early in the second half of the final to snuff out Catonsville's best scoring opportunity.

Meramec's championship was the third for a St. Louis juco women's team in four years, coming on the heels of Flo Valley's titles in 1988 and 1990.

Meramec 4, Catonsville (MD) 0

NJCAA women's championship game at Mercer Community College, Trenton, NJ

SUMMARY: Full recap unavailable

GOALS: Katie Kluba (Jamie Casillas) 2:53, Jacki Verity (Kim Winterer) 19:18, Chris Fernandez (Winterer) 61:27, Nicole Lamia (UA) 63:45

SHOTS: M 23, C 4. Saves: Kelly Hearne (M) 2, Michele Burns (C) 2

ATTENDANCE: Unknown

NOVEMBER 6, 1992

AMBUSH FOILED IN FIRST-EVER GAME

THE AMBUSH, St. Louis's new indoor soccer team, lost their opener, 13–10, to the Dayton Dynamo.

The Ambush represented the third try for St. Louis at pro indoor soccer, following the Steamers (1979–88) and the Storm (1989–92). Fans noticed a big difference in the Ambush's National Professional Soccer League: scoring. Power-play and penalty-kick goals counted as one, most others for two, and long-range goals for three.

Dayton Dynamo 13, St. Louis Ambush 10

NPSL regular-season opener at Ervin J. Nutter Center, Wright State University, Dayton, OH

FIRST PERIOD: Scoring—1. Tony Bono (D, 2 points) (R.C. Campagnolo) 4:55, 2. Bono (D, 2 points) (Scott Cook) 5:11, 3. Kirk Moser (S, 2 points) (Daryl Doran) 7:49, 4. Campagnolo (D, 2 points) (Cook) 9:23, 5. Doran (S, 2 points) (UA) 14:18

SECOND PERIOD: Scoring—6. Bono (D, 2 points) (Cook) 3:28, 7. Bobby Harmon (D, 2 points) (Dennis Brose) 5:59

THIRD PERIOD: Scoring—8. Tim Walters (S, 2 points) (Mark Moser) 7:51, 9. Brose (D, 2 points) (Cook) 8:23

FOURTH PERIOD: Scoring—10. John Klein (S, 2 points) (Mark Santel) 9:28, 11. Kevin Sloan (D, 1 point PPG) (UA) 13:03, 12. Doug Kriska (S, 2 points) (UA) 13:11

SHOTS: St. Louis 44, Dayton 40

SAVES: Jeff Robben (S) 28, Carlos Pena (D) 20

ATTENDANCE: 3,729

The Ambush marked the third St. Louis professional indoor team for Indoor Soccer Hall of Famer Daryl Doran (7).
DAVID W. PRESTON

The Ambush never led in their opener. Doug Kriska, John Klein, Indoor Soccer Hall of Famer Daryl Doran, Kirk Moser, and Tim Walters scored two-point goals.

All the Ambush's opening-game players were St. Louis residents, as was head coach and former Steamers star Steve Pecher. The Ambush included Dan O'Keefe, who had led the NPSL with 144 points with Detroit in 1991–92. Dr. Abe Hawatmeh, part-owner of the Storm, was the Ambush's president and chairman of the board. He and Dr. Richard Rende bought the Tulsa, Oklahoma, NPSL franchise and moved it to St. Louis.

The Ambush posted a 19–21 record in 1992–93. The franchise continued until 2000 and reached the NPSL finals four times. They won the 1995 title, the only pro soccer championship for a St. Louis team, indoors or outdoors.

NOVEMBER 22, 1992

IT GETS EVEN BETTER FOR MERAMEC

MERAMEC'S LADY Warriors dominated in 1991. They were better in 1992—maybe the best to that point in the 11-year history of women's junior college soccer.

Meramec put the exclamation point on a 21–0 season by swamping four-time NJCAA champion Monroe of Rochester, New York, 3–0. Combined with their national championship season in 1991, Meramec ran its winning streak to an NJCAA-record 35 games.

Win number 35 saw Kim Winterer score nine minutes into the match. Jenni Burton made it 2–0 15 minutes later. Monroe had practically no chance to come back against the Lady Warriors, who blanked all three of their national tournament opponents and had 12 other shutouts during the season. Meramec goalkeeper Shelli Kleba made sure of that with a diving save on a point-blank shot from Anna Lynah early in the second half.

"They're just a superior team," Monroe coach Dan Perritano said. "The first 30 minutes, we played the best we have all week, but they are a better team."

Local rival and two-time NJCAA champion Florissant Valley dashed Meramec's hopes of a third straight title, winning 2–1 in the 1993 regional final. Flo Valley lost in the 1993 national semifinals.

Meramec 3, Monroe (NY) 0

NJCAA women's championship game at Mercer Community College, West Windsor, NJ

SUMMARY: Full recap unavailable

GOALS: Kim Winterer (Tina King) 9:19, Jenni Burton (UA) 24:39, King (UA) 79:18

SHOTS: Meramec 20, Monroe 12. Saves: Shelli Kleba (Meramec) 6, Tare DeFilippo (Monroe) 13

ATTENDANCE: Unknown

A 21–0 season and a second consecutive national championship gave the Lady Warriors reason to celebrate. ST. LOUIS COMMUNITY COLLEGE

APRIL 27, 1994

AMBUSH CAUGHT IN A CRUNCH

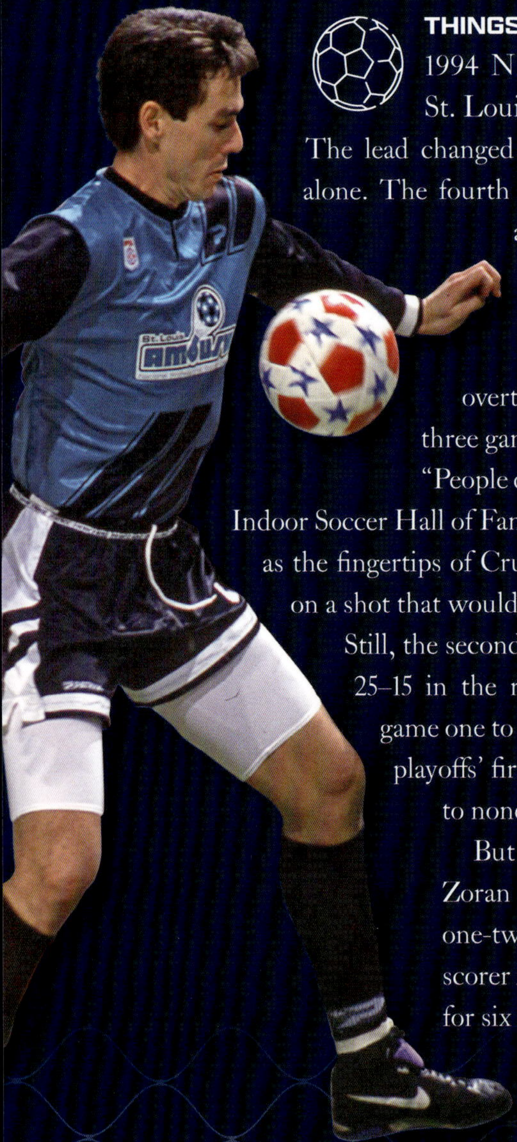

THINGS CHANGED quickly in game four of the 1994 NPSL championship series between the St. Louis Ambush and the Cleveland Crunch. The lead changed hands seven times in the third quarter alone. The fourth quarter saw Cleveland come back from a 15–10 deficit to take the match into overtime. The last lead change, and the NPSL championship, went to Cleveland on Hector Marinaro's goal in the second overtime. The Crunch clinched the series, three games to one.

"People don't realize how close we came," Ambush Indoor Soccer Hall of Famer Daryl Doran said. They came as close as the fingertips of Crunch goalkeeper Otto Orf, who got them on a shot that would have won the game in the first overtime.

Still, the second-year Ambush had a big year. They were 25–15 in the regular season. They rallied after losing game one to oust Milwaukee, two games to one, in the playoffs' first round, then blitzed Detroit, two games to none, in the semifinals.

But no one had bigger years than Cleveland's Zoran Karić and Hector Marinaro, who finished one-two in NPSL scoring. Marinaro, a 113-goal scorer in the regular season, burned the Ambush for six goals, including the winner, in game four.

Cleveland Crunch 17, St. Louis Ambush 15 (2 OTs)

NPSL best-of-five championship series at CSU Convocation Center, Cleveland. Cleveland won series, three games to one.

FIRST PERIOD: Scoring—1. David Doyle (S, 2 points) (UA) 11:44, 2. Andy Schmetzer (C, 1 point, PPG) (Shawn Medved) 13:26. Penalty—Laposha (S) tripping 12:51

SECOND PERIOD: Scoring—3. Schmetzer (C, 2 points) (Zoran Karić) 4:03. Penalties—None

THIRD PERIOD: Scoring—4. Kevin Hundelt (S, 2 points) (Doyle) :39, 5. Hector Marinaro (C, 2 points) (Tom Tanner) :50, 6. Joe Reiniger (S, 2 points) (Ted Eck) 3:13, 7. Marinaro (C, 2 points) (Karić) 6:37, 8. Eck (S, 2 points) (Doyle) 8:19, 9. Tim Tyma (C, 2 points) (Karić) 9:27, 10. Doyle (S, 2 points) (Eck) 12:24, 11. Eck (S, 2 points) (Kuntz) 13:05. Penalties—Glen Carbonara (C) misconduct 8:19

FOURTH PERIOD: Scoring—12. Doyle (S, 1 point) (UA) :10, 13. Marinaro (C, 1 point) (UA) :10, 14. Mark Moser (S, 2 points) (UA) 2:19, 15. Tanner (C, 1 point, PPG) (Medved) 4:24, 16. Marinaro (C, 2 points) (Karić) 8:13, 17. Marinaro (C, 2 points) (Karić) 8:55. Penalties—Karić (C) holding :10, Karić (C) major misconduct :10, Dev Reeves (S) holding :10, Reeves (S) major misconduct :10, S bench too many men 3:34, Doyle (S) tripping 5:48

FIRST OVERTIME: Scoring—None. Penalties—None

SECOND OVERTIME: Scoring—Marinaro (C, 2 points) (Schmetzer) 1:30. Penalties—None

SHOTS: St. Louis 61, Cleveland 43. Saves: Bill Cowie (S) 16, Doyle (S) 0, Otto Orf (C) saves unknown

REFEREES: Terry Campbell, Steve Olson, Blaz Pesorda

ATTENDANCE: 11,162

Steve Maurer had 42 goals and 33 assists in the 1993–94 season.
DAVID W. PRESTON

JULY 4, 1994

SORBER UNOFFICIAL MVP OF USA'S BEST WORLD CUP SINCE 1930

US COACH Bora Milutinovic christened St. Louisan Mike Sorber the MVP of the United States' best World Cup in 64 years after the US gained the round of 16. Eventual Cup winner Brazil defeated the USA, 1–0, in the Round of 16 on July 4.

"When you analyze the World Cup, Sorber was probably our MVP," Milutinovic said. "It is difficult for me to explain what I feel about him. He is disciplined and intelligent."

Sorber came off the field only once, in the 75th minute of the USA's final group stage match.

Milutinovic invited Sorber, son of Flo Valley coach Pete Sorber, to a national team camp in December 1991 after seeing him play for Saint Louis University in the NCAA semifinals. Sorber earned his first of 67 caps a month later. Only one other St. Louisan, Tim Ream, has more US Men's National Team appearances.

Sorber capitalized on his 1994 Cup performance with Mexico's UNAM Pumas, where he became the first US player to earn Mexican all-league honors. Five years with three MLS teams followed. He was USMNT assistant coach from 2007 to 2011, including at the 2010 World Cup. He also served as an MLS and college assistant coach and as U-16 St. Louis CITY head coach.

St. Louisan Mike Sorber challenges Alberto Garcia Aspe of Mexico during a 1–0 victory for the USA in a friendly at the Rose Bowl in Pasadena on June 4, 1994. Sorber appeared in 67 games for the US Men's National Team, more than any other St. Louisan except Tim Ream. **GETTY IMAGES/AL BELLO/GETTY IMAGES SPORT**

Brazil 1, United States 0

World Cup round of 16 at Stanford Stadium, Palo Alto, CA

UNITED STATES: GK Tony Meola. Field players: Thomas Dooley, Hugo Pérez (Roy Wegerle 66), Earnie Stewart, Tab Ramos (Eric Wynalda 46), Cobi Jones, Mike Sorber, Marcelo Balboa, Paul Caligiuri, Fernando Clavijo, Alexi Lalas

BRAZIL: GK Claudio Taffarel. Field players: Jorge Campos Jorginho, Aldair Santos, Márcio Santos, Leonardo de Araujo, Mauro Silva, Carlos Verri Dunga, Mazinho do Nascimento, Crizam de Oliveira Zinho (Marcos de Moraes Cafu 69), Jose Oliveira Bebeto, Romário de Souza Faria

GOALS: Bebeto (Romário) 74. Shots: United States 4, Brazil 16

REFEREE: Joël Quiniou

LINESMEN: Mikael Everstig, Hae-Yong Park; fourth official Bo Karlsson

ATTENDANCE: 84,147

APRIL 25, 1995

AMBUSH SWEEPS UP FIRST PRO TITLE FOR ST. LOUIS

THE AMBUSH overcame an 11–0 deficit to capture St. Louis's first pro soccer national league championship, indoors or outdoors, beating the Harrisburg Heat, 14–11.

St. Louis Ambush 14, Harrisburg (PA) Heat 11

NPSL best-of-seven championship series at Farm Show Arena, Harrisburg, PA. St. Louis won series, four games to none.

FIRST PERIOD: Scoring—1. Scott Henderson (H, 2 points) (Danny Kelly) :11, 2. Bill Becher (H, 2 points) (Tarik Walker) 8:02. Penalties—None

SECOND PERIOD: Scoring—3. Mark Pulisic (H, 2 points) (Richard Chinapoo) :17, 4. Nassim Olabi (H, 2 points) (UA) 3:09, 5. David Bascome (H, 1 point, shootout) (UA) 6:49, 6. Bob Lilley (H, 1 point, PPG) (Kelly) 7:32, 7. Kelly (H, 1 point, shootout) 8:55, 8. Daryl Doran (S, 2 points) (Maurer) 14:04. Penalties—Doran (S) boarding 6:49, Walker (H) misconduct 8:55, Greg Sczurek (S) striking 8:55, Sczurek (S) misconduct 8:55

THIRD PERIOD: Scoring—9. Mark Moser (S, 3 points) (Jamie Swanner) 3:28, 10. Mike LaPosha (S, 2 points) (Moser) 6:59, 11. Steve Maurer (S, 2 points) (UA) 13:44. Penalties—None

FOURTH PERIOD: Scoring—11. Kevin Hundelt (S, 3 points) (UA) 2:16, 12. Maurer (S, 2 points) (Doran) 14:40. Penalties—None

SHOTS: St. Louis 41, Harrisburg 32. Saves: Bill Cowie (S) 6, Swanner (S) 6, Scoop Stanisic (H) 20, Chinapoo (H) 0

REFEREES: Joe Rudy, Richard Herron, Mike Lukashunas

ATTENDANCE: 4,013

The Ambush swept the best-of-seven series, four games to none.

The title avenged the Ambush's loss to the Cleveland Crunch in the 1994 NPSL finals.

The Heat, coached by St. Louis native Jim Pollihan, were less than a minute away from a first-half shutout when player-coach and Indoor Soccer Hall of Famer Daryl Doran finally broke through with a two-point goal. The second half was all Ambush: Mark Moser and Kevin Hundelt netted three-pointers, Mike LaPosha had a two-pointer, and Steve Maurer scored two two-pointers.

Hundelt's three-point goal at 2:16 of the fourth quarter proved to be the game winner. His shot caromed off the head of a defender and into the net. Jamie Swanner took over from Bill Cowie in goal during the second half and faced only 11 shots after Cowie was bombarded with 21, 17 of which came in the second quarter.

Mark Moser had a career year with 195 points, third-best in the NPSL, during the 1994–95 season.
DAVID W. PRESTON

MAY 12, 1998

WAVE SWAMPS AMBUSH

THE MILWAUKEE Wave outscored the St. Louis Ambush 14–0 in the second half and drowned the Ambush, 21–10, to clinch the best-of-seven NPSL championship series, four games to one.

The Ambush overcame a 5–0 deficit to lead 10–7 at halftime. The Wave cut the lead to 10–9 on a two-point goal by Michael King, then pulled away on consecutive three-pointers from Chris Jahr.

Milwaukee Wave 21, St. Louis Ambush 10

NPSL best-of-seven championship series at Bradley Center, Milwaukee. Milwaukee won series, four games to one.

FIRST PERIOD: Scoring—1. Rusty Troy (M, 3 points) UA :36, 2. Mike Richardson (M, 2 points) (Troy) 2:06, 3. Scott McDoniel (S, 2 points) (Mark Moser) 11:00. Penalties—None

SECOND PERIOD: Scoring—4. Moser (S, 2 points) (Joe Reiniger) 3:59, 5. Brandon Ward (S, 2 points) (Steve Kutnz) 4:59, 6. Kevin Hundelt (S, 2 points) (Reiniger) 7:28, 7. Kuntz (S, 2 points) (UA) 10:18, 8. Steve Morris (M, 2 points) (UA) 11:30. Penalties—None

THIRD PERIOD: Scoring—9. Michael King (M, 2 points) (David Moxom) 5:07, 10. Chris Jahr (M, 3 points) 9:44, 11. Jahr (M, 3 points) (UA) 12:16. Penalties—None

FOURTH PERIOD: Scoring—12. Tarik Walker (M, 2 points) (UA) :37, 13. Richardson (M, 2 points) (Peter Hattrup) 7:22,14. Morris (M, 2 points) (King) 8:09. Penalties—None

ATTENDANCE: Unknown

Joe Reiniger was fourth in the NPSL in scoring in 1997–98.
DAVID W. PRESTON

Meanwhile, Milwaukee goalkeeper and NPSL most valuable player Victor Nogueira held the Ambush scoreless over the final 30 minutes.

The Ambush rolled through two earlier playoff rounds, ousting Kansas City two games to none in a best-of-three set, then eliminating Wichita three games to one in the best-of-five semifinals. The championship series matched the teams with the two best regular-season records. The Wave, who topped the NPSL with 28 regular-season victories, won the first three games of the series. The Ambush, who had 27 wins in the regular season, stayed alive, winning 12–8 in game four.

Joe Reiniger, a native of Collinsville, Illinois, who scored more than 600 goals during his pro indoor career, racked up 61 in 39 games for St. Louis and finished fourth in the league in scoring in the 1997–98 season.

NOVEMBER 14, 1998

DOZEN STATE TITLES FOR DRAKE-COACHED TEAMS

AQUINAS-MERCY'S FALCONS scored two goals in the dying minutes to beat Park Hill South, 3–2, in the Missouri Class 1A–3A boys' high school championship game. The Falcons won their third consecutive state title and gave coach Vince Drake his 11th boys' and 12th overall state championship.

Both are records for Missouri high school soccer coaches. Drake began coaching in 1968 after playing at Saint Louis University. He retired in 2015 after coaching boys to 737 wins and 11 state titles in 48 seasons, and girls to 349 wins and one state title in 29 seasons. Perhaps the most memorable championship came against CBC in the 1985 final, when all schools played in a single classification. Tom Kearns's goal with 17 seconds left for the Falcons sent the game into overtime. Jeff Horton scored the winner 7 seconds into overtime.

The Falcons also rallied for Drake's last title. Trailing 2–0 at halftime, the Falcons got on the board via Ryan Buckley's penalty kick early in the second half. Ano Costello made the score 2–2 with eight minutes left. Jason Gittemeier executed a give-and-go with Justin Laramie and put Laramie's return pass into the net for the winner.

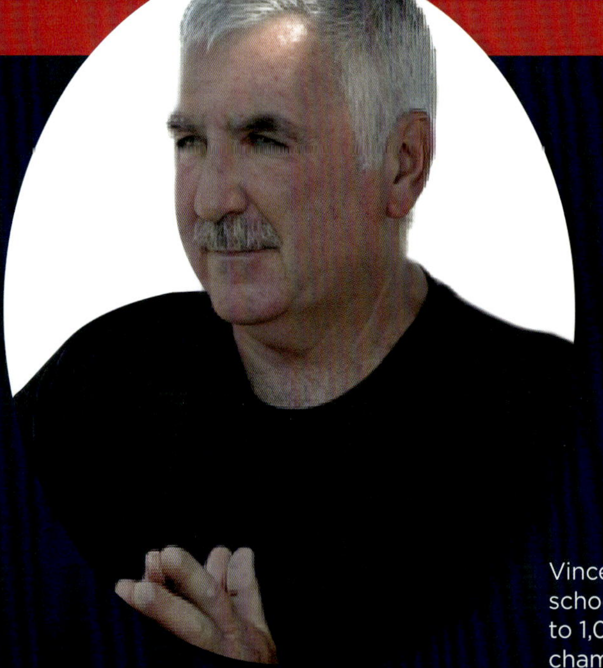

Vince Drake coached high school boys' and girls' teams to 1,086 victories and 12 state championships.
VINCE DRAKE COLLECTION

Aquinas-Mercy 3, Park Hill South (Riverside, MO) 2

Missouri Class 1A–3A boys state championship game at Anheuser-Busch Conference & Sports Centre

SUMMARY: Full recap unavailable

SCORING (first-half times unknown): First half—Ben Boehner (P) (Kyle Sebus), Daren Steward (P) UA. Second half—Ryan Buckley (A) PK 49, Ano Costello (A) (assist unknown) 72, Jason Gittemeier (A) (Justin Laramie) 77

MAY 14, 1999

AMBUSH OUSTED IN FINALS SECOND STRAIGHT SEASON

THE ST. Louis Ambush and the Cleveland Crunch played even through the first four games, and the first 45 minutes of the deciding fifth game, of the NPSL finals. But the Crunch cracked the Ambush for three unanswered two-point goals over the last 15 minutes, winning the game, 18–12, and their third NPSL championship.

The Ambush lost in the finals for the second consecutive season.

A crowd of 12,726 helped boost the Crunch to their 13th straight home victory. The home field likely was the deciding factor. The Crunch won the first two games in Cleveland, and the Ambush prevailed in the next two at the Kiel Center.

Cleveland pulled away in the fourth quarter of game five on two-point goals from three defenders, Scott Schweitzer, Troy Dusosky, and John Ball. Zoran Karic assisted on six of Cleveland's goals in the game. Mark Moser scored the Ambush's first three goals and finished the game with four.

The 1998–99 season was the last playoff hurrah for the Ambush. They reached the NPSL finals four times, winning in 1995, and qualified for the playoffs every season but their last. The Ambush folded after the 1999–2000 season, their eighth in St. Louis.

Cleveland Crunch 18, St. Louis Ambush 12

NPSL best-of-five championship series at CSU Convocation Center, Cleveland

Cleveland won series, three games to two.

FIRST PERIOD: Scoring—1. Hector Marinaro (C, 2 points) (Zoran Karic) 3:31, 2. Mark Moser (S, 2 points) (Steve Kuntz) 13:10. Penalties—None

SECOND PERIOD: Scoring—3. Moser (S, 2 points) (Chris Kenny) :54, 4. Schmetzer (C, 2 points) (Karic) 1:25, 5. Marinaro (C, 2 points) (Karic) 10:48, 6. Moser (S, 2 points) (Joe Reiniger) 12:01, 7. Daryl Doran (S, 2 points) (Hernandez) 14:54. Penalties—None

THIRD PERIOD: Scoring—8. John Ball (C, 2 points) (Karic) :41, 9. Troy Dusosky (C, 2 points) (Ball) 4:05, 10. Moser (S, 2 points) (Reiniger) 10:00, 11. Vasic (C, 2 points) (Karic) 11:20, 12. Kuntz (S, 2 points) (Reiniger) 12:36. Penalty—Hundelt (S) five-minute misconduct 7:03

FOURTH PERIOD: Scoring—13. Scott Schweitzer (C, 2 points) (Ristic) 4:31, 14. Dusosky (C, 2 points) (Karic) 7:47, 15. Ball (C, 2 points) (Tanner) 13:03. Penalties—None

SHOTS: St. Louis 36, Cleveland 58. Saves: Hernandez (S) 24, Hundelt (S) 1, Orf (C) 16

REFEREES: Joe Rudy, Ted Griforiou, Jason Krnac

ATTENDANCE: 12,726

Kevin Hundelt was the 1999 NPSL Defender of the Year.
DAVID W. PRESTON

NOVEMBER 21, 1999

ANGIE BODE SWELL FOR LEWIS & CLARK

ANGIE BODE, who thought she was through with soccer after high school, capped a stellar career at Lewis & Clark Community College by scoring both goals in the Trailblazers' 2–1 upset of No. 1-ranked Monroe in the NJCAA women's final.

Bode's goals, her 39th and 40th of the season, boosted the Trailblazers to a 2–0 lead. They hung on to win the first NJCAA championship for L&C. Tim Rooney, a St. Louis native and L&C's men's coach since 1986, started the women's team in 1993. With the Godfrey, Illinois, school less than 15 miles from north St. Louis County, he built both programs with St. Louis players.

Bode was a good example. A star player at Francis Howell North, she had decided not to play in college, but Rooney convinced her otherwise. The outcome: Bode scored 62 goals, had 37 assists, and was a two-time first-team NJCAA All-American. Her last award was her best one: 1999 NJCAA player of the year.

After an early-season loss, the Trailblazers won 23 straight and finished 25–1 in 1999. Freshman Jamie Dienell joined Bode as a first-team All-American, an honor Dienell received again in 2000. Bode, Dienell and teammate Debra Aaron made the 1999 all-tournament team.

Lewis & Clark 2, Monroe (Rochester, NY) 1

NJCAA women's championship game at Essex Community College, Baltimore

SUMMARY: Full recap unavailable

GOALS: Angie Bode (L) 23, Bode (L) 63, Beth Henley (E) 75

SHOTS: Lewis & Clark 14, Monroe 12

ATTENDANCE: Unknown

Angie Bode, the 1999 NJCAA Player of the Year, with Lewis and Clark coach Tim Rooney on her induction into the NJCAA Hall of Fame in 2017. **JAN DONA/ LEWIS AND CLARK COMMUNITY COLLEGE**

AUGUST 5, 2000

STEAMERS BACK IN BUSINESS

A NEW St. Louis pro indoor soccer team with an old name—the Steamers—lost its first game, 8–5, to the Arizona Thunder.

Arizona Thunder 8, St. Louis Steamers 5

World Indoor Soccer League regular-season opener at Veteran's Memorial Coliseum, Phoenix

(penalty information unavailable)

FIRST PERIOD: Scoring—1. Donny Galliard (A) :14, 2. Sasha Hunter (A) 6:49, 3. Kevin Groark (S) 9:14

SECOND PERIOD: Scoring—4. Hunter (A) 6:28, 5. Jeff DiMaria (S) 11:25, 6. Daryl Doran (S) 14:54

THIRD PERIOD: Scoring—7. Kevin Berry (A) PPG 4:04, 8. Mark Moser (S) 5:06

FOURTH PERIOD: Scoring—9. Milos Tomic (A) 3:30, 10. Ziad Allen (A) time unknown, 11. Rick Soderman (A) time unknown, 12. Kevin Koetters (S) time unknown, 13. Berry (A) time unknown

SHOTS: Arizona 47, St. Louis 27. Saves: Juan De La O (A) 13, Brett Phillips (S) 15

ATTENDANCE: 2,519

The Steamers leveraged the heritage of the original Steamers, who often drew sellout crowds in the early years of their existence from 1979 to 1988.

The new Steamers included an old one, Indoor Soccer Hall of Famer Daryl Doran, who also played on the city's other predecessor indoor teams, the Storm and the Ambush. Other new Steamers from the old Ambush included Kevin Hundelt and Mark Moser.

The new Steamers started badly. A shot by Arizona's Donny Galliard ricocheted off two players for a goal 14 seconds after kickoff. The Steamers rallied to tie, 4–4, after three quarters, but Arizona thundered in the fourth to win.

Unlike past indoor teams based at the Arena or Kiel Center, the Steamers called the Family Arena in St. Charles their home in 2000. They played at the Savvis Center in later seasons. The Steamers ended their first season with a 9–15 record and were 11–13 in 2001. They did not play in 2002. Their best season was their last, when they posted a 23–7 record and lost in the 2006 league finals.

St. Louisan Jeff DiMaria played for the Steamers throughout their six years of existence.
STLDIGITAL

NOVEMBER 23, 2004

LINDENWOOD LATCHES ON TO NAIA TITLE

THE LINDENWOOD Lions' men's soccer team didn't win their conference title or their regional playoff.

All they won was the NAIA national championship.

A national tournament entrant via an at-large bid, the Lions outscored their four opponents 9–1, including a 1–0 victory over Auburn Montgomery in the final. Milivoje Cecaric netted the game winner. Against a wind approaching 20 miles per hour in subfreezing temperatures during a rainstorm, Cecaric redirected Radi Zaprynof's pass over the goalkeeper in the 61st minute. Goalkeeper Edin Sabic preserved the win with a save with eight seconds left.

Lindenwood completed a 19–3–1 season with a mix of local, national, and international players. The NAIA title was the first for a "St. Louis" school since Quincy College dominated the NAIA with 11 titles from 1966 to 1981, fielding almost all St. Louis players.

Above: Lindenwood team captain Martin Barreiro (left), Pedro Chain (center), and Almir Hot. Below: Lindenwood honors its 2004 NAIA champions.
LINDENWOOD UNIVERSITY

Sangamon State of Springfield, Illinois, won NAIA titles in 1986 and 1988 with a contingent of St. Louisans. One of them, Bill Becher, scored the only goal on a penalty kick as Sangamon defeated Simon Fraser in the 1986 final. St. Louisans scored all Sangamon State's goals in the 1988 final, two from Tim Amlong and one from Joe Becher, in a 3–1 victory over Alderson-Broaddus.

Lindenwood 1, Auburn Montgomery (AL) 0

NAIA men's championship game at College Boulevard Activity Center, Olathe, KS

SUMMARY: Full recap unavailable

GOAL: Milivoje Cecaric (Radi Zaprynof) 60:54

GOALKEEPERS: Edin Sabic (L), Bjarki Gudmundsson (A)

ATTENDANCE: 200 (estimated)

FEBRUARY 19, 2005

KENNEDY FIRST ST. LOUIS WOMAN TO PLAY MEN'S PRO SOCCER

LINDSAY KENNEDY became the first St. Louis woman to play in a men's professional soccer game when she entered the St. Louis Steamers–Milwaukee Wave match with 76 seconds remaining.

She is believed to be the fourth woman to play in a men's professional indoor game.

Her debut resulted from a remark to Steamers president Michael Hetelson during a postgame gathering earlier in February. Asked for ideas to increase attendance, the 24-year-old forward suggested signing a woman—herself.

She had credentials to back her up. With no first-division women's pro league, Kennedy played in the WPSL after college. She was a three-time NAIA honorable mention All-American at Harris-Stowe and the *Post-Dispatch* player of the year at Alton High School. Invited to a tryout, she scored on her first touch at her first Steamers' practice and signed a five-game contract soon after. Her signing generated the largest home crowd of the season on February 19. She played in two more games for the Steamers.

She returned to the WPSL through 2006. Eversmeyer—her married name—later coached collegiate men's and women's soccer and started, owned, and coached the WPSL's Fire and Ice. She led the team to the 2017 WPSL championship.

Milwaukee Wave 7, St. Louis Steamers 3

MISL regular-season game at Savvis Center

FIRST PERIOD: Scoring—1. Shaun David (S) (Daryl Doran) 1:12, 2. Doran (Joe Reiniger) PPG 7:50, 3. Giuliano Oliviero (M) (Matt Schmidt) 9:10, 4. Reiniger (S) (Doran) 10:06, 5. Greg Howes (M) (Johnny Torres) 10:41, 6. Semir Mesanovic (M) 11:57. Penalties—Angel Rivillo (M) tripping 7:40; Sterling Westcott (S), Rivillo (M) altercation 10:06; Matt Caution (S) tripping time unknown

SECOND PERIOD: Scoring—7. Chris Morman (M) (Oliviero) PPG 5:38. Penalties—D.J. Newsom (S) boarding two minutes, dissent five minutes 4:26; Howes (M) dissent five minutes 13:58

THIRD PERIOD: Scoring—None. Penalties—None

FOURTH PERIOD: Scoring—8. Howes (M) PPG 5:56, 9. Michael King (M) 13:52, 10. Marcelo Fontana (M) time unknown. Penalties—Randy Soderman (S) boarding 5:15, Torres (M) tripping 9:16

ATTENDANCE: 13,798

Lindsay Kennedy plays the ball in her history-making appearance for the men's professional St. Louis Steamers on February 19, 2005.
MISSOURI SPORTS HALL OF FAME

APRIL 30, 2006

LIGHTS OUT AFTER STEAMERS LOSE CHAMPIONSHIP GAME

MACHEL MILLWOOD'S goal at 6:33 of overtime lifted the Baltimore Blast past the St. Louis Steamers to win the MISL championship.

Steamers goalkeeper Brett Phillips was the MISL goalkeeper of the year in 2006. STLDIGITAL

The finals were formatted as a home-and-home series with a golden-goal overtime to decide the champion immediately after game two if the series ended with each team winning once. The Blast won the opener, 4–2, on April 28. The Steamers thoroughly dominated the second game in St. Louis and won, 4–1.

As 16,061 fans watched the overtime that followed game two, Millwood took a pass from his left and one-timed the ball with his left foot into the top near corner of the net, beating MISL goalkeeper of the year Brett Phillips.

The Steamers, who had a league-best 23–7 regular-season record, folded after the season. Their demise ended a golden era of indoor pro soccer in St. Louis that began in 1979.

St. Louis Steamers 4, Baltimore Blast 1

Steamers tied two-game MISL finals at one game apiece at Savvis Center. Baltimore won on golden-goal overtime played immediately after game two.

FIRST PERIOD: Scoring—1. Jeff DiMaria (S) (Carlos Farias) 6:37. Penalties—None

SECOND PERIOD: Scoring—None. Penalties—Robbie Aristodemo (B) holding 2:12; Mike Kirchoff (S) holding 6:10

THIRD PERIOD: Scoring—2. Shaun David (S) (Brett Phillips) 1:50, 3. Jamar Beasley (S) (Rey Martinez) PPG 6:21, 4. Danny Kelly (B) (Adauto Neto) 13:40, 5. Martinez (S) (Mariano Bollella) 14:42. Penalty—Sanaldo Freitas de Carvalho (B) tripping 6:17, D.J. Newsom (S) holding 7:43

FOURTH PERIOD: Scoring—None. Penalties—None

SHOTS: St. Louis 31, Baltimore 22. Saves: Phillips (S) 13, Sanaldo (B) 18, Lee Tschantret (B) 1

REFEREES: Kelly Mock, Ted Grigoriou, Tim Tyma

ATTENDANCE: 16,061

Golden Goal Game

FIRST PERIOD: Scoring—Machel Millwood (B) (Giuliano Celenza) 6:33. Penalties—None

SHOTS: St. Louis 3, Baltimore 2

NOVEMBER 19, 2006

"TODAY WAS OUR DAY": JEFFCO MEN WIN NJCAA IN OT

JEFFERSON COLLEGE'S Vikings reversed roles in the NJCAA men's Division I final, defeating the team that had ousted them in the 2005 tournament.

Rhamon Silva dramatically ended the 2006 final when he scored late in the first sudden-death overtime period for a 2–1 win over Mercer. Mercer had eliminated Jeffco, 4–0, in the first round of the 2005 NJCAA national tournament.

Mercer outshot Jefferson by a wide margin in the 2006 final but missed capitalizing on several prime opportunities. "We got lucky and they missed some shots with an open net earlier in the game, but today was our day," Jefferson coach Stephen Peck Jr. said.

Tournament most valuable player Claudio Dantas set up the winning goal with what was described as a "perfect pass" to Silva. Silva hit an eight-yard shot past goalkeeper Shawn Carr.

The victory wrapped up a 21–3–1 season for the Vikings. The national title came in only the second year for men's soccer at the Hillsboro, Missouri, school.

Jefferson College 2, Mercer (Trenton, NJ) 1 (OT)

NJCAA Division I men's championship game at Pat Hartley Field, Tyler (TX) Junior College

SUMMARY: Full recap unavailable

GOALS: Rafael Segal (M) (assist unavailable) 65, Judner Joseph (J) (Samuel Drummond) 74, Rhamon Silva (J) (Claudio Dantas) 98:58

SHOTS: Mercer 10, Jefferson 3

ATTENDANCE: Unknown

Jefferson College coach Stephen Peck Jr. (right) holds the national championship trophy with Jefferson College president Wayne Watts. **JEFFERSON COLLEGE**

NOVEMBER 23, 2008

WHAT A YEAR FOR L&C AND KAYLEE

IT DIDN'T take long for Lewis & Clark women's soccer coach Tim Rooney to see he had someone special when freshman midfielder Kaylee Neutzling decided to attend L&C just before the start of the season.

"It was huge," Rooney said. "You don't get a player of her ability often."

Four months later the Trailblazers were the NJCAA Division I women's champions, they had set an NJCAA record with 26 victories (against one loss), and their last-minute addition in midfield was named NJCAA player of the year. An Edwardsville High graduate, Neutzling amassed 39 goals and 17 assists despite missing four games with an injury.

Two of Neutzling's goals came in the NJCAA final as the second-seeded Trailblazers defeated top-seeded and previously unbeaten Darton. Midfielder Kristen Pelley scored L&C's other goal.

Neutzling, Pelley, and midfielder Kelly Muesenfechter, all freshman, combined for 81 goals. Muesenfechter finished fifth in the nation, just behind Neutzling, with 91 points on 35 goals and 21 assists. Another freshman, goalkeeper Taylor Bivens, ranked eighth in the nation with a 0.625 goals-against average.

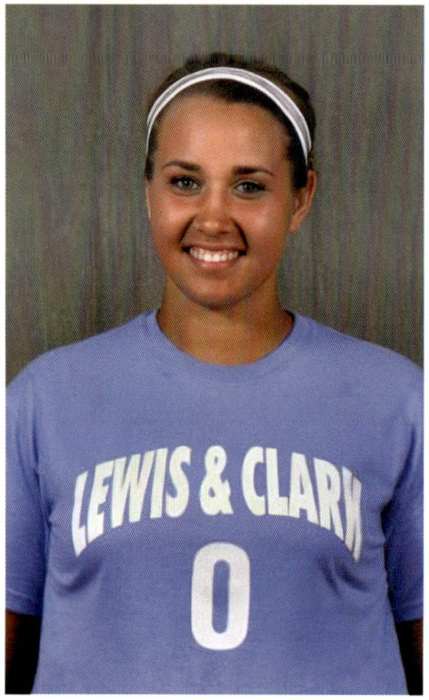

Goalkeeper Taylor Bivens (0) ranked eighth in the nation in goals-against average, Kelly Muesenfechter (11) was fifth in the nation in scoring, and Kaylee Neutzling (8) was NJCAA Player of the Year. **LEWIS AND CLARK COMMUNITY COLLEGE**

Lewis & Clark 3, Darton (Albany, GA) 2

NJCAA Division I women's championship game at Chandler-Gilbert Community College, Chandler, AZ

SUMMARY: Full recap unavailable

GOALS (assists and times unavailable): Kaylee Neutzling (L) 2, Kristen Pelly (L), Stephanie Daniels (D), Shakira Duncan (D)

APRIL 4, 2009

ST. LOUIS'S FIRST WOMEN'S PRO TEAM DEBUTS

THE ATHLETICA, St. Louis's first professional women's soccer team, opened with a 1–0 loss to the Chicago Red Stars.

The Athletica conceded in the 78th minute when Lindsay Tarpley headed in a rebound off a save from Hope Solo on a hard shot by Carli Lloyd.

"Even if the outcome had been different tonight our goal remains to get better," Athletica captain and St. Louis native Lori Chalupny said. "You'll see a completely different team at the end of the year."

Chicago Red Stars 1, St. Louis Athletica 0

WPS regular-season opener at Ralph Korte Stadium, SIU-Edwardsville

ST. LOUIS: GK Hope Solo. Field players: Kerri Hanks, Sara Larsson, Kia McNeil, Lisa Stoia, Tina Ellertson, Eniola Aluko, Daniela, Angie Woznuk, Melissa Tancredi, Lori Chalupny. Subs: Sheree Gray 65, Francielle 80

CHICAGO: GK Caroline Jonsson. Field players: Marian Dalmy, Ifeoma Dieke, Frida Östberg, Nikki Krzysik, Brittany Klein, Megan Rapinoe, Carli Lloyd, Karen Carney, Ella Masar, Lindsay Tarpley. Sub: Danesha Adans (85)

GOAL: Tarpley 78. Shots on goal: St. Louis 4, Chicago 4. Saves: Solo (S) 3, Jonsson (C) 4. Corner kicks: St. Louis 5, Chicago 2

REFEREE: Margaret Domka

ATTENDANCE: Capacity crowd of 5,008

The St. Louis Athletica's Eniola Aluko (right) pursues Chicago's Nikki Krzysik in the Athletica's first-ever match.
GETTY IMAGES/ICON SPORTS WIRE

Chalupny's prediction was on target. The Athletica, featuring a roster loaded with international stars such as Chalupny and Solo, found its stride and finished 10–6–4 and second in Women's Professional Soccer. The season ended abruptly when New Jersey Sky Blue upset the Athletica, 1–0, in the semifinals.

A new team in a new league, the Athletica were the women's side of local attorney Jeff Cooper's Saint Louis United soccer operations. United intended to build an 18,500-seat stadium for an MLS and a WPS team in Collinsville, Illinois. But investors added for the 2010 season pulled out, and the Athletica folded just six games into their second season. WPS lasted one more season before it, too, went out of business.

JUNE 7, 2009

TAYLOR TWELLMAN TOPS CENTURY MARK

TAYLOR TWELLMAN reached the century mark in MLS goal-scoring faster than anyone, driving in No. 100 (and 101) as a halftime sub in his 174th and last MLS game. His two goals, and one from fellow St. Louisan Steve Ralston, helped the New England Revolution blank the New York Red Bulls, 4–0.

Twellman, a talented multisport athlete at Saint Louis University High, was limited to two appearances in 2009 in the aftermath of a head injury suffered August 30, 2008. The New England Revolution placed him on the disabled list on June 26 because of post-concussion issues. Twellman never played again. He retired in November 2010 at age 30.

Asked his biggest career disappointment, he said: "Not playing longer. It is hard for any athlete who does not get the most out of their ability."

In addition to his career in MLS, Twellman scored six goals in 30 appearances for the US National Team, including three in a friendly against Norway in January 2006. Despite scoring a hat trick, he was not selected to the 2006 US World Cup team.

Twellman transitioned to soccer broadcasting after retirement. Twellman supports better education about concussion-related issues through his "Think Taylor" foundation, thinktaylor.org.

New England Revolution 4, New York Red Bulls 0

MLS regular-season game at Gillette Stadium

NEW ENGLAND: GK Matt Reis. Field players: Jay Heaps, Emmanuel Osei, Darrius Barnes, Kevin Alston, Jeff Larentowicz, Pat Phelan (Taylor Twellman 46), Abdoulie Mansally, Sainey Nyassi (Wells Thompson 73), Steve Ralston (Michael Videira 82), Shalrie Joseph

NEW YORK: GK Jon Conway. Field players: Kevin Goldthwaite (Carlos Mendes 80), Danleigh Borman, Mike Petzke (Sinisa Ubiparipovic 55), Jeremy Hall, Albert Celades, Dane Richards (John Wolyniec 79), Nick Zimmerman, Seth Stammler, Juan Pablo Angel, Luke Sassano

GOALS: Heaps 45 + 2; Ralston 52; Twellman 57, 64. Shots on goal: New England 2, New York 3. Saves: Reis (NE) 2, Conway (NY) 2. Corner kicks: New England 4, New York 5

REFEREES: Hilario Grajeda, SAR Daniel Belleau (bench), JAR Jason Cullum (opposite), 4th Niko Bratsis

ATTENDANCE: 11,183

Taylor Twellman attacks the New York Red Bulls' defense during his record-setting game on June 7, 2009. GETTY IMAGES/ ICON SPORTS WIRE

APRIL 10, 2010

SHORT-LIVED AC ST. LOUIS LOSES OPENER

MEN'S PROFESSIONAL soccer returned to St. Louis briefly after a 33-year absence with the start of Athletic Club St. Louis. AC opened its first and only season with a 2–0 loss to the Carolina RailHawks.

AC started the game with 10 men because AC lacked the player identification card for the 11th starter, Manuel Kanté. A frantic trip to the team's hotel yielded the missing card in time for Kanté to enter the match in the 30th minute with AC already losing, 2–0.

Caroline RailHawks 2, AC St. Louis 0

USSF Division 1 Pro League regular-season opener at WakeMed Soccer Park, Cary, NC

CAROLINA: GK Eric Reed; Defenders: Matt Bobo, Amir Lowery, Mark Schulte, John Gilkerson, Josh Gardner, Greg Shields; Midfielders: Joseph Kabwe (Matt Watson 73), Cory Elenio (Jun Marques Davidson 76), Dan Paladini; Forward: Etienne Barbara (Andriy Budnyi 80)

ST. LOUIS: GK Alec Dufty; Defenders: Zach Bauer, Tim Velten, Troy Cole, John Lesko, Manuel Kanté, John Traynor, Mark Bloom; Midfielder: Ryan Moore; Forwards: Elvir Kafedzic (Christian Nzinga 79), Jeff Cosgriff

GOALS: Barbara (UA) 4, Barbara (Elenio) 25

REFEREE: Andrew Chapin

ATTENDANCE: 2,013

St. Louisan Mike Ambersley beats Portland Timbers goalkeeper Steve Cronin for the first of three goals Ambersley scored for AC St. Louis in a 3-0 victory at the Soccer Park on July 28, 2010.
ZUMA PRESS, INC./ALAMY

The club was part of local attorney Jeff Cooper's soccer operations, which included the St. Louis Athletica in Women's Professional Soccer. Club investors in England yanked their funds in May, and the Athletica folded six games into its 2010 season. AC, which played in the USSF Division 2 Pro League (the forerunner of the USL Championship), went out of business after the season.

AC went 7–15–8 and finished second-to-last in its six-team conference. AC's most notable personality was player–assistant coach, midfielder, and St. Louis native Steve Ralston, a former US National Team player who appeared in 378 MLS matches. He was named one of the top 25 players in the first 25 seasons of MLS.

FEBRUARY 25, 2012

REAM FIRST ST. LOUISAN TO PLAY IN PREMIER LEAGUE

TIM REAM became the first St. Louisan to appear in a Premier League match. Signed by Bolton from the MLS New York Red Bulls on January 26, 2012, Ream played the entire match at left center back in Bolton's 3–0 loss at Chelsea.

Ream started a 12-year stint in England that served as a springboard to a key role with the US Men's National Team.

At Bolton, and later at Fulham, Ream was named his team's player of the year. He logged 438 appearances in all competitions until 2024, when he returned to MLS with Charlotte.

Ream rejoined the USMNT in 2013 after a two-year absence, playing an ever-larger part that led to becoming the team's captain and starting all four of the USA's games in the 2022 World Cup. He began 2022 with 46 USMNT appearances. By the summer of 2025, that total exceeded 80, more caps than any other St. Louisan who has played for the USMNT.

Chelsea 3, Bolton 0

English Premier League regular-season game at Stamford Bridge, London

CHELSEA: GK Petr Cech, RCB David Luiz, LCB Gary Cahill, LOB Ashley Cole, ROB Branislav Ivanovic, LMF Michael Essien, CMF Frank Lampard, RMF Ramieres (John Obi Mikel 88), LF Juan Mata, CF Didier Drogba (Fernando Torres 76), RF Daniel Sturridge (Salomon Kalou 80)

BOLTON: GK Adam Bogdan, LCB Tim Ream, RCB David Wheater, LOB Sam Ricketts, ROB Grétar Steinsson, LMF Frabrice Muamba, CMF Darren Pratley, RMF Nigel Reo-Coker, LF Rye Miyaichi, RF Tunclay Sanli (Chris Eagles 75), CF David N'Gog

SCORING: Luiz (UA) 48, Drogba (Lampard) 61, Lampard (Mata) 79. Shots on goal: Chelsea 13, Bolton 1

REFEREE: Michael Oliver

ATTENDANCE: 40,999

Tim Ream (left) defends against Chelsea's Salomon Kalou in Ream's Premier League debut. GETTY IMAGES/ADAM DAVY - EMPICS

MAY 23, 2013

MANCHESTER CITY, CHELSEA DRAW FULL HOUSE AT BUSCH

INTERNATIONAL MEN'S soccer returned to St. Louis after a 16-year absence when Premier League giants Manchester City and Chelsea met in a friendly at Busch Stadium. A standing-room crowd of 48,263, the largest to date for a sporting event at the seven-year-old stadium, watched.

Manchester City 4, Chelsea 3

International friendly at Busch Stadium

CHELSEA: GK Peter Cech (Jamal Blackman 61); Defenders: Branislav Ivanovic (David Luiz 45), Gary Cahill (Ramires 45), Andreas Christensen, Ashley Cole; Midfielders: Ruben Loftus-Cheek (Nathan Aké 80), Jon Obi Mikel, César Azpilicueta (Paulo Ferreira 45), Juan Mata (Oscar 45), Yossi Benayoun; Forward: Demba Ba (Fernando Torres 45)

MANCHESTER CITY: GK Joe Hart (Richard Wright 45); Defenders: Pablo Zabaleta (Maicon 62), Vincent Kompany (Micah Richards 45), Karim Rekik (Dedryck Boyata 80), Gael Clichy; Midfielders: Javi Garcia, Albert Rusnak (James Milner 62), Yaya Touré (Emyr Huws 45); Forwards: David Silva (Samir Nasri 45), Sergio Agüero (Edin Džeko 45), Carlos Tevez

GOALS: Ba (C) 22; Azpilicueta (C) PK 45; Oscar (C) 53; Garcia (M) 63; Džeko (M) 64, 85; Richards (M) 90 + 1

REFEREE: George Gansner

ATTENDANCE: 48,263 (sellout)

Chelsea plays Manchester City in a packed Busch Stadium.
GETTY IMAGES/DARREN WALSH

The game sold out 20 minutes after tickets went on sale to the public, although thousands of tickets had been bought earlier in a presale.

Manchester City rallied from a 3–0 deficit to win, 4–3. Edin Dzeko tallied twice for Manchester City, and Micah Richards scored the winner in added time.

While the game seemed meaningless, the spirited reaction of the local soccer community built momentum that encouraged more international matches for St. Louis. Just 79 days later, on August 10, Real Madrid played Inter Milan at the Edward Jones Dome before 54,184, the largest crowd up to that time for a soccer game in Missouri.

Large turnouts for subsequent matches demonstrated that St. Louis could support professional soccer. Local investors took notice. Jim Kavanaugh of World Wide Technology helped start minor-league St. Louis FC in 2014. Kavanaugh and the Taylor family of Enterprise Mobility teamed up to secure an MLS franchise for St. Louis in 2019.

OCTOBER 15, 2013

IBISEVIC SENDS BOSNIA TO WORLD CUP

FORMER ST. Louisan Vedad Ibisevic sent the soccer fans of Bosnia and Herzegovina into ecstasy by scoring the only goal of the game against Lithuania in the 68th minute to qualify Bosnia and Herzegovina for its first trip to the World Cup.

Exactly eight months later, Ibisevic tallied Bosnia's first-ever World Cup goal in the 84th minute of a 2–1 loss to Argentina.

Ibisevic traveled a long and dangerous road to his history-making games against Lithuania and Argentina. He and his family were among tens of thousands who fled genocidal war for St. Louis and created the largest Bosnian community outside of Bosnia and Herzegovina. They included many skillful soccer players, Ibisevic first and foremost.

Ibisevic was quick to establish himself after reaching St. Louis as a teenager. He demonstrated his proclivity for scoring goals, first at Roosevelt High School and then as a freshman at Saint Louis University. He turned pro after being named NCAA freshman of the year following an 18-goal season.

His pro career took him to seven different European teams, primarily in Germany. By the time of his retirement in 2020, he was tied for 27th in all-time scoring in the Bundesliga with 127 goals.

Bosnia and Herzegovina 1, Lithuania 0

World Cup qualifier at Dariaus and Gireno Stadium, Kaunas, Lithuania

LITHUANIA: GK Giedrius Arlauski. Field players: Tadas Kijanskas, Marius Zaliukas, Egidijus Vaitkunas, Valdemar Borovskij, Mindaugas Kalonas, Gedeminas Vichyus, Mindaugas Panka, Deivydas Matulevicius (Evaldas Razulis 78), Saulius Mikoliunas (Nerijus Valskis 69), Fiodor Cernych (Gratas Sirgedas 86)

BOSNIA AND HERZEGOVINA: GK Asmir Begovic. Field players: Emir Spahic, Ermin Bicakcic, Haris Medunjanin, Sejad Salihovic, Avdija Vrsajevic (Adnan Zahirovic 71), Zvjezdan Misimovic, Senad Lulic, Miralem Pjanic, Edin Džeko, Vedad Ibisevic

GOALS: Ibisevic (Džeko) 68. Shots on goal: Lithuania 2, Bosnia and Herzegovina 7. Saves: Arlauski (L) 6, Begovic (BH) 2

REFEREE: Felix Zwayer

ATTENDANCE: 6,239

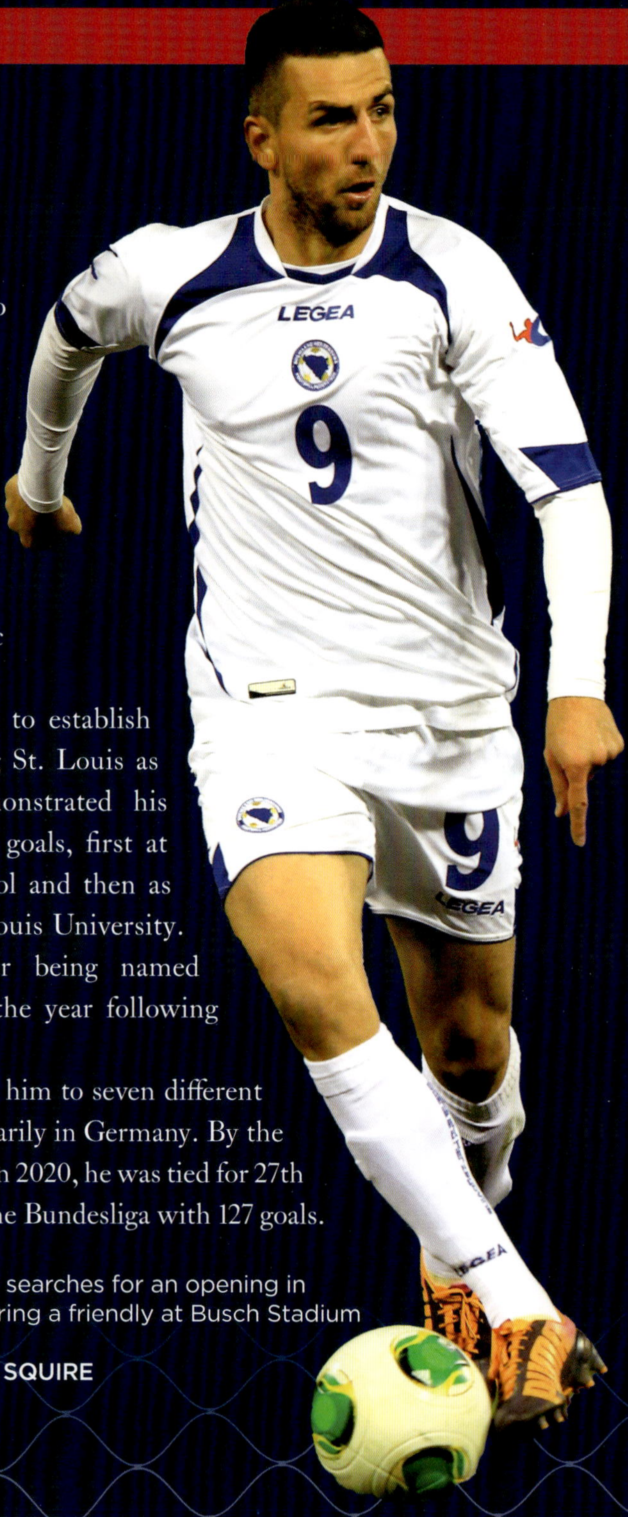

Bosnia's Vedad Ibisevic searches for an opening in Argentina's defense during a friendly at Busch Stadium on November 18, 2013.
GETTY IMAGES/JAMIE SQUIRE

NOVEMBER 22, 2013

AMBUSH BRING BACK PRO INDOOR SOCCER

PROFESSIONAL INDOOR soccer returned after a seven-year absence with a new team using an old name, the Ambush. Floridian Andrew Haines, whose indoor football team kicked off at the Family Arena in St. Charles in March 2013, headed a group that formed the new Ambush.

St. Louis Ambush 17, Pennsylvania Roar (Reading, PA) 4

MISL regular-season opener at the Family Arena

FIRST PERIOD: Scoring—1. Corey Adamson (S, 2 points) (Odane Sinclair) 11:27, 2. Daniel Antoniuk (S, 2 points) (Michael Roach) 11:58, 3. Antoniuk (S, 2 points) (Kory Dowell) 13:16, 4. Sinclair (S, 2 points) (UA) 13:54. Penalties—Adamson (S) holding 14:10

SECOND PERIOD: Scoring—5. Kyle Martyn (P, 2 points PPG) (Patrick Thompson) 1:43, 6. Jerjer Gibson (P) (Corey Maret) 4:08, 7. Chris Mattingly (S, 2 points PPG) (UA) 14:54. Penalties—Bench (S, served by Brian Soell) illegal substitution :19, Eric Puls (P) elbowing 13:26

THIRD PERIOD: Scoring—8. Dowell (S, 3 points) (Mike Mesle) 5:25, 9. Chad Vandegriffe (S, 2 points) (Roach) 6:10. Penalties—Gibson (P) boarding 2:28, Thompson (P) holding 9:46

FOURTH PERIOD: Scoring—10. Antoniuk (S) (Mesle) 14:08. Penalties—None

SHOTS ON GOAL: St. Louis 27, Pennsylvania 12. Saves: Jeff Richey (S) 10, Peter Pappas (P) 19

CREW CHIEF: Ron Cory

ASSISTANT REFEREES: Shane Butler, Doug Wolff

ATTENDANCE: 7,109

Ambush head coach Daryl Doran talks to his team during a timeout in the Ambush's first game on November 22, 2013.
DAVE LANGE COLLECTION

Haines couldn't lose when the Ambush opened the 2013–14 season against another expansion team, the Pennsylvania Roar. Haines and his wife, Leah, were majority owners of both teams.

The Ambush, featuring 10 St. Louis players and coached by St. Louisan and Indoor Soccer Hall of Famer Daryl Doran, routed the Roar, 17–4. Dan Antoniuk, a 32-year-old Philadelphia native and a veteran of 14 pro teams, led the Ambush with three goals.

The rest of the season went badly. The Ambush stumbled to a 4–16 record. But they survived, unlike the Roar, who folded after the season. Despite coaching and ownership changes and only one winning record over the years, the Ambush became the longest-running pro indoor soccer franchise in St. Louis history. The 2025–26 season was the Ambush's 14th. Two constants throughout those seasons were Shelly and Will Clark, part of the ownership group since the beginning and majority owners since 2016.

MAY 1, 2014

ST. LOUIS FC OPENS FOR BUSINESS

RIDING THE rebound of pro soccer in St. Louis begun by big crowds for international friendlies in 2013, St. Louis Scott Gallagher unveiled St. Louis Football Club (SLFC).

St. Louis Football Club

(USL PRO League, 2015–17; USL, 2018; USL Championship, 2018–20)

FIRST GAME: March 28, 2015, at Louisville Slugger Field; Louisville City 2, SLFC 0

(A: 6.067)

LAST GAME: October 17, 2020, at Lynn Family Stadium; Louisville City 2, SLFC 0 (A: 4,900)

YEAR	RECORD	STANDINGS	PLAYOFFS
2015	8-11-9	9th, Eastern Conf.	Did not qualify
2016	8-12-10	14th, Western Conf.	Did not qualify
2017	9-14-9	12th, Eastern Conf.	Did not qualify
2018	14-9-11	8th, Western Conf.	Quarterfinals: Orange County 4, SLFC 0
2019	11-14-9	11th, Eastern Conf.	Did not qualify
2020	7-5-4	2nd; Eastern	Group E Conf. quarterfinals: SLFC 1, Hartford 0; Conf. semi-finals: Louisville City 2, SLFC 0

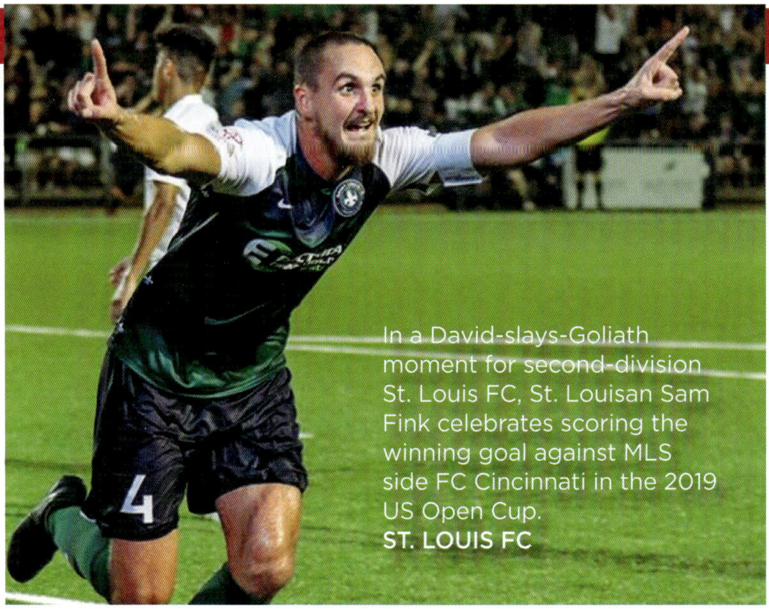

In a David-slays-Goliath moment for second-division St. Louis FC, St. Louisan Sam Fink celebrates scoring the winning goal against MLS side FC Cincinnati in the 2019 US Open Cup.
ST. LOUIS FC

The new men's outdoor team operated as a nonprofit under the St. Louis Scott Gallagher (SLSG) Foundation. SLSG, one of the nation's premier youth clubs, makes its home at the World Wide Technology (WWT) Soccer Park, which features a 5,500-seat lighted stadium.

Jim Kavanaugh, cofounder of WWT, and Tom Strunk, WWT's chief financial officer, personally financed the purchase of the Soccer Park in 2011, gave the park to SLSG, and became SLSG's president and treasurer/secretary, respectively.

The United Soccer Leagues courted SLSG to obtain a team in the USL's third-division PRO league. The team took the field in 2015, drew well throughout its history, and defeated two MLS teams in the 2019 US Open Cup. Meanwhile, Kavanaugh helped lead the successful charge for bringing an MLS team to St. Louis and served as one of the MLS team's investors.

Operational difficulties from the 2020 COVID-19 pandemic and the 2019 award of the MLS franchise to St. Louis contributed to putting SLFC out of business after the 2020 season.

APRIL 4, 2015

LORI CHALUPNY ELECTRIFIES HOMETOWN CROWD

LORI CHALUPNY made a triumphant homecoming with a second-half goal that sparked the US Women's National Team to a 4–0 win over New Zealand.

A total of 35,817 fans—a then-record crowd for a USWNT stand-alone friendly in the United States—saw the United States dominate play but lead only 1–0 after 75 minutes. Chalupny, inserted into the game in the 57th minute at left back, left-footed a pass from Megan Rapinoe for a goal in the 76th minute.

She had been an integral part of the USWNT until US Soccer decided in 2010 that she no longer could play on the team because of concussion aftereffects. Reinstated to the team in late 2014—she continued to play professionally in the interim and was widely regarded as one of the best players in the NWSL—she was a member of the 2015 World Cup champions.

Chalupny retired in late 2015 with 106 caps, the most by any player, male or female, in St. Louis soccer history. Becky Sauerbrunn, who started at center back against New Zealand, surpassed Chalupny's total in 2016.

United States Women's National Team 4, New Zealand 0

International friendly at Busch Stadium

USA: GK Hope Solo. Field players: Ali Krieger (Kelley O'Hara 83), Becky Sauerbrunn, Julie Johnston, Meghan Klingenberg (Lori Chalupny 57), Christen Press (Tobin Heath 56), Lauren Holiday, Carli Lloyd, Megan Rapinoe (Morgan Brian 79), Amy Rodriguez (Sydney Leroux 57), Alex Morgan (Abby Wambach 73)

NEW ZEALAND: GK Erin Nayler. Field players: Abby Erceg, Rebekah Stott, Kaite Duncan, Ria Percival, Ali Riley, Annalie Longo, Katie Brown (Kirsty Yallop 85), Amber Hearn, Sara Gregorius (Jasmine Pereira 65), Hannah Wilkinson (Rosie White 74)

GOALS: Klingenberg 14, Chalupny (Rapinoe) 76, Johnston (Holiday) 78, Brian (Leroux) 18. Shots on goal: USA 11, New Zealand 0. Saves: Solo (U) 0, Nayler (N) 6

OFFICIALS: Referee Carol Anne Chenard, assistant referee 1 Marie-Josée Charbonneau, assistant referee 2 Suzanne Morisset, fourth official Marie-Soleil Beaudoin

ATTENDANCE: 35,817

Teammates, including St. Louisan Becky Sauerbrunn (4), mob Lori Chalupny (16) after she scored at Busch Stadium. **GETTY IMAGES/DILIP VISHWANAT**

JUNE 2, 2016

DUCHESNE GIRLS GO FOUR-FOR-FOUR

Duchesne 4, Pembroke Hill (Kansas City) 1

Missouri girls' Class 2 state high school championship game at Swope Park Soccer Village, Kansas City

SUMMARY: Full recap unavailable

GOALS: Ryan Kielty 2, Amy Jung, Maria Wilder. Pembroke Hill—Caroline Salzman. Assists: Duchesne—Megan McDonald 2, Emily Bennett. Pembroke Hill—Julia Rosher

ATTENDANCE: Unknown

DUCHESNE HIGH School's girls' soccer team became the first boys' or girls' team to win four consecutive Missouri state high school soccer championships by defeating Pembroke Hill, 4–1, in the Missouri Class 2 championship game.

Seniors Courtney Reimer, Emily Bennett, Ryan Kielty, and Hannah Shambro were veterans of all four state championship teams. "We're the only people that can say that they've ever done that, so that feels awesome," Kielty said. "We just made history." Kielty, a four-year starter, led the 2016 Pioneers with 19 goals and 14 assists. Reimer, another four-year starter, had 15 goals and six assists and was named the state Class 2 player of the year.

Kielty scored two second-half goals against Pembroke Hill. Amy Jung and Maria Wilder netted the Pioneers' other goals. Reimer scored two goals and Kielty had one in Duchesne's 4–0 semifinal victory over St. Pius X of Kansas City. Bennett assisted on four goals in the semifinal and final.

Their fourth straight title capped a 17–4–0 season. The Pioneers, who also won a state title in 2009, won their sixth state championship in 2019.

Duchesne's record-setting 2016 state champions. Front (L-R): Rebecca Linck, Courtney Haggerty, Payton Bodden, Amy Jung, Shannon Ryan. Middle: McKenzie Struckhoff, Hannah Shambro, Ryan Kielty, Mary Gould, Meghan Neuner, Maria Wilder. Back: Head Coach Patrick Turner, Emily Bennett, Maddie Goeke, Courtney Reimer, Katie Sportsman, Meg McDonald, Sam Muska, Jen Kinworthy **DUCHESNE HIGH SCHOOL**

OCTOBER 23, 2016

BRAD DAVIS ENDS STELLAR MLS AND INTERNATIONAL CAREER

ST. LOUISAN Brad Davis retired, capping a 15-year pro career that included six MLS All-Star selections, one MLS Best XI selection, two MLS Cup championships, 17 caps, and one start for the United States in a group-stage match at the 2014 World Cup.

A midfielder, Davis played on the Scott Gallagher team that won the US Under-18 national title in 2000. He was a second-team All-American at Saint Louis University. At the professional level, Davis retired with 57 goals and the fourth-highest number of assists (123) in league history. Davis finished second in the 2011 MLS MVP voting.

Among Davis's many soccer talents, his deadliest was a lethal left foot that proved particularly effective whether during the run of play or on corner kicks and free kicks. His service from the wings gifted goals to many fortunate forwards.

Coming from a military family and deeply affected by the experience of a cousin who was wounded in Iraq, Davis started "Brad's Brigade" while with the Houston Dynamo and began "Military Appreciation Nights" at designated Dynamo matches. Davis also started Banded Brigade Outdoors, a nonprofit organization that took veterans and active-duty personnel on all-expenses-paid hunting trips and other nature activities.

Brad Davis cuts to his right for the USA in a 2–1 victory over Turkey in a friendly on June 1, 2014. USA coach Jurgen Klinsmann shouts encouragement.
GETTY IMAGES/TIM CLAYTON

DECEMBER 3, 2016

FIRST WOMEN'S FOUR-YEAR COLLEGE CHAMPIONSHIP FOR ST. LOUIS

MEGAN WOLF scored on the deciding penalty kick to lift Washington University to the NCAA Division III women's championship. The title was the first for a St. Louis women's four-year college soccer team.

WashU won in a shootout over five-time champion Messiah after regulation and overtime ended in a 1–1 tie. Washington U. prevailed, 5–4, on PKs for the school's first NCAA title in men's or women's soccer.

Washington U. led in regulation on Taylor Cohen's goal in the 72nd minute. She headed down a service from Lexie Sprague and drove an 18-yard shot past Messiah goalkeeper Sara Yunez. Messiah drew even in the 84th minute.

Goalkeeper Lizzie Crist, the United Soccer Coaches' player of the year, saved the Bears in the 109th minute. She dove to stop a shot from Kate Shults with 25 seconds left in the second 10-minute overtime.

The Bears made all five of their PKs in the shootout that followed. Messiah's only miss came when Sunny Gelnovatch hit the crossbar in the second round.

WashU, which lost in the 2015 Division III final to Williams, went undefeated in its last 14 games of 2016 and finished the season with a 19–2–3 record.

Washington University 1, Messiah (Mechanicsburg, PA) 1 Washington University won in PK shootout 5–4

NCAA Women's Division III championship game at Kerr Stadium, Salem, VA

WASHINGTON U: Starters—GK Lizzy Crist; D Lexie Sprague, Hannah Rosenberg, Kelly Von Zup, Megan Nicklay, Caroline Dempsey; M Mia Mastroianni, Maggie Crist; F Katie Chandler, Darcy Cunningham, Taylor Cohen. Substitutions—Alison Cerny, Megan Wolf, Megan Renken, Jessica Kovach, Mariana Alisio, Kat Kerska, Elise Brown, Gillian Myers, Rachel Mickelson

MESSIAH: Starters—GK Sara Yunez; D D.J. Cole, Sarah Strachan, Summerly Merson, Kayla Deckert, Skyler Ulry; M Olivia Snare, Sunny Gelnovatch, Missy Biener; F Marisa Weaver, Erin Sollenberger. Substitutions—Ellie Lengacher, Julia Kyne, Courtney Wagner, Kate Shults, Lilly Shover, Brooke Firestone, Emily Lockwood

GOALS: Cohen (W) (Sprague) 72, Sollenberger (M) (Cole) 84. PKs: First round—Weaver (M) made, Dempsey (W) made. Second round—Gelnovatch (M) miss, Von Zup (W) made. Third round—Firestone (M) made, Kovach (W) made. Fourth round—Ulry (M) made, Myers (W) made. Fifth round—Deckert (M) made, Wolf (W) made

SHOTS ON GOAL: Washington U. 5, Messiah 7. Saves: Crist (W) 6, Yunez (M) 4

REFEREE: Elivs Mahmutovic; assistant referees Rebekah Friedrich, Jasmine Peralta

ATTENDANCE: 847

Previous page: Lizzie Crist, the United Soccer Coaches' Player of the Year, stretches for the ball. This page: Washington University's players are all smiles after winning the NCAA Division III championship.
WASHINGTON UNIVERSITY ATHLETICS

MAY 19, 2017

ROBBEN COACHES 1,125TH AND LAST WIN

OAKVILLE HIGH School's girls blanked Lindbergh, 2–0, for the 1,125th and last victory for a Dave Robben–coached high school soccer team. His boys' and girls' victory total leads all St. Louis area high school soccer coaches.

Robben, who played at Saint Louis University and Harris Teachers College, spent his entire coaching career at Oakville. He coached the girls to 594 victories starting in 1978, and the boys to 531 wins starting in 1981. The girls won a state championship in 1991 and the boys captured a Missouri title in 2000.

Robben earned state coach of the year honors twice and was National Soccer Coaches Association of America Midwest girls coach of the year in 1991. He was inducted into the Missouri State High School Soccer Coaches and St. Louis Soccer halls of fame.

Oakville 2, Lindbergh 0

Missouri Class 4 District 7 final at Oakville High School

SUMMARY: Full recap unavailable

GOALS: Chelsea Morris (assist unknown) 17, Morris (McKenna Books) approximately midway second half. GK: Emily Jackson (O), Hanna Groh (L)

ATTENDANCE: Unknown

Dave Robben (right) coached Oakville High School's boys and girls' teams to 1,125 victories.
TARA VOGLER/OAKVILLE HIGH SCHOOL JOURNALISM PROGRAM

Senior midfielder Chelsea Morris helped seal Robben's final victory with both goals on long-range shots against Lindbergh. The Tigers won their fifth consecutive game and ninth of their last 10. Their season, and Robben's high school coaching career, ended in their next match, a 4–1 loss to St. Joseph's in the Section 4 playoffs May 23. The Tigers finished the season with a 13–6–2 record.

JULY 30, 2017

FIRE AND ICE CAPS PERFECT YEAR WITH WPSL TITLE

FIRE AND Ice of Belleville, Illinois, won the championship of the second-division, 112-team Women's Premier Soccer League with a come-from-behind 2–1 victory over the Gulf Coast Texans.

Kelsey Dinges scored on a penalty kick in the 38th minute. Dinges netted the winner in the 68th minute on an assist from Tara Sullivan. An Althoff High School and Miami of Ohio player, Dinges had decided before the 2017 season that it probably would be her last. She went out with five goals in the final three games. The victory capped a 12–0 season for Fire and Ice.

Belleville's Lindsay Kennedy Eversmeyer founded Fire and Ice in 2013 as a summertime amateur club fielding current and recent collegiate players. She was its owner and head coach. A standout collegiate player, she became the fourth woman to play in a men's professional soccer game when she appeared three times with the indoor St. Louis Steamers in 2005. She continued as Fire and Ice's owner and head coach until the team folded after the 2022 season.

Fire and Ice left a legacy of three conference and two regional championships and two WPSL final four appearances. The team never had a losing season.

Kelsey Dinges scored both goals in Fire and Ice's WPSL championship victory.
FIRE AND ICE SOCCER CLUB

Fired-up Fire and Ice players and coaches enjoy their WPSL championship.
FIRE AND ICE SOCCER CLUB

Fire and Ice (Belleville, IL) 2, Gulf Coast Texans (Pensacola, FL) 1

WPSL final at SilverLakes Sports Complex in Norco, California

SUMMARY: Full recap unavailable

GOALS: Kelsey Dinges (F) PK 38, Dinges (F) (Tara Sullivan) 68. Gulf Coast scorer unknown

AUGUST 31, 2017

ROONEY RACKS UP 400TH WIN FOR SECOND TIME

ST. LOUIS native Tim Rooney gained his 400th men's junior college coaching victory as Lewis & Clark blanked Lincoln Land, 6–0.

The landmark victory came a year after Rooney had notched his 400th women's junior college victory at L&C. He retired after the 2021 season as the winningest women's coach in NJCAA history with 476 victories and two national titles.

While the 6–0 win at Lincoln Land for Rooney's 400th win as men's coach might have seemed easy, the road to get there was not. Rooney spent a dozen years as an assistant coach at various clubs, most notably the original St. Louis Steamers, before becoming the men's head coach at L&C in 1986. He started the women's program at the Godfrey, Illinois, school in 1993.

Rooney built both Trailblazers' programs with players from nearby St. Louis. In later years, L&C included some foreign players, such as Morapeli Lesoesta. The freshman from Maseru in the African nation of Lesotho scored four goals in Rooney's 400th men's victory against Lincoln Land.

During his 32 seasons as L&C men's coach, Rooney developed 20 NJCAA All-Americans. The women's program produced 27 NJCAA All-Americans during Rooney's 30 years as women's coach.

Lewis & Clark 6, Lincoln Land 0

Men's junior college regular-season game at Lincoln Land Community College, Springfield, Illinois

LINCOLN LAND STARTERS: GK Kyle Bugay. Field players: David Pope, Devin Compton, Matheus Sobucki, Nathan Makolo, Nkululeko Mkhonto, Kyle Goetz, Dmitrije Antonijevic, Jefferson Brito, Alan Rivera, Logan York

LEWIS & CLARK STARTERS: GK Isaac Hdingson. Field players: Michael Drake, Osvaldo Guerrero, Ethan Mayberry, Morapeli Lesoesta, Paul Amponsah, Skylar Funk, Camarri Johnson, Drew Moser, Ahmed Mahdi, A.J. Underwood

GOALS (times unavailable): C.J. Nasello (Darcy Madden), Lesoesta (Mahdi), Lesoesta (Johnson), Lesoesta (Funk), Lesoesta (UA), Johnson (Amponsah). Shots on goal: Lincoln Land 4, Lewis & Clark 18. Saves: Bugay (LL) 8, Grant Flynn (LL) 4, Hidingson (LC) 4

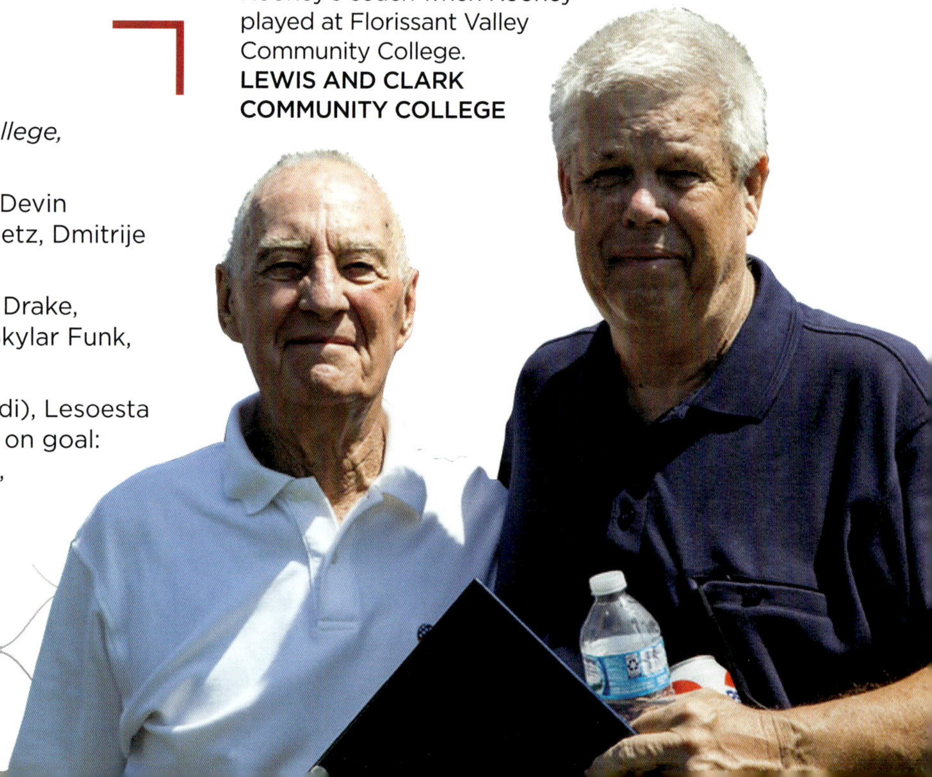

Tim Rooney (right) shares an emotional moment with Pete Sorber, Rooney's coach when Rooney played at Florissant Valley Community College.
LEWIS AND CLARK COMMUNITY COLLEGE

OCTOBER 5, 2018

TOCCO BECOMES SECOND MEN'S COLLEGE COACH TO WIN 700

ROCKHURST UNIVERSITY coach and St. Louis native Tony Tocco recorded his 700th coaching victory as the Hawks defeated William Jewell, 3–1.

The Hawks came from behind with three unanswered goals from Pablo Salvador Lopez, Chandler Peterson, and St. Louisan Andrew Patke to make Tocco the second collegiate men's soccer coach to reach 700 victories. All came at Rockhurst.

Tocco became the Kansas City school's head coach in 1970 after two years as the Hawks' assistant coach. Tocco's early teams consisted almost entirely of St. Louis players. Tocco guided the Hawks to NCAA Division II national semifinal appearances in 2013, 2015, 2016 and 2017. The Hawks were NAIA national tournament runners-up four times before the Hawks moved to the NCAA in 1998. He guided the Hawks to eight seasons with more than 20 victories, all from 1986 to 1997.

Tocco, an accounting teacher, also became the longest-serving professor in Rockhurst's Helzberg School of Management.

Tocco grew up in downtown St. Louis. He was a goalkeeper on Saint Louis University's only unbeaten and untied team in 1964. Tocco also pitched for the Billikens in the 1965 College World Series.

Rockhurst 3, William Jewell 1

Men's NCAA regular-season game at Greene Stadium, Liberty, MO

WILLIAM JEWELL: GK Quinn Ruggeri; D Tyler Walker, Chris Cotton, Keaton Wiley, Matthew Martel; MF Blake Lines, Cody Benedict, Teddy Gifford, Charlie Parrish, Blake Dessell; F Noah Espinosa. Subs: Will Davis, Griffin King, Drew Dempsey, Alex Trinidad, Dakota Hayes, Sam Gettings

ROCKHURST: GK Peter Baker; D Vincent Swann, Filippo Santandrea, Preston Mboob; M Marco Cora, Pablo Salvador Lopez, Federico Verlicchi, Nandor Benucci, Jordan Andrews; F Andrew Patke, Chander Peterson. Subs: Tylor Pisoni, Fabio Reato, Dylan Brown, Umoh Ufot, Chandler Parrish, Noah Mabry, Collin Chrun

GOALS: Gifford (W) (UA) 18, Salvador Lopez (R) (Patke) 19, Patke (R) (Peterson) 52, Peterson (R) (Benucci) 83. Shots on goal: William Jewell 2, Rockhurst 5. Saves: Ruggeri (W) 2, Baker (R) 1

REFEREE: Denis Zijadic; assistant referees Ken Bartkowski, Ryan Cook

ATTENDANCE: 196

Rockhurst's men's soccer team gathers around Coach Tony Tocco (holding white jersey) after his 700th career coaching victory. ROCKHURST UNIVERSITY

AUGUST 20, 2019

MLS COMES TO THE LOU

A DECADE-LONG saga ended happily with the announcement that Major League Soccer had awarded a franchise to St. Louis.

The successful effort was the third known attempt to bring an MLS team to St. Louis. Local attorney Jeff Cooper had come up short in his efforts to land an MLS team 10 years earlier. A second group of local and out-of-town investors failed to win approval of partial public funding for a soccer stadium in a St. Louis City vote in April 2017. The vote effectively killed that attempt.

The third effort began just 18 months later. The Taylor family, owners of Enterprise Holdings (today's Enterprise Mobility), headquartered in St. Louis and the world's largest car rental company, and Jim Kavanaugh, a former professional soccer player and cofounder and chief executive officer of World Wide Technology, led the ultimately successful drive for an expansion team.

The reported expansion fee of $200 million represented a fraction of the ownership group's total investment over the next few years. They built a privately funded stadium, training facilities, and a youth academy; signed players; and hired coaching and administrative staffs. Christened St. Louis CITY SC, the club played its first MLS game on February 25, 2023.

That's a wrap: St. Louis's Carolyn Kindle and MLS commissioner Don Garber announce the award of an MLS franchise to St. Louis. Kindle and the Taylor family, along with Jim Kavanaugh and his family, formed the team's ownership group. **ST. LOUIS CITY SOCCER CLUB**

SEPTEMBER 9, 2019

DAN FLYNN FINISHES INFLUENTIAL TENURE LEADING US SOCCER

DAN FLYNN, a native of St. Louis, concluded a remarkable 19-year tenure as the chief executive of US Soccer, transforming the federation into a global leader in the sport and one of the most financially stable governing bodies in international soccer.

As CEO and secretary general, Flynn implemented a strategic vision that increased US Soccer's budget fivefold, enabling expansive growth across both the sporting and business sides of the organization. Under his leadership, the US Women's National Team won two Olympic gold medals and two FIFA Women's World Cup titles while the US Men's National Team reached the World Cup quarterfinals in 2002 and advanced to the Round of 16 in 2010 and 2014. The Federation's Youth National Teams expanded from U-14 through U-20 on the girls' and boys' sides, and national training centers were established in Carson, California, and Kansas City, Kansas.

The *New York Times* once described Flynn as the man who "transformed US Soccer from a small-time governing body into a financial juggernaut with a $100 million annual budget and reserves of nearly twice that amount."

A standout on Saint Louis University's 1973 NCAA championship team, Flynn launched a successful business career at Anheuser-Busch, ultimately leading its international operations by age 31. He later served as venue director for the 1994 FIFA World Cup in Chicago, a role that paved the way for his long-term service to US Soccer.

A year after "retiring," Flynn took on another big job: serving as a special advisor for FIFA in the lead-up to and during the 2026 World Cup in North America.

Dan Flynn led US Soccer through two decades of financial and competitive growth.
GETTY IMAGES/NED DISHMAN

OCTOBER 18, 2019

1,000 BOYS' COACHING WINS FOR TERRY MICHLER

TERRY MICHLER, the winningest boys' high school soccer coach in US history, reached 1,000 career victories when Christian Brothers College defeated Nixa, 3–0.

The milestone came in Michler's 49th season, all at CBC. As St. Louis sportscaster Frank Cusumano said, "No one will ever break this record. Go ahead and try and win 20 games a year for 50 years."

The 1,000th victory came with an asterisk. Michler coached for two seasons at Bishop Hogan in Kansas City before moving to CBC, his alma mater. But it's unknown how many games Bishop Hogan won. CBC captured nine state championships under Michler, the last in 2018. Those nine titles are second only in Missouri to the 11 boys' championships taken by St. Louis teams coached by Vince Drake. Drake's girls' teams also won one state title.

Needing 10 victories at the start of the 2019 season to reach 1,000, the Cadets struggled through their first 21 games with a 9–10–2 record. But Luca Bartoni, a third-generation student at CBC, got the Cadets untracked with three second-half goals against Nixa.

Michler's head coaching career at CBC ended after 52 seasons with a record of 1,053–312–119.

CBC 3, Nixa 0

Boys' high school Art Firley Shootout at Art Firley Soccer Complex, Jefferson City, MO

SUMMARY: Full recap unavailable

GOALS (times unavailable): Luca Bartoni 3, all in second half. Assists: Ethan Mayo 2, Alex Peters

SHOTS: CBC 16, Nixa unavailable. Saves: Riley Carron (C) 2, Sean Stenger (C) 0, Nixa unavailable

CBC players and staff mark 1,000 coaching victories for Terry Michler (center, holding CBC shirt). CHRISTIAN BROTHERS COLLEGE HIGH SCHOOL

DECEMBER 9, 2020

RALSTON RATED ONE OF MLS'S 25 GREATEST

MAJOR LEAGUE Soccer asked a panel of 200 "MLS experts" to take on the monumental task of picking the 25 biggest stars from among the thousands of players in the league's first 25 seasons. One St. Louisan made the cut: midfielder Steve Ralston.

Joining the likes of David Beckham, Landon Donovan, and Preki on the all-time MLS team, Ralston made his mark as a consistent playmaker, scorer, and winner over a 15-year career, mostly with the New England Revolution. Ralston's achievements included 135 assists (second all-time as of 2020), 76 goals (23rd all-time), 378 games (sixth all-time), seven MLS All-Star appearances, and selections to the MLS Best XI. He helped the Revolution reach four MLS Cup finals and a US Open Cup championship.

A graduate of Oakville High School, Ralston blossomed under the coaching of US Soccer Hall of Famer Pat McBride at Forest Park Community College. Ralston transferred to Florida International, where he scored 40 goals.

Ralston made the first of 36 appearances for the United States on January 7, 1997. His game-winning goal against Mexico on September 3, 2005, qualified the US for the 2006 World Cup. An injury kept Ralston off the final World Cup roster.

MLS 25 Greatest

Selected by a panel of 200 "MLS experts" as the best 25 players in the first 25 seasons of Major League Soccer.

Jeff Agoos, Kyle Beckerman, David Beckham, Carlos Bocanegra, Dwayne De Rosario, Clint Dempsey, Landon Donovan, Marco Etcheverry, Robin Fraser, Sebastian Giovinco, Kevin Hartman, Cobi Jones, Robbie Keane, Chad Marshall, Josef Martinez, Tony Meola, Jaime Moreno, Edie Pope, Preki, Steve Ralston, Nick Rimando, Carolos Valderrama, Diego Valeri, Chris Wondolowski, Bradley Wright-Phillips.

Steve Ralston runs down the ball for the USA in a scoreless draw with Costa Rica on July 12, 2005.
GETTY IMAGES/MATTHEW ASHTON - EMPICS

JANUARY 21, 2022

SARGENT FIRST ST. LOUISAN TO SCORE IN PREMIER LEAGUE

JOSH SARGENT scored the first goal by a St. Louisan in England's Premier League, then added a second goal 23 minutes later as Norwich City sank Watford, 3–0.

The 21-year-old from O'Fallon, Missouri, scored first with a spectacular "scorpion kick" in the 51st minute. Reacting to a pass behind him, he lunged back with his right foot and redirected the ball from six yards out into the top near corner of the net. His second goal came on a header.

Norwich City 3, Watford 0

Premier League game at Vicarage Road, Watford, England

WATFORD: GK Daniel Bachman, LCB Samir, RCB Christian Kabasele, LOB Hassane Kamara (Ken Sema 84), ROB Kiko Femenía (Juraj Kucka 89), CM Edo Kayembe, LM Moussa Sissoko, RM Tom Cleverley (Cucho Hernández 59), CF Josh King, RF João Pedro, RF Emmanuel Dennis (ejected 78th minute)

NORWICH CITY: GK Angus Gunn, LCB Ben Gibson, RCB Grant Hanley, LOB Brandon Williams, ROB Max Aarons, LM Jacob Lungi Sørensen (Kenny McLean 21), RM Pierre Lees-Melou, LW Milot Rashica (Przemyslaw Placheta 90+6), RW Josh Sargent, LF Temmu Pukki (Sam Byram 87), RF Adam Idah

GOALS: Sargent (N) (Pukki) 51, Sargent (N) (Rashica) 74, Kucka (W) OG 90+2. Shots on goal: Watford 4, Norwich City 2. Saves: Bachman (W) 0, Gunn (N) 3

REFEREE: Mike Dean

ATTENDANCE: 20,782

Josh Sargent redirects the ball with his back foot and scores the first goal by a St. Louis player in the Premier League.
GETTY IMAGES/CHARLOTTE WILSON/OFFSIDE

Sargent's two-goal outburst demonstrated his knack for scoring. He tallied 34 times in 56 appearances for US youth teams. At age 17, he became the youngest player to score in the U-20 World Cup. He turned professional with the Bundesliga's Werder Bremen, scoring on his first touch in his first match with the senior team on December 7, 2018. Injuries plagued him at his next stop, Norwich City. Nevertheless, he scored 15 goals for Norwich in the 2024–25 season.

With the US Men's National Team, he scored in his first appearance on May 28, 2018, against Bolivia. He played in all three group-stage matches of the 2022 World Cup but missed the round of 16 with an ankle injury.

FEBRUARY 17, 2022

SAUERBRUNN PLAYS 200TH TIME FOR USA

BECKY SAUERBRUNN added another to a long list of milestones by appearing in her 200th game with the US Women's National Team. The Ladue High School graduate became the 12th player in USWNT history to reach 200 caps during a scoreless tie with the Czech Republic.

Few players, male or female, can approach Sauerbrunn's accomplishments: two-time World Cup champion; two-time Olympic medalist (gold in 2012, bronze in 2020); four-time NWSL Defender of the Year; six-time selection to the NWSL Best XI; three-time collegiate All-American. Respect for her is reflected in her being named one of six defenders among the top 20 USWNT players of all time by goal.com.

All her achievements at the pro and international levels came after her 26th birthday. A turning point in her career came when she made the 2011 World Cup team as a substitute for an injured player. Her only minutes of the tournament came as a replacement starter in the semifinals of the USA's 3–1 win over France. "That was the moment I realized I could do this soccer thing," Sauerbrunn said.

She did it well for the next 13 years.

St. Louis honors Becky Sauerbrunn at Energizer Park on June 3, 2025. She retired in 2024 with 219 appearances for the USA, most of any St. Louis man or woman. **GETTY IMAGES/BILL BARRETT/ISI PHOTOS/USSF**

United States Women's National Team 0, Czech Republic 0

International friendly at Dignity Sports Health Park, Carson, CA

USA: GK Casey Murphy. Field players: Kelley O'Hara, Alana Cook, Tierna Davidson (Becky Sauerbrunn 72), Emily Fox (Emily Sonnett 46), Andi Sullivan, Morgan Gautrat (Kristie Mewis 46), Rose Lavelle (Ashley Sanchez 72), Sophia Smith (Margaret Purce 60), Catarina Macario, Mallory Pugh (Trinity Rodman 60)

CZECH REPUBLIC: GK Barbora Votíková. Field players: Anna Dlasková, Petra Bertholdová, Simona Necidová, Gabriela Šlajsová; Tereza Krejčiříková (Franny Cerny 79), Klára Cahynová, Kamila Dubcová (Aneta Pochmanová 90+2), Kateřina Svitková; Andrea Stašková (Klára Cvrčková 90), Lucie Martínková (Michaela Khýrová 79)

SHOTS ON GOAL: USA 8, Czech Republic 0. Saves: Murphy (U) 0, Votíková (C) 8

OFFICIALS: Referee Laura Fortunato, assistant referee 1 Mariana De Almedia, assistant referee 2 Daiana Milone, fourth official Maria Belen Carvajal

ATTENDANCE: 7,333

OCTOBER 8, 2022

SCHULTE SHUTS DOWN CITY2 IN MLS NEXT PRO FINAL

BIDDING TO become the first St. Louis team to win a professional nationwide outdoor league championship, St. Louis CITY2 found its way blocked, ironically, by a St. Louisan: goalkeeper Patrick Schulte.

The Francis Howell High School graduate manned the nets for the Columbus Crew 2 in a 4–1 defeat of St. Louis CITY2 in the inaugural MLS NEXT Pro final. MLS NEXT Pro was formed as a Division III league primarily for MLS reserve teams such as CITY2.

Columbus Crew 2 4, St. Louis CITY2 1

MLS NEXT Pro championship game at Lower.com Field, Columbus, OH

COLUMBUS: GK Patrick Schulte, LB Philip Quinton, CB Justin Malou (Jacob Erlandson 88), RB Tristan Weber (Jordan Knight 82), LW Jake Morris (Coleman Gannon 74), LM Sean Zawadzki, RM Isaiah Parente (Isaac Angking 88), RW Abdi Mohamed, LF Ryan Telfer, CF Jacen Russell-Rowe, RF Marco Micaletto (Noah Fuson 82)

ST. LOUIS: GK Michael Creek, LOB Akil Watts, LCB Kyle Hiebert, RCB Josh Yaro, LOB Ben Di Rosa (Dida Armstrong 84), LM Max Schneider (Selmir Pidro 46), RM A.J. Palazzolo (Ezra Armstrong 68), LW Isak Jensen (Wan Kuzain 55), CM Tomas Ostrák (Vitor Dias 68), RW Célio Pompeu, CF Josh Dolling

SCORING: Parente (C) PK 45, Micaletto (C) (Mohamed) 45+3, Russell-Rowe (C) PK 58, Pompeu (S) (UA) 80, Telfer (C) (Russell-Rowe) 83. Shots and saves unavailable

REFEREE: Malik Badawi

ATTENDANCE: 7,446

CITY2's Dida Armstrong and Ben Di Rosa thank supporters who journeyed to Columbus, Ohio, for the MLS NEXT Pro championship game.
ST. LOUIS CITY SOCCER CLUB

The game was scoreless until the final minutes of the first half. A controversial handball call on CITY2's Max Schneider led to Isaiah Parente's goal on the resulting penalty kick. The winner came three minutes into first-half stoppage time when CITY2 keeper Michael Creek misplayed Marco Micaletto's cross.

CITY2 enjoyed an otherwise memorable season, finishing first in the Western Conference. CITY2 helped acclimate first-team players, such as goalkeeper Roman Bürki, forward João Klauss, and midfielder Eduard Löwen, who reported to St. Louis in the summer and trained with CITY2.

Schulte, named the league's goalkeeper of the year, used NEXT Pro as a springboard to become the Crew's first-team keeper in 2023 and earn call-ups to the US National and Olympic Teams.

NOVEMBER 16, 2022

MARKET STREET MASTERPIECE STAGES GRAND OPENING

THE GRANDEST stage in St. Louis soccer history opened for business. While not a smash hit on the score sheet—Germany's Bayer Leverkusen licked the hometown side, CITY2, 3–0—CITYPARK sold out on a 32-degree night.

The $458 million stadium served as the centerpiece of a Downtown West complex that included a training facility and team store across Market Street and would eventually house the club's administrative headquarters four blocks south of the stadium. St. Louis CITY became the first MLS team to concentrate its stadium and training grounds together.

The first kick is taken in St. Louis CITY Soccer Club's 22,500-seat stadium on November 16, 2022.
DAVE LANGE COLLECTION

The party at CITYPARK began early. The new first-team jerseys went on sale at noon. The St. Louligans, vocal supporters of St. Louis soccer for more than a decade, marched to the stadium an hour before kickoff and filled the standing-only section at the north end.

As for the game, the 118-year-old Bundesliga team tossed the newcomers aside by scoring twice in eight minutes late in the first half. Although the home team was billed as third-division CITY2, some who played, such as goalkeeper Roman Bürki, rostered with first-team CITY. Two youthful St. Louisans, 15-year-old Caden Glover and 17-year-old Miguel Perez, played in the second half.

Bayer Leverkusen 3, St. Louis CITY2 0

International friendly at CITYPARK

ST. LOUIS: GK Roman Bürki, LCB Josh Yaro, RCB Kyle Hiebert, LOB Selmir Pidro (Ezra Armstrong 45), ROB Benjamin Di Rosa (A.J. Palazzolo 75), CM Tomas Ostrák (Aaron Heard 74), LM Eduard Löwen (Miguel Perez 61), RM Akil Watts, CF Josh Dolling (João Klauss 45, Dida Armstrong 84), LW Isak Jensen (Wan Kuzain 45), RW Célio Pompeu (Caden Glover 75)

BAYER LEVERKUSEN: GK Andrey Lunev (Niklas Lomb 45), LCB Joshua Eze (Madi Monamay 45), RCB Jonathan Tah, LOB Mitchel Bakker, ROB Ayman Azhi, LM Kerim Demirbay (Nadiem Amiri 45), RM Robert Andrich, LW Callum Hudson-Odoi, RW Karim Bellarabi (Moussa Diaby 45), LF Adam Hlozek, RF Zidan Sertdemir

SCORING: Hudson-Odoi 36; Hlozek 44, 51. Shots on goal: St. Louis 5, Bayer Leverkusen 4. Saves: Bürki (S) 1, Lunev (B) 1, Lomb (B) 4

REFEREE: Jervis Atagana

ATTENDANCE: 22,500

MARCH 25, 2023

RECORD-SETTING START FOR CITY

THE NEWEST team in MLS became one of only three clubs to win their first five games of the season. But this win was no sure thing. The last play of the first half required an incredible stop from Roman Bürki, the MLS Goalkeeper of the Year, on Brayan Vera to keep the game scoreless.

The second half was all CITY. Nicholas Gioacchini one-timed Indiana Vassilev's corner kick for a goal just 85 seconds after play resumed. João Klauss scored his fourth and fifth goals of the season five minutes apart. Klauss helped set up the final tally with his pass to Eduard Löwen, who in turn laid off the ball to his right for a goal by Rasmus Alm.

CITY went 1–4–1 over its next six games. But the team rebounded and became the first expansion team in MLS history to win a regular-season conference championship. The team's 17–12–5 record gave CITY 56 points, fourth best in the league. CITY sold out every home game in 22,453-seat capacity CITYPARK.

The season ended abruptly. Sporting Kansas City, which finished eighth in the conference, stunned CITY by winning the first two games of a best-of-three playoff series.

João Klauss scored twice as St. Louis CITY Soccer Club won its fifth consecutive game to open its inaugural season.
ST. LOUIS CITY SOCCER CLUB

St. Louis CITY 4, Real Salt Lake 0

MLS regular-season game at America First Field, Sandy, UT

REAL SALT LAKE: GK Zac MacMath, LCB Brayan Vera, RCB Justen Glad, LOB Andrew Brody, ROB Emeka Eneli, CM Damir Kreilach, LM Pablo Ruiz, RM Jasper Löeffelsend, CF Anderson Julio (Maikel Chang 72), LW Justin Meram (Jefferson Savarino 60), RW Andres Gomez (Daniel Musovski 72)

ST. LOUIS: GK Roman Bürki, LCB Tim Parker, RCB Lucas Bartlett, LOB John Nelson, ROB Jake Nerwinski, LM Eduard Löwen (Njabulo Blom 77), RM Indiana Vassilev (Akil Watts 77), LW Tomas Ostrák (Rasmus Alm 61), RW Jared Stroud (Isak Jensen 61), LF João Klauss, RF Nicholas Gioacchini (Célio Pompeu 86)

SCORING: Gioacchni 47; Klauss 61, 66; Alm 76. Shots on goal: St. Louis 8, Real Salt Lake 7. Saves: MacMath (R) 4, Bürki (S) 7

REFEREE: Mark Allatin

ATTENDANCE: 19,508

MARCH 16, 2024

PFEIFFER SETS RECORD IN NWSL DEBUT

ST. LOUISAN Alex Pfeiffer became the youngest player to score a goal in the 12-year history of the National Women's Soccer League when she tallied in the 68th minute for the Kansas City Current against the Portland Thorns. Aged 16 years, 3 months and 20 days when she scored, Pfeiffer surpassed the previous record set by Olivia Moultrie in 2022.

Pfeiffer scored in her NWSL debut.

Pfeiffer already had established herself as one of the most promising female players in US Soccer's youth system. She scored eight goals in six appearances for the U-17 US Women's National Team.

Her goal against Portland came as a second-half substitute at center forward. Pfeiffer ran on to the ball and one-timed it with her left foot at the edge of the penalty area past goalkeeper Shelby Hogan. Pfeiffer's goal gave the Current a 5–1 lead but ended up as the game winner as the Thorns scored three more times.

Pfeifer suffered a knee injury three months later, causing her to miss the 2024 U-17 Women's World Cup. She did not play again until July 13, 2025.

Kansas City Current 5, Portland Thorns 4

NWSL regular-season opener at CPKC Stadium, Kansas City, MO

KANSAS CITY: GK Adrianna French, LCB Gabrielle Robinson, RCB Elizabeth Ball, LOB Hailie Mace, ROB Ellie Wheeler, CMF Vanessa DiBernardo (Temwa Chawinga 63), LMF Claire Hutton, RMF Lo'eau LaBonta, CF Bia Zaneratto (Alex Pfeiffer 45), LF Alexa Spaanstra (Claire Lavogez 63), RF Debinha (Kristin Hamilton 32, Stine Balisager Pedersen 88)

PORTLAND: GK Shelby Hogan, LCB Isabella Bryld Obaze, RCB Kelli Hubly, LOB Marie Müller, ROB Nicole Payne (Reyna Reyes 75), CMF Sam Coffey (Olivia Wade-Katoa 75), LMF Olivia Moultrie (Hina Sugita 62), RMF Jessie Fleming, CF Sophia Wilson (Izzy D'Aquila 75), LF Morgan Weaver, RF Christine Sinclair (Janine Sonis 45)

SCORING: DiBernardo (K) 22, Wheeler (K) 25, Zanaretto (K) 34, Wilson (P) 43, Hamilton (K) 64, Pfeiffer (K) 68, Sonis (P) 71, Wilson (P) 74, Sonis (P) 90+1. Shots on goal: Kansas City 7, Portland 8. Saves: French (K) 4, Hogan (P) 2

OFFICIALS: Referee Alex Billeter, assistant referee 1 John Krill, assistant referee 2 Jennifer Garner, fourth official Velimir Stefanovic

ATTENDANCE: 11,500 (sellout)

Alex Pfeiffer (second from left) accepts congratulations from her teammates after becoming the youngest player to score in NWSL history. GETTY IMAGES/JAMIE SQUIRE

JUNE 20, 2024

DiMARIA FIRST FRESHMAN TO WIN US GATORADE PLAYER OF YEAR

A TOTAL of 383,895 girls participated in high school soccer in 2023–24, according to the National Federation of State High School Associations. St. Louisan Maddie DiMaria was one of them. In fact, she was *the* one, winning the Gatorade national girls' high school soccer player of the year award—as a freshman.

She was the first freshman to receive the girls' soccer award in its 26-year history.

She led Cor Jesu to the Missouri Class 3A state championship and a 21–4 record. She amassed 30 goals and 21 assists, including two goals and an assist in Cor Jesu's 3–0 victory over Rockwood Summit in the state final. She was even better as a sophomore, collecting 45 goals and 19 assists. She had two goals and an assist in Cor Jesu's 4–0 victory over St. Dominic in the state championship game.

Her high school accomplishments, combined with her performance for US Soccer youth national teams, led PrepSoccer.com and TopDrawerSoccer.com to call DiMaria the No. 1 recruit in the high school class of 2027.

DiMaria is the first St. Louis girls' soccer player to win the national Gatorade award. St. Louisans

Cor Jesu's Maddie DiMaria scores past St. Dominic defender Sophia Catalano in Cor Jesu's 4–0 victory in the 2025 Missouri Class 4A state championship game at World

DECEMBER 8, 2024

UNBEATEN BEARS BRING BACK SECOND TITLE

WASHINGTON UNIVERSITY put the final brushstroke on a dominant season by defeating William Smith College, 3–0, in the NCAA Division III women's championship game. The victory left the Bears with a 23–0–2 record and their second NCAA title in eight years.

Leading 1–0 on an Ally Hackett penalty kick, the Bears blew the game open with two goals one minute apart. Freshman Olivia Clemons made it 2–0 in the 77th minute, beating three defenders and breaking in alone on goalkeeper Kirsten Nelson for her 22nd goal of the season. Gaelen Clayton sealed the deal when she scored following a corner kick.

The national championship came just a year after the Bears lost, 1–0, in the NCAA Division III final to California Lutheran.

Washington University 3, William Smith 0

NCAA Division III women's championship game at Peter Johann Memorial Field, Las Vegas

WILLIAM SMITH: Starters—GK Kirsten Nelson; D Lexi Hasbrouck, Ireland Krawczyk, Ava Brazie; M Kaleigh Darby, Majorie Plants, Moira van der Putt, Marissa Mastracco, Ruth Hotaling; F Anna Nichols, Nell Dwyer. Substitutions—Hanna Goodness, Ava Ruppersberger, Grace Metzler, Emily Blight, Lily Pryzwansky, Lindsay Ringbloom, Kelsey Otridge, Izzy Thors

WASHINGTON UNIVERSITY: Starters—GK Sidney Conner; D Olivia Foster, Emma Riley McGahan, Ally Hackett; M Sophie Viscovich, Gaelen Clayton, Jadyn Aling, Kacie Karl, Meryl Mckenna, Grace Ehlert; F Ella Koleno. Substitutions—Sam McKibben, Nicole Schmidt, Regan Cannon, Olivia Clemons, Cami Colpitts, Sara Giannotti, Madi Foley, Kate Martin

SCORING: Hackett PK 51, Clemons 77, Clayton 78. Shots on goal: William Smith 5, Washington U. 10. Saves: Nelson (WS) 7, Conner (WU) 5

OFFICIALS: Lila Remache; assistant referees Audra Fullen Balcer, Hao Guo; alternate official Erin Patterson

ATTENDANCE: 252

Sam McKibben advances the ball during the NCAA Division III championship game. **ALON SOWELL**

Goal coming up: Olivia Clemons attacks on a play that ended with her scoring the second goal of the NCAA Division III championship game. **ALON SOWELL**

The 2024 Bears made a strong case as the best team in the 35-year history of WashU women's soccer. The 2025 team went 20–0–2 in its first 22 games, was ranked first nationally throughout the season, and reached the Division III semifinals as this book went to press.

JULY 11, 2025

CITY2 SOARS TO LEAGUE-RECORD EIGHTH STRAIGHT WIN

CITY2 WASTED little time in setting a league record with its eighth consecutive victory. St. Louisan Miguel Perez headed in the first goal in the 12th minute, and CITY2 added three more to lead, 4–0, 39 minutes into the match.

Eight straight wins broke the previous record in the four-year-old MLS NEXT Pro league, which competes in the third division of US soccer.

Mykhi Joyner moved CITY2 to a 3–0 lead with a penalty kick in the 17th minute and on a left-footed shot seven minutes later. The two goals gave him 11 for the season and tied him for first in the league's scoring race.

CITY2's win streak ended in the team's next outing, which ended in a 1–1 tie after regulation time with Ventura County FC on July 16. CITY2 won the ensuing penalty shootout, 4–2, but the game counted as a tie for purposes of CITY2's victory streak. CITY2 went on to have an 18-game unbeaten streak and finished the regular season with a league-best 62 points.

St. Louis CITY2 4, Austin (TX) FC II 2

MLS NEXT Pro regular-season game at Parmer Field, Austin, TX

AUSTIN: GK Charlie Farrar; D Riley Thomas, Antonio Gomez, Jules Bery, Rubén Bonachera; MF Ervin Torres (Adrián González, 46), Jorge Alastuey, Djakaría Barro; F Bryant Farkarlun (Chris Avila, 88), Peter Grogan (Diego Abarca, 65); Micah Burton (Vlad Dănciuțiu, 46)

ST. LOUIS: GK Christian Olivares; D Miguel Perez, Gabriel Mikina, Cam Cilley, Jay Reid (Joey Zalinsky 46); MF Seth Antwi (Matteo Kidd 60), Wan Kuzain (Jack DiMaria 77), Mykhi Joyner, Caden Glover, Brendan McSorley (Lorenzo Cornelius 81); F Emil Jääskeläinen (Edin Clark, 77)

SCORING: Perez (S) (Kuzain) 12, Joyner (S) PK 17, Joyner (S) (McSorley) 24, Kuzain (S) (Jääskeläinen, Reid) 39, Torres (A) (Alastuey) 79, Alastuey (A) (Torres) 90+4. Shots on goal: Austin 3, St. Louis 7. Saves. Farrar (A) 3, Olivares (S) 1

OFFICIALS: Referee Benjamin Mayer; assistant referees Matt Trotter, Benjamin Davis; fourth official William Hale

ATTENDANCE: Unknown

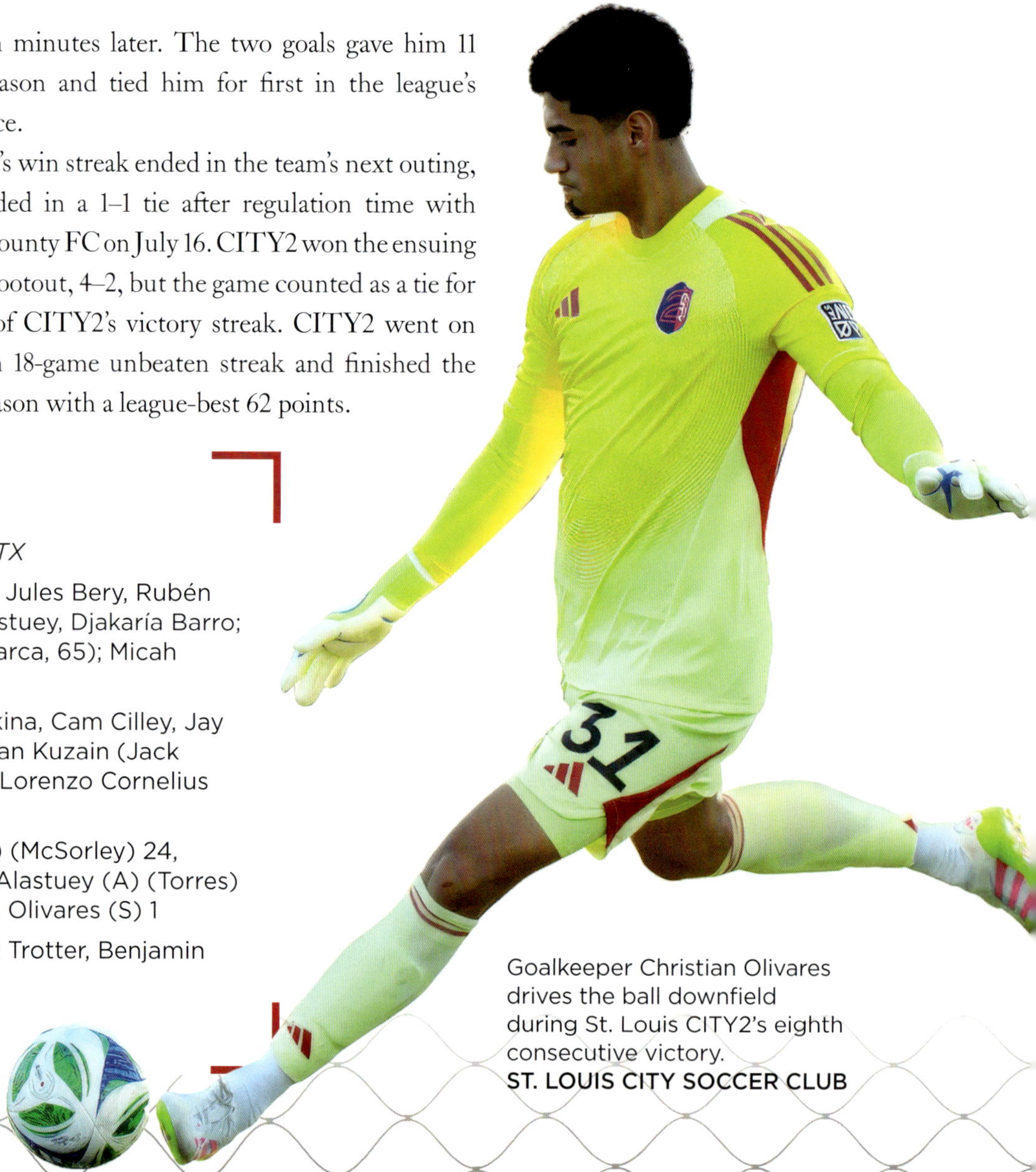

Goalkeeper Christian Olivares drives the ball downfield during St. Louis CITY2's eighth consecutive victory.
ST. LOUIS CITY SOCCER CLUB

INDEX